WORK, RETIRE, REPEAT

WORK, RETIRE, REPEAT

The Uncertainty of Retirement in the New Economy

Teresa Ghilarducci

WITH A FOREWORD BY
E. J. DIONNE JR.

THE UNIVERSITY OF CHICAGO PRESS
Chicago and London

The University of Chicago Press, Chicago 60637
The University of Chicago Press, Ltd., London
© 2024 by The University of Chicago
Published 2024
Printed in the United States of America

33 32 31 30 29 28 27 26 25 24   1 2 3 4 5

ISBN-13: 978-0-226-83146-6 (cloth)
ISBN-13: 978-0-226-83147-3 (e-book)
DOI: https://doi.org/10.7208/chicago/9780226831473.001.0001

Library of Congress Cataloging-in-Publication Data

Names: Ghilarducci, Teresa, author. |
Dionne, E. J., Jr., writer of foreword.
Title: Work, retire, repeat : the uncertainty of
retirement in the new economy / Teresa Ghilarducci ;
with a foreword by E. J. Dionne Jr.
Description: Chicago ; London : The University
of Chicago Press, 2024. | Includes bibliographical
references and index.
Identifiers: LCCN 2023032852 | ISBN 9780226831466 (cloth) |
ISBN 9780226831473 (ebook)
Subjects: LCSH: Retirement—Economic aspects—United States. |
Older people—United States—Economic conditions. |
Older people—Employment—United States. | Older people—
Pensions—United States. | Social security—United States. |
Equality—United States.
Classification: LCC HQ1063.2.U6 G55 2024 |
DDC 332.024/0140973—dc23/eng/20230804
LC record available at https://lccn.loc.gov/2023032852

♾ This paper meets the requirements of ANSI/NISO Z39.48-1992
(Permanence of Paper).

*To Joseph Ghilarducci O'Rourke and
Julian Rowan O'Rourke—to your futures.*

Contents

Acknowledgments

Like planning for your old age, it's impossible to thank all the students, teachers, coworkers, scholars, friends, family, and professionals who have helped inspire and teach me.

My colleagues at the New School's Schwartz Center for Economic Policy Analysis and Retirement Equity Lab deserve first mention—I leaned heavily on Tony Webb, Sia Radpour, Michael Papadopoulos, Aida Farmand, Bridget Fisher, Monique Morrissey, and Chris Cook—I simply couldn't have done this work without them. Kate Bahn, Owen Davis, Ismael Cid-Martinez, Kyle Moore, Drystan Phillips, Steve Pressman, Barbara Schuster, Lauren Schmitz, and University of Notre Dame PhDs Kevin Neuman and Sharon Hermes. Thank you, E. J. Dionne, Jared Bernstein, Ross Eisenbrey, and Kathleen Kennedy Townsend.

My deep gratitude goes to Tony James, a writing partner and friend, and to Bernard Schwartz for his support and wisdom. I thank the seminars at the University of Notre Dame and the New School, University of Michigan, Harvard History Seminars, Harvard Kennedy School, and at my second home University of California, Berkeley, Labor Center, thanks to Clair Brown, Michael Reich, and Jesse Rothstein.

I am grateful to my colleagues at the University of Chicago Press: Charles Myers for his patience, encouragement, and belief in the book. Chad Zimmerman for his energy and wisdom. Elizabeth Ellingboe for her expert editing and stewardship.

My fierce commitment to the book and subject would not have been possible without my dearest friends and family: David Ghilarducci,

Sally Ghilarducci, Chris Tiedemann, Marcia Marley, Lisa Veglahn, Peter Rappoport, Darrick Hamilton, Will Millberg, Kathleen Gerson, John Mollenkopf, Carol Willis, Mark Willis, David Howell, Lydia Tugendrajch, Andy Stern, and Jennifer Johnson Stern. The next generation provides energy, passion, and love for the work—Jay and Ben Ghilarducci and Margaret and Robbie Veglahn. Thank you, Joe O'Rourke, Emily Kirkland, Genevieve McGahey, and, of course, little Julian Rowan O'Rourke.

Rick McGahey, my husband, comes last, but is first in his steadfast support and love. He knows the book and the author better than anyone; Rick's love and attention to my fears and hopes has made my happy life possible. Gratitude and love are different words that barely encompass our relationship. Thank you, Rick, for giving me your best, which is better than I could have imagined.

Foreword

E. J. DIONNE JR.

In recent decades, our society has largely given up on the idea that a dignified retirement should be the right of every worker in our affluent nation. Most private-sector workers are no longer guaranteed fixed pensions—not because they chose that option, but because employers and government policy have pushed almost everyone into a system where there are no guarantees.

Our debates over retirement rarely look at what this means for middle- and especially lower-income workers—people whose life expectancies, on the whole, are shorter than those who earn higher incomes. In fact, to the extent that these issues are discussed, the arguments are heavily tilted toward proposals to cut back Social Security, typically by raising the retirement age.

Oh, yes, and the elderly who are being told to work late into their lives are also told that they have to live with widespread, informal (if technically illegal) age discrimination.

This book is aimed at shaking up the debate over retirement and shining the bright light of research and analysis on a problem that is so often misdescribed and misunderstood. Teresa Ghilarducci is an economist who has always looked at the world from the bottom up. This perspective allows her to see dimensions of the issues surrounding pensions and savings that often elude those who examine these questions from comfortable quarters and abstract spreadsheets alone.

Ghilarducci, it should be said, is highly skilled when it comes to spreadsheets and data. In fact, she knows that in this argument, good data, properly understood, is her friend. But there is humanity—and at times righteous fury—in these pages, so often missing from bloodless policy arguments. Innovatively, she focuses intensely on how economic inequality shapes the experience of people to the very end of their lives. The result: readers are encouraged to look afresh at problems they thought they already understood.

"We have both a tale of two retirements and two old-age labor markets," she writes, adding that "where you sit completely shapes which policies you think should be passed." "At the top," she continues, "people are living longer and healthier and choosing meaningful jobs in old age. Meanwhile, the middle and lower economic classes have much smaller increases in longevity, and they are either struggling in retirement without enough income or trying but failing to find good jobs."

It's important to take note of what Ghilarducci is saying here. She is emphatically *not* against people continuing to work after they are 62 or 65 or 70—or even older. In both theory and practice, I emphatically agree. Being able to do meaningful work later in life is an enormous blessing. It's good for individuals and for society alike.

But she is rightly against pension and retirement policies that *force* those who often live shorter lives to scramble in their final years to find even bad jobs just to keep the lights on and their pharmaceuticals and groceries paid for. Those modest goals are often a challenge for those at the bottom of the wealth and income structure. "Nearly half of all families in the U.S. have no retirement savings," she writes, "and the cost-of-living Elder Index reveals that about 50 percent of older adults living alone are in precarious financial situations."

Implicit in her argument is a critique of the "three-legged stool" theory that elders get sufficient income from a combination of Social Security, employer-based pensions, and personal assets. Americans at the top and some in the middle of the income distribution may have a sturdy-enough perch. But for many, the stool is missing two of its three legs.

Our system's "poor design," she notes, means that "most workers don't voluntarily save for retirement, because it is simply not economically feasible." Exacerbating this inequality, government subsidies—the tax incentives for various savings options—mostly go to higher-income groups.

As for those who think it's easy for older Americans to find work, she urges readers to consider the research of journalist Peter Gosselin and Urban Institute economist Rich Johnson. They found that the labor market for older workers is filled with "discrimination and desperately low wages."

Her conclusion is that "working longer is not the solution to bad retirement policy. In fact, working longer is causing an insidious problem—eroding both the quantity and quality of older people's years. Not only is retirement—which is precious time before death—slipping away but also retirement time is also becoming more unequal."

For Ghilarducci, it's time to make a commitment to "an adequate pension" part of our social bargain.

Note, by the way, the modesty of her demand, which would nonetheless be transformative. She is talking about "adequate," not lavish. But adequate income at retirement would make a big difference: "An adequate pension is crucial . . . to whether one has a choice to spend their sixties and seventies working for pay or not. It is this time of life and the quality of time in old age for low-income and middle-class workers that is rigorously contested."

The choice she poses is stark: "We can continue pushing older people to work longer out of sheer necessity—risking their health, keeping them precarious, and destabilizing the larger economy—or we can embrace and reinvigorate a universal pension system that enables old folks to retire in dignity and comfort if they wish."

This book is important for another reason. Too often, rationalizations for paltry or nonexistent pensions and big Social Security cuts are rooted in contrived generational warfare. The (false) claim is that providing a decent retirement for workers across classes forces cuts in needed programs for children, such as universal childcare and preschool, and help for pregnant women and young parents. Surely you've heard the ugly phrase "greedy geezers," as if every older person were enormously affluent, rolling across magnificent fairways on a golf cart?

Moving the discussion toward generations is a way of evading the deeper issue of class inequality. For starters, policies that assist low- and middle-income people early in their lives (by, for example, tilting the tax code in their favor and providing savings incentives geared toward those with the least rather than the most) would strengthen the capacity of workers to save for old age.

It's also no accident that those who call for cuts in social spending for the aged often oppose programs to help kids from poor and middle-income households, too, such as an expanded Child Tax Credit. It's entirely true that health-care costs for the aged are high and largely assumed by the government through Medicare (and often Medicaid). Yet so many who complain about those costs often oppose efforts to push down the prices of prescription drugs and other reforms in the system.

Does the retirement of the baby boomers cause fiscal challenges? Of course it does. It is painting with far too broad a brush to say that anyone who worries about deficits is automatically an enemy of a decent retirement for all. But the solution to these problems cannot rest on the shoulders of low- and middle-income elderly Americans who already live with policies that delay the age of maximum benefits under Social Security to 70. The answer to inequities in government policies as they affect poor children and wealthy seniors is not to trash retirees but to insist on a more progressive structure of taxes and tax incentives across generations. It's odd that those who complain about those retirees in golf carts when they make a case for Social Security or Medicare cuts are often not at all enthusiastic about proposals that might tax the wealthiest, including seniors, a bit more heavily.

And those who are worried about the nation's fiscal position need to pay close attention to a key component of Ghilarducci's argument: the retirement crisis cannot be handled by Social Security alone, with the entire cost of a decent old age for all placed on the shoulders of taxpayers. One of the central purposes of this book is to show how we have let private pensions atrophy and have provided far too few savings incentives for those who need them most. Ghilarducci is critical of the three-legged stool metaphor not because she's against stools but because they collapse when one or more of the legs are defective or missing entirely.

My hope is that this eloquent, strongly argued, and well-documented book will provoke a broad new debate. Many readers—including some sympathetic to Ghilarducci's overall perspective—may disagree with some of her specific and admirably detailed policy proposals. Let them join the constructive fray. But a warning: her critics will (or at least should be) compelled by her case to describe what they think old age should look like and to explain whether they believe that a longer work life is fair to those likely to have a shorter life expectancy. Also this: if they really want seniors to work longer, how they will provide them with the decent work opportunities they claim are available?

I suspect that for some readers, Ghilarducci's analysis will come as a surprise: They will be taken aback by the extent to which our retirement policies have moved backward. But they and many others will experience a sense of relief in encountering a powerful case for reform, social decency, and a vision of retirement rooted in respect for the humanity and aspirations of us all.

E. J. Dionne Jr. is university professor at Georgetown's McCourt School of Public Policy, senior fellow at the Brookings Institution, and a columnist for the *Washington Post*. His books include *100% Democracy* (with Miles Rapoport), *Code Red*, *Our Divided Political Heart*, and *Why Americans Hate Politics*.

PART I

How the Working-Longer Consensus Made the Retirement Crises Worse

1

The Erosion of Retirement and the Rise of Retirement Inequality

Around Christmas time in 2022, a local businessman from Cumberland, Maryland, chatted with an 82-year-old US Navy veteran, Warren Marion, who was working at Walmart.[1] The younger man, Rory McCarty, had seen a fundraising campaign helping another 82-year-old Walmart worker to retire, Mrs. Carman Kelley, who used a shopping cart as her cane. So, he made a TikTok video and started a GoFundMe page, where he wrote: "I was astounded seeing this little older man still grinding. Working 8- to 9-hour shifts." The money flowed in, and because of it, with over $100,000, Marion said he could retire: "What else can I say? I can't wrap my mind around it. What this is going to do for me at 82 years old is allow me to pay all my bills off, including my house, and I will have nothing but my utility bills. I'll be able to travel to Florida whenever I feel like going and to see my kids. I'm very, very blessed."

Is this what America's retirement system has come to? People work until someone does a random act of kindness and collects money on TikTok. Are we heading for a TikTok pension system? If we are, we would need millions more GoFundMe accounts for working people older than age 75 who can't retire.

Long, Deep Cracks in the Retirement System

In 2019, even before the pandemic and subsequent economic meltdown, when jobs were plentiful, many older workers faced downward mobility—over 40 percent of older middle-class workers were on the path to becoming poor or near-poor retirees.[2] In the midst of the pandemic, I was quoted in a front-page story in the *New York Times* noting that older workers weren't retiring by choice. For workers with earnings at or below the national median, 52 percent of retirements were involuntary: "By contrast, among the top 10 percent of earners, only 10 percent of exits were involuntary." "It's a tale of two retirements," I said.

If older workers had good pensions, then taking a dignified off-ramp to retirement would make good sense. Pensions may seem like a throwback to an earlier, grittier age when jobs were hard and people were less educated and died sooner. The truth is pensions are needed now more than ever. Working longer is not the "freebie" it is made out to be. Working longer means giving up well-earned rest in old age. Older workers are in warehouses or doing home health care and other jobs that require a great deal of physical labor and intense concentration. For some, working longer means aging more quickly and dying sooner.[3] For most people, the only way working longer boosts retirement finances is grotesque: when they finally retire, they are closer to death.

We have both a tale of two retirements and two old-age labor markets.[4] Where you sit completely shapes which policies you think should be passed. At the top, people are living longer and healthier and choosing meaningful jobs in old age. Meanwhile, the middle and lower economic classes have much smaller increases in longevity, and they are either struggling in retirement without enough income or trying but failing to find good jobs.

Diana Sanger (profiled by *NBC Nightly News* in October 2021), who helps takes care of a grandson with autism, spent all her free time searching for a job after being laid off during the COVID-19 pandemic. "Do you know what it's like to find a job when you are 70, no one wants to hire you, and you can't find a job with benefits and some paid time off?" Diana may be facing discriminatory prejudice, but employers also avoid older workers because they face higher costs for employing them.[5] Average monthly health spending per worker is twice as great for those aged 60–64 than it is for those aged

30–34.[6] On *NBC Nightly News*, the journalist Harry Smith asked Diana if she would ever retire: "I will die at my job; that's when I'll be able to retire."[7]

Sanger's story is in deep contrast to Howard Lieberman, age 69, who told the *New York Times* in 2022 that he is winding down his consulting business because his wife retired from teaching during the pandemic, and they want to go camping and volunteer.[8] Now, post-COVID-19, that the economy has recovered, why can't these folks just jump back into the labor market? Getting a new job when the economy recovers is not so simple for older workers.[9] The pandemic recession may have produced more Sangers than Liebermans. The COVID-19 recession may push an additional 1 million older workers into poverty in old age.[10]

As we might expect, low-wage older workers (aged 50–60 and earning less than $47,600 in 2020)—such as those toiling in retail, janitorial services, and health care—were more likely to lose their jobs in the recession.[11] Two-thirds had no savings, and for those who did, their average retirement savings were just about $42,000.[12] Middle-class older workers (earnings greater than $48,000 and lower than the Social Security earnings cap of $137,700 in 2020) did a little better, but not very well.[13] Of them, 41 percent had no savings, and those who did had median savings of $101,000. Those who lost their jobs were worse off: they will have less than $5,000 in savings at age 65.[14] It is no surprise poverty rates for middle-income older workers who lose their jobs will increase from 38 percent to 42 percent between 2020 and 2030.

Higher-earning older workers were safer from recession's harm but not completely safe. A whopping 27 percent of these better-off folks—with earnings above $137,700—have nothing but Social Security to rely on in retirement.[15] Astoundingly, the COVID-19 recession is expected to double the number of high earners who end up in poverty in old age.

Moreover, 40 percent of the 21 million people who live in households with an older worker but aren't poor yet will be if they must retire at age 62. Even if all those middle-class older workers delayed retirement until age 65, the number of downwardly mobile would still be substantial, about 5 million.[16] And these households are more in debt than they were a decade ago. An Urban Institute study showed that 61 percent of households with people aged 65 and older had debt in 2016, up from 38 percent in 1989.[17] When people's debt rises, they become more economically desperate and thus more vulnerable to need work of any sort.

Needing to work in old age marks our times. Nearly half of all families in the United States have no retirement savings, and the cost-of-living Elder Index, developed by the Gerontology Institute at the University of Massachusetts Boston, reveals that about 50 percent of older adults living alone are in precarious financial situations.[18] The relentless erosion of pensions and the unreliability of other kinds of retirement accounts tied to fluctuating financial markets heightens inequality between people as they age. The retirement crisis also dooms us to watch many more millions of elderly people ending up in poverty, struggling in a job, and adding to the unemployment lines.[19] This humanitarian and economic crisis is on the boil.

So, with such a large and financially precarious American older worker population, you would think that the president and Congress would be facing a national outcry. But politically, the grim reality is that this situation has elicited a big shrug. I think I know why.

The prevailing view is that individuals should save for their retirement—and if they don't have enough money in retirement, it's their own fault—after all, they can work more. Working more and longer is, not surprisingly, a mantra emanating from industry and many policy makers. In lionizing a fall 2019 report, *Working Better with Age*, published by the Organisation for Economic Co-operation and Development (OECD), the pro-business magazine the *Economist* concluded uncritically that "employment of older workers is vital if prosperity is to be maintained."[20] In this starry-eyed scenario, elders should retrain to become the economy's "silver surfers"—"surfing" for computer technology—to save prosperity. Retraining advice is often paired with a shaming message: "If you don't have enough money to retire, it is your fault for not having kept up."

But it turns out that working longer is not the solution to bad retirement policy. In fact, working longer is causing an insidious problem, eroding both the quantity and the quality of older people's years. Not only is retirement—which is precious time before death—slipping away, but also retirement time is becoming more unequal.

I can already hear the pushback from elites. After all, in 2024, the president of the United States is 81; and the most powerful Republican in the Senate, Mitch McConnell, is also 81. If they can do it, shouldn't we all? Elon Musk's septuagenarian mother is a super-model—it may seem we are all living longer, we can all be beautiful as we age, and we all can work more. From Washington's perspective, 64—about the age most Americans are retiring now—seems just the right age to launch your presidential and congressional career. A third act for a rather elite bunch.

But the truth is, over the past seventy years, life expectancy for Americans at age 65 has inched up more slowly than in other nations, and all that added longevity went to those at the top.

Working longer solves the problem of inadequate retirement accounts funding retirement only because the length of retirement just shrinks. And working longer may even hasten death for workers in subordinate positions and in other stressful situations, making the funding of retirement not a problem because, gruesomely, there is no retirement to fund when people work until they die.

The nation should not depend on people working longer to make up for inadequate retirement-income security. Doing so only exacerbates inequalities in wealth, health, well-being, and retirement time. Even in purely economic terms, compelling people to work longer is not likely to pay dividends. As a rule, more grannies laboring wearily for longer at McDonald's diminishes average productivity, shortens retirement life for the vulnerable, and may suppress wages and working conditions for younger workers. Working longer doesn't even improve a person's Social Security benefits: most older workers collect Social Security benefits to supplement their wages, forgoing any delayed retirement credit. Perhaps the only beneficiaries of older people working longer—beyond the few older workers with good jobs and adequate wealth—are employers who benefit from the increased labor supply. Yes, Granny deserves a good job if she wants one, but working until you drop is not a civilized plan for a civilized society.

Everyone needs a dignified way to retire. Despite the limited benefits, the push for elderly people to work longer is everywhere.

....

BOX 1.1 Doomsday for Pensions and the Rise of Older Workers

The do-it-yourself American pension system is failing. For instance, the median holding in a retirement account for all workers aged 55–64 is only $15,000, but the average worker needs $600,000 to supplement Social Security and maintain their standard of living. The bottom 50 percent have nothing but need $300,000; the next 40 percent have $60,000 but need $600,000; and the top 10 percent need at least $1 million but have $200,000.

As all this evidence tells us, it's past time to banish the myth that America has a "three-legged stool" supporting the elderly; that is, that elders get income from Social Security, employer-based pensions, and personal assets. Only elders at the top of the income distribution have anything resembling a stool.

The Urban Institute's "This Is Not Your Parents' Retirement" predicted that by 2020, middle-class Generation Xers would receive 37 percent of their retirement income from Social Security when they reach age 67; about 24 percent will come from working; 22 percent from personal assets (mainly from owning a house); and, bringing up the rear, 18 percent from employer pensions. So that means for our three-legged stool, the Social Security leg is 37 inches; the earnings-from-work leg is 24 inches; the personal-assets leg is 22 inches; and the employer-pension leg is just 18 inches. That's an awfully wobbly stool.

I offer an alternative to cutting pensions and forcing work on elders. A work plan that is pro-worker enforces anti-age-discrimination laws, institutes effective job training, and pays for good pensions and more Social Security benefits. In contrast, the working-longer consensus is a recipe for creating a group of elders desperate to work. The pro-worker plan for retirement helps elders choose work on their own terms.[21]

The Age-Old Controversy: Who Deserves to Retire?

While I was on a panel of retirement finance experts, we were all asked to call retirement something else—the moderator said it was a bad word. Earlier, I had asked a friend about her retirement plans, and she mumbled defensively, "I'm not really going to retire; I am not going to nothing." Her defensive response made me think I, indeed, had said a bad word. On the panel, I responded a bit tersely, why a new name for retirement and not for holidays, vacation, bathroom breaks, and the weekend? Is retirement bad because it is "time off"? Couldn't the same arguments marshaled against retirement be made against the weekend and holidays? After all, we would increase economic output if people worked seven days a week all year long. OK, maybe people have leave to take care of children—but that is still work. We haven't had to seriously defend the weekend and paid holidays just yet, but widespread shaming for wanting time away from work causes us to defend and justify the word *retirement*, which for our purposes only means controlling the pace and content of your time at the end of a working life.

Who deserves to retire, and who gets to retire? The answer to this question has changed dramatically over time. Back in 1935, when President Franklin Delano Roosevelt and Congress established Social Security, most working men died in their boots—they never retired. Women were not prevalent in the paid workforce, so we do not have reliable statistics about how many died on the job. Only the well-off got to retire. Although some might romanticize the family spirit of those times, the elderly did not generally live in the bosoms of their extended families. Instead, they filled poorhouses and lonely boardinghouses.[22] Then, as now, the poor elderly were less likely than other elderly to have financially stable adult children with extra income or in-law suite to help them out.

For decades—in the more than eighty years since the Great Depression—Social Security and workplace pension and retirement plans only expanded. An economically secure retirement became a staple of American life and a commonplace expectation among most workers. But since the 1980s, fewer people have access to decent pensions, and even fewer have enough financial assets to spend down in their retirement. As a result, access to retirement itself has become a luxury and viewed as an economic privilege rather than a normal expectation for someone who worked their entire life. In this, the distribution of retirement time, as well as the average time in retirement, tells the story. On average, American elders are working more and further into old age. Between 1985 and 2016, the labor-force participation rate for men at age 65 shot up from 31 percent to 46 percent, and for women from 15 percent to 23 percent.[23] But the work circumstances of these millions of older workers are very different—some are working out of abundance and interest, and others are working because they can't afford to retire.

And there is more to the story than fairness in retirement time and the well-being of elders. The circumstances under which elderly people work matter to everyone, regardless of age. The sheer scale of the aging population poses huge questions for the balance of power between employers and workers.

Economists project that over 6 million jobs will likely be added to the US economy by 2026—and more than 4 million will be filled by workers older than age 55.[24] That's a lot of older workers. Their sheer numbers, low pay, and weak pensions affect all workers' bargaining power. The size of the boomer cohort coupled with their insecure pensions—and by "pensions," I mean a source of income in retirement, such as assets in an employer-based defined-contribution or 401(k)-type plan, an employer traditional defined-pension plan, and/or government-based Social Security—will cause a flood of impoverished elders, many of whom were once middle class, and a stark increase in elderly workers. The quality of their pensions—if they have any at all—will create spillover effects on the overall labor market.

As the aging economy barrels ahead, how we pay for pensions and Social Security depends on how we answer basic quality-of-life questions: When can workers catch a break? What is the ideal retirement age anyway? That a nineteenth-century German leader tagged 65 as a retirement age is irrelevant to our twenty-first-century question of what workers deserve. A nation's retirement age—whether age 65 or 62 or 70—is never determined on the basis of longevity, working capacity, or optimal career trajectory. Retirement ages and decent pensions are born of union contracts, political negotiations, social norms, struggles for retirement, public employment activism, and employer practices that changed according to employers' own needs.[25] So age 65 is not scientific; it is a political number set by convention and consensus.

The choices we make about funding pensions and Social Security— and about who gets to retire and when—also have a huge bearing on younger workers. How much do Generation X, Generation Y, and Generation Z owe their parents' and grandparents' generations? Should younger populations subsidize older workers working less, either by retiring completely or working part-time? How many years of retirement leisure should a worker get? These questions are deceptively simple.

How Long Should People Work before They Retire?

At one extreme of defining who deserves to retire is Yale law professor Anne Alstott. In her provocative 2016 book *A New Deal for Old Age*, Alstott encourages an average retirement age of 76 based on evidence that, on average, older people can work longer.

The attempt to pick a retirement age based on science is typically based on so-called work ability, not on improving people's lives. Extending the scientific approach to paid time off could lead to a ridiculous rethink of the "scientific" number of holidays, weekend days, and so on. It's clear that all those decisions are based on struggle, won by workers' political leverage and market power. Retirement policy has shifted ground away from improving workers' lives to a science-based length of working time.

Another problem is the widespread notion that retirement is not something workers deserve. The notion is that someone either accumulates hundreds of thousands of dollars and can supplement their Social Security retirement or must work into their older years to cover retirement costs. In *Working Longer*, the well-respected Boston College retirement researcher Alicia Munnell and coauthors argue that unless they work longer, older people will fall short of a secure retirement.[26] But there is evidence to suggest this is simply not true. In one study, my coauthors and I were surprised to find that working longer did not increase financial preparedness for retirement as much as these experts had expected.[27] Working longer makes retirement more affordable only because a person has less retirement. It is like making lunch affordable by skipping it. Yet despite the oxymoronic policy, promoting work to solve the retirement-income crisis persists. In a July 2019 interview, Munnell advocates age 70 as the new retirement age: "With people starting to work at 22 and retiring at 62, that's 40 years of work. They then have 20 years in retirement, so you must put away enough in those 40 years—after paying for housing, educating your kids and other big expenses—to support yourself for at least 20 more years. That just is not feasible. If you can add eight years to your work life by delaying retirement, suddenly the ratio of work to retirement years changes dramatically. 70 should be the goal now."[28]

The advice to work until age 70 is presented as "pragmatic." The recommendation ignores politics and inequality and concedes to diminishing the value of human labor by diminishing paid time off. I call this blithe promotion of working-longer policies the "working-longer consensus." The working-longer consensus hides behind a veneer of science. In a 2012 report, the prestigious National Research Council proposed that average work lives be at least forty-five years long and that people retire after age 70, because, on average, people were living longer and were healthier.[29]

The National Research Council's conclusion represents the regrettable view that US retirement is overly generous because healthier Americans are not working longer than they were in the past. This alleged problem, the report claims, is caused by too-high FICA taxes—that's for the Federal Insurance Contributions Act—on older workers and the legacy of defined-benefit retirement plans, like those in the public sector, which encourage Americans to retire too early. "Too early," though, is subjective; it points to science that shows that retiring in one's 60s is "too early" because people in their 60s today can work longer than those in their 60s could in the past. The academy's report focuses on the less educated, arguing that their ability to work far exceeds their "work effort." Thus, it identifies reluctant older workers as the problem rather than scrutinizing the kinds of jobs elders can get. Many older workers' jobs offer low pay, inflexible conditions, and bad hours. Older workers without a college degree face worse conditions. The National Research Council's report does not address older workers' meager leverage in the labor market and how that little bargaining power compels most to accept low pay and bad working conditions.

A so-called science-based age of retirement would be convenient. If economists and physicians could come up with a formula to determine how many years people should work before they receive decent pensions, we wouldn't need to make value-based judgments, politics, and economic struggles about what workers deserve. Finding this scientific answer—with codas that some workers in especially dangerous jobs, such as mining and the military, should be able to retire after fewer years—is the goal of many scholars working in this field. But there is no such thing as a scientific answer about the proper age of retirement. Retirement is moral, political, and social, not scientific. The most influential economist of the twentieth century, John Maynard Keynes, wrote—after reordering the global monetary system and revolutionizing the way governments stave off recessions—that prosperity would bring future generations less work and more healthy time to do what they please.[30]

An example of the struggle is what unionized workers and their employers have worked out. When workers have bargaining power, they bargain for a particular retirement-age target. Forced retirement is illegal in the US. That means that an automatic retirement age isn't established; instead, a pension or retirement fund design is bargained over. "Thirty and out," for example, is the defined-benefit pension deal for union miners with the United Mine Workers. If they want, they have access to a pension for life that pays out about 80 percent of their pre-retirement income after working full-time for thirty years. The UAW, which represents auto, aircraft, and other industry manufacturing employees, has a similarly designed pension plan. It's twenty and out for the military, police, and firefighters. There is no science behind this, only market power.

Another way to understand the politics of retirement age is to take a close look at national policies surrounding retirement age for a clue about what rich countries have worked out about how long people should work. In the United States, the age at which a person receives a maximum benefit from Social Security is age 70. I used a simple method to compare the socially determined retirement age in the US with other nations. For each nation, I compare the age of retirement (i.e., the age at which national pension systems stop increasing benefits) and subtract from that the age people start work to get a "policy work-life norm." By this method, the US policy work-life norm is forty-eight years for college graduates and fifty-two years for people who start work at age 18. And it may not be a surprise that the "policy-target work life" in the United States is the highest among our national peers who belong to the OECD. Norway, Poland, Italy, and Israel have target work lives between forty-four and forty-five years. Turkey, Korea, France, and Greece have target work lives shorter than forty years.[31]

Americans work longer because of our stingy pensions. American men work an average of 46 years, compared to 43 years for men in the OECD countries. Women in the US work an average of 45 years, compared with 42 years for women in the OECD countries.[32] The United States ranks ninth out of the thirty-eight OECD nations in average work life for men and second behind Japan among the large G-7 nations in work time for women.[33] The United States ranks fourth out of thirty-four nations and second behind Japan in the G-7 in working time for women.

When nations choose the age at which workers get full retirement benefits, they are also making a choice about who effectively gets full benefits. Retirement-age policy is a value statement about the value of work and elders' quality of life. In most nations, the so-called full retirement age is typically much higher than when people retire. That means the average worker doesn't get a maximum pension benefit. In the OECD countries, men get the maximum benefit in only thirteen of thirty rich nations, and women collect the maximum benefit in only ten of thirty.

Whose choice is it to retire before age 70—the worker's or someone else's or something else's? In the United States, most retirees lament retiring earlier than planned because they were laid off, forced out, or their health or their spouse's health drove them out of the labor force.[34] Fewer than 10 percent of Social Security claimants wait until age 70. Setting ages for maximum benefits much higher than actual retirement age means nations essentially penalize workers for claiming benefits before the maximum age and reward those who can wait—those with brighter employment prospects or more wealth.

We are left with an unhealthy (and unsustainable) contradiction. Many older workers are forced out of the labor force in their mid-60s or earlier. Many other retirees are forced back into the labor force or to work longer because of inadequate pensions. All the while, the nation sets policies as if working and waiting to claim benefits until age 70 were a personal choice, or even a possibility.

The Cultural Emergence of the Greedy Geezer

A sinister consequence of policies that target a high retirement age is that retirees younger than, say, age 70, feel they must be apologetic and explain why they aren't working and why they retired "too early."

With a cultural norm of 70 as a retirement age, a needy retiree younger than that is being moved from the "deserving" to the "undeserving" category. As I pointed out earlier, most people don't work as long as the "policy norm," which automatically makes those who retire before the target retirement age socially on the defensive.

A mandated retirement age is now unthinkable in the US, yet a ban on forced retirement weakens claims to pensions. Retirees had a more socially acceptable claim to pensions when retirement was mandated. Now, work is the new pension.

For the half century between the 1930s and the 1980s, the elderly worker had the two characteristics required for a socially legitimate claim to pensions: being blameless and needy. Mandatory retirement (which was legal in the US before 1978) meant that being retired was through no fault of one's own, and elderly poverty rates were so high their need was not questioned.[35] I do not favor bringing back mandatory retirement, but mandatory retirement legitimated providing decent Social Security and pensions.

Being "deserving retirees" would give workers stronger claims to secure, adequate pensions. But sometimes, being legitimate and deserving is not enough. Obtaining a claim to income after a lifetime of work may require threats. Workers organized into unions that mobilized and pressured politicians and employers to provide pensions and expand Social Security. The Gray Panthers, a name that echoes the militant group Black Panthers, was formed in 1970 and aimed to inspire more fierceness into old-age advocacy. (In 2022, the scholar and activist Bill McKibben's started the Third Act political movement to recruit elders for progressive social change.[36])

Age 62 is the youngest age at which an eligible person can claim Social Security benefits, which acknowledges that many older households need income supplements and that work lives get cut short before people are in their mid-60s. But monthly benefits are reduced substantially before "full retirement age," the age Social Security targets as the age at which one gets 100 percent of a monthly benefit that is neither reduced for early claiming nor increased for "delaying" claiming.[37] Collecting early has become less common: in 2000, about 45 percent of men and 27 percent of women applied for benefits at age 62, and by 2020 those shares fell further, to 24 percent for men and 26 percent for women. But Social Security amendments in 1983 intended to cut benefits and change social norms by raising the "full retirement age." Age 62 remained the "early" retirement age, but the 1983 law raised the full retirement age—which had been 65 since 1935—from 65 to 67 for people born between 1943 and 1960. The age for maximum benefits became age 70.[38]

By 1983, legal mandatory retirement was out, and anti-age-discrimination protections were in. Banning age discrimination is obviously a good thing, although, combined with Social Security cuts, a side effect is the diminished social legitimacy of retiring before age 70, because one isn't forced to retire and is rewarded for working longer. Both the rise of the 401(k) plan—the do-it-yourself pension—and the push to work longer have caused those who reach retirement age without enough money to be seen as undeserving of sympathy or help.[39] Add a third factor, the "forever young" movement—for example, the 2008 World Science Festival claimed "90 is the new 50"—and changing cultural norms, and struggling older Americans become people who have created their own predicament by not saving enough or investing better or working long enough.[40] The DIY retirement system promotes shaming and blaming older economic victims, and it effectively suppresses the idea that older folks are deserving of retirement income.

THE RISE OF THE WORKING-LONGER CONSENSUS

You will recognize the working-longer consensus everywhere. One aspect of the working-longer consensus is the popular portrayal of older workers featured in feel-good human-interest stories. Another aspect is academics and policy makers treating working longer as a free-lunch policy—all gain, no pain. In the media, it's a cliché that reporters always highlight the bad. But reporting on older workers is a consistent exception. Older workers in grinding jobs without protection are hardly mentioned; instead, the media is filled with one-sided profiles of delighted older workers.

My favorite examples are the 100-year-old yoga teacher profiled by AARP's magazine who wondrously declared, "I start every day an optimist," and the *Huffington Post*'s report on 90-year-old Alice Pirnie, of Broken Bow, Nebraska, who had worked as a greeter and cashier at a McDonald's since she was 64.[41] Too bad Alice met only a feel-good-seeking reporter and not a Good Samaritan with a TikTok account.

A probing journalist would have asked Alice what her financial situation would be if she didn't work. "Oh, I don't need the money; I have a large pension and Social Security" might mean we could presume her fallback position was strong and she genuinely liked working at McDonald's. But if Alice answered, "Without McDonald's wages I would skip dinner most nights," we could assume her fallback position is grim and her bargaining power low.

The labor market for older workers is two-sided. On the one hand, older workers face discrimination and desperately low wages, and most retirements are involuntary.[42] On the other hand, involuntary retirement often diminishes people's self-regard for the rest of their lives. Although in surveys Americans often say they want to work longer, most practically cannot do so because of their own personal circumstances or employers not wanting to hire them. The COVID-19 recession exaggerated the mismatch between the age at which one wants to retire and the age at which they are forced to.[43]

The erosion of guaranteed pensions and the "legitimate" retiree, and the rise of the media portrayal of the happy older worker, makes adequate pensions seem like some artifact from the past. But the need for better pensions and more secure income in old age is greater than ever.

Why Do We Even Have Pensions?

The current American do-it-yourself pension system, which essentially tells workers they are on their own, runs counter to some of the core principles behind pensions. Nations set up pension systems for two practical reasons.

First, most people in market societies are workers, and their well-being depends on them selling their labor (or depends on their family members' labor). This means the risk of superannuation—that is, becoming unemployable before the age one wants to retire—is shared by most everyone who works and is not a capital owner. In the face of this universally shared risk, nations promote various forms of public or social insurance to protect against worker obsolescence.[44]

Second, nations establish pensions because as societies grow richer, so does the demand for paid time off. In the United States and other market economies, workers and unions fought for paid time off, a victory encapsulated by a favorite slogan: "Don't Thank God It's Friday, Thank the Labor Movement."[45] Universal public education for children under age 16, paid vacations, paid family leave, and retirement came about thanks to collective bargaining, political pressure, and societies reaching together for a good life.

Economists describe the social demand for retirement as a form of paid time off. The demand for more paid time off increases with a nation's wealth, meaning the political demand is sensitive to the level of income people have (the nerd term for this is *income elastic*, the demand for time increases as the income of a person in a household increases). In other words, as income goes up, demand for paid time off, such as retirement, increases. What good is having money to buy roses if you don't have time to smell them? Humans like paid time off, and retirement is a special form of paid time off—the time is taken at the end of our working lives.

With income elasticity, when pay increases, we buy more of what we like and fewer cheaper substitutes. As nations grow richer, demand rises for pasta and falls for potatoes; it goes up for houses and declines for mobile homes. As countries boost wealth, they make more arrangements for vacations, holidays, weekends, and shorter workdays and workweeks.[46] The economic historian Dora Costa has shown that as economies grow, people's demands for retirement time increase, and the long hours of work required to obtain subsistence goods and services fall.[47]

Although it's clear that we all want time off and that economic riches expand that possibility, the distribution of this freedom—who gets it and when—is hotly contested. The prevailing concern expressed in this debate, that working families don't have enough paid time, carries the unfortunate implication that retirees have too much time, as if age were the central feature of the time-off conflict rather than class and inequality.

Two progressive feminist scholars have asked whether society allocates individuals' time off efficiently. Kathleen Gerson and Jerry Jacobs argue for reallocating time off so it is not bunched up at the end of people's working lives because young families need paid time off. But paid time off is not a fixed good.[48] Economist Heather Boushey argues what workers and employers want is often in conflict.[49] The distribution of pay and time is not a reflection of what people want; it is what they are compelled to accept. Household demand alone, then, does not drive the distribution of paid time off. The pioneer in feminist, political economy of aging studies, Carroll Estes, turns the question of efficient time allocation on its head. The allocation of time has little to do with efficiency but rather is about dominance. Aging is a women's issue because the combination of patriarchy and the market as a dominant institution affecting women's life supports a gendered system that puts women in a dependent role socially and financially to men or to state programs.[50]

Economists, sociologists, anthropologists, psychologists, and historians all wrestle with how societies get people on the off-ramp from paid work into retirement. They all agree on one thing, at least: humans need a period at the end of their lives for personal narrative, to derive a meaning for their life, and to control the pace and content of their lives. The psychologist Erik Erikson described the last stage of life as one of integrity and wisdom.[51]

No one seriously disputes the care and respect that elders need beyond their productive years. But how do we ensure this happens? A modern and humanistic idea of old age and retirement emerged in the 1970s that claimed everyone—poor, middle class, rich—deserves a life stage of integration that requires hope and economic security to ward off despair. An adequate pension is crucial, though, to whether one has a choice to spend their 60s and 70s working for pay or not. It is this time of life and the quality of time in old age for low-income and middle-class workers that is rigorously contested.

How Long Do People Live after Retirement?

Even before the COVID-19 vaccine was widely available, several polls found that older workers, especially those in the middle class, were planning to work more to survive the pandemic recession. Both high- and low-income older workers told surveys that they were retiring earlier than they had planned. A December 2020 consumer survey revealed that 59 percent of boomers planned to keep working during their retirement because of the pandemic recession.[52] A November poll reported that 19 percent of people in their 50s planned to work full-time in retirement.[53] Did you just blink? Yes, you read that right. Working full-time in "retirement." These plans come at a cost. Since life expectancy has not kept up with the increase in work, working longer reduces access to some of the best years of life. And economic strife only makes work at older ages worse. In recessions, employers write the rules on wages, hours, and labor conditions. Employer power tilts the retirement playing field even more against workers.

And the loss of pensions is made worse by the loss of life expectancy. The US is one of the few OECD nations in recent years that has seen reduced life expectancy among people in the lowest-income groups. This means that Americans experience less time not working in their later years.

We can chart this back to policy decisions made in the 1980s. In 1983, President Reagan and Congress faced an emergency. Within just a few years, Social Security would not be able to pay full benefits. To achieve full funding for the next seventy-five years, Congress passed a combination of benefit cuts and revenue increases.

The cut in future Social Security benefits came about mainly by gradually raising the "full retirement age"—the age at which beneficiaries could collect "full" Social Security—from 65 to 67 for people born after 1960. Notably, the "full benefit" is different from "maximum" Social Security benefits, which kick in at age 70. Congress, for reasons of complex calculations and politics, has hopelessly confused the full benefit with the maximum benefit. The maximum benefit is obtainable at age 70. Reduced monthly Social Security benefits are available as early as age 62.

In 1983, raising the age to get maximum benefits seemed fair—lawmakers held out the likelihood that life expectancy would continue to improve and workers would not miss a bit of retirement time. But growth in American life expectancy did not keep up with the growth in retirement ages. A nation will shrink the retirement time for its workers by making the pensionable age increases faster than life expectancy. And in making things worse for American workers' prospects in old age, the US almost stands alone. While only a few nations in the OECD raised full retirement ages faster than their life expectancy growth—notably the US, Hungary, and Poland—most

OECD nations improved their residents' life expectancy faster than they raised the full pensionable age.

The US is also home to stark and growing differences in the amount and quality of healthy retirement experienced by whites and nonwhites, women and men, and disparities by geographic region (more on this in later chapters). While the US has reduced retirement time over the past sixty years, between 1958 and 2020, the average OECD country created more retirement time by setting the pensionable age at 62, thus increasing life expectancy after pensionable age. I calculate the life expectancy after pensionable age by subtracting elder life expectancy from the nation's established pensionable age.

Throughout OECD countries, during the years 1958 and 2020, the average increase in life expectancy after retirement age is just over six years for women and just over five years for men. This rise of five to six years in retirement time after age 62 is a tremendous achievement worthy of celebration—it is concrete economic and social progress that boosted demand for leisure in people's final years.[54]

If we scan the century from 1958 to a projected 2050, we see even more glaring disparities in nations' progress on retirement time. For all OECD countries, the projected average increase in time in retirement during this period is about 56 percent for men and 51 percent for women. Meanwhile, by comparison, the US increase in retirement time was much lower, just a 38 percent increase for both men and women. (The US reduction in retirement time would be even worse if I incorporated the negative life expectancy effects of the COVID pandemic and opioid addiction.[55]) Even this miserly rise might be much smaller or nonexistent if OECD researchers used the current American "unofficial" retirement age of 70 in calculations. In stark contrast, other nations have expanded retirement as their economies and national wealth expanded. For example, with different policy choices and better life expectancy, Canada's retirement time is expected to double for men and to grow 71 percent for women from 1958 to 2050. Norway and France will have expanded their national expected retirement time by about 92 percent; Spain,

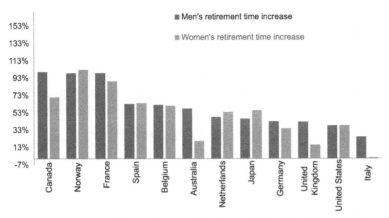

FIGURE 1.1 US Lagged Projected Increases in Retirement Time in Rich, Large Nations, 1958–2050

Note: "Rich, large nations" have per capita gross domestic product over $30,000 and more than twelve million people. Retirement time is the time between life expectancy and actual pensionable age. Life expectancy is calculated using data from 1960 for the pensionable ages applicable in 1958, the earliest dates these data are available. Historical data on life expectancy are taken from the OECD Health Database 1960–1995. Recent data and projections of life expectancy in the future are based on the UN Population Division Database, *World Population Prospects—The 2008 Revision*, and the OECD's *Pensions at a Glance 2011: Retirement-Income Systems in OECD and G20 Countries* (OECD Publishing, 2011).

Belgium, Australia, and the Netherlands expanded by about 50 percent (fig. 1.1).

In closing, the picture for Americans' retirement is dismal. The US did not always rank near the bottom of retirement time. In 1958, the US ranked eighteenth among nations in the OECD in retirement time. Over the following decades, pension plans and health improved, so the US ranked fourteenth in 1983, before the Reagan administration's policy shifts took hold. But with longevity gains slowing and anti-pension policy decisions since then, the US has fallen backward. By 2050, the US is expected to rank twenty-fifth, near the bottom of retirement time after pensionable age. Let's peel back another layer of the bitter story: if we take the US pensionable age to be 67 instead of 70, then the US would be dead last among rich nations in providing people with retirement time. The US is a rich nation, and it can do better for its workers' old age.

This book fully rejects the working-longer consensus and proposes the Gray New Deal in its place. Gray New Deal policies create genuine choices to work or retire and recognize that civilized democratic societies provide adequate pensions and enable people to retire or work in dignity.[56] The dignity part is vital. The problem is not that people do work in their late 60s, 70s, and 80s; the problem is that very few work at older ages for the right reasons.

2

The Shift to Retirement Insecurity

The US retirement system is broken. Most elders need to supplement their meager retirement income with work. And worries about insecure old-age finances are not isolated to low-income workers. After 2020, even many high-income older workers earning $170,000 or more per year will retire into poverty because they lost their jobs and were pushed into an early, underfunded retirement. Faced with low incomes and meager savings, many elders will need to turn to gig work to maintain their material conditions; for many, this will be a matter of survival. This pressure to work longer in old age, combined with unequal socioeconomic class-based life spans and top-heavy wealth accumulation, will worsen inequality in well-being in old age. This inequality is not only financial—many of today's older workers will have less time before infirmity and death to enjoy productive physical and social activities than their counterparts in the past and in other nations.[1]

Retirement used to be a social norm, a good thing, sought out and respectable. Retirement was something both the rich and the poor aimed for and a legitimate goal for working people to plan. Ending mandatory retirement was a good thing; age discrimination is wasteful and violates human dignity. But the stealth attack on a decent retirement that most people can count on is a big loss to society. It is also unfair and unnecessary. But I am getting ahead of myself. How did we get to such an impoverished and unequal American retirement landscape?

A Short History of Retirement in America

A bit of history is in order. The Social Security program, launched in the 1930s, aimed to help off-ramp older workers to a dignified old age. Through the 1950s, labor unions and employers that agreed to union demands developed retirement plans, enabling more pensions and less work. Advanced capitalist nations created ways for workers to save while working to fund retirement without dropping off a cliff. The alternative to pensions was no or meager pensions, which created a pool of desperate elderly workers clinging to their jobs to survive.

In the late 1970s, the legal end to mandatory retirement and the rise of a new way to save for retirement through the 401(k)-type plan promised workers two good options: in old age they could continue working or could retire with adequate income. But forty years later, most workers can't expect even one of those options.

The rise in old-age inequality and old-age poverty is rooted in the prolonged period of stagnating wages and job quality. Over the past thirty years, living standards have fallen for a large share of elderly workers because increasingly inadequate retirement-income sources will fall short for more workers to maintain pre-retirement living standards. Researchers at Boston College compute a retirement adequacy indicator every year, and it always falls.[2]

The reality of failure contradicts the widely repeated myth that Americans are living longer and have easier jobs. The well-off are doing well, of course, but the boomer generation and the generations following will do relatively worse than their parents and grandparents did in older age.

Since 1980, wage patterns created economic inequality: the earnings of the top 1 percent increased 158 percent, whereas hourly compensation for most workers increased by less than 12 percent.[3] Wealth inequality trends are even worse.[4] Those in the top 1 percent in 2022—that's about 1.3 million households out of 130 million—have 22 percent of the country's wealth in comparison to 7 percent in 1978. You could fit those elite households in either the small neighborhood of Soho or Greenwich Village in New York or Presidio Heights in San Francisco.

The American retirement system contributes to the growing and extreme distribution of American wealth: high-paid workers save a lot more, they get the bulk of available tax breaks for saving, and they get high rates of return on their assets. As the economist Thomas Piketty has pointed out in his best-selling book, on average, financial market rates of return have exceeded wage increases and economic growth over the past four decades.[5]

The once-sturdy pension and retirement systems that emerged after World War II were built by policy makers, unions, and employers. They secured middle-class stability for generations of older Americans who were covered by these pensions. Even so, about 40 percent of families were untouched by them. In contrast, the retirement plans that emerged during and after the Reagan era were mainly guided by the financial industry. The 1980s ushered in dramatic shifts in retirement plans and policies, marked by the rise of do-it-yourself, individual-directed, market-based, voluntary retirement, as well as the now-ubiquitous 401(k) and Individual Retirement Account.

Retirement itself is a dynamic ecosystem that involves work, Social Security, workplace retirement plans, tax codes, and culture. The good retirement systems are flexible and can weather disturbances like recessions and politics. A good retirement system helps employers and workers both. In contrast, the current retirement system is driven by the financial industry's profit interests and the needs of upper-income workers. The current retirement system is also part of the reason people's old-age security is upside down. Despite heaps of hype about the power of the market and the individual to shape a retirement future, huge shifts in the design of retirement plans have made it more difficult for older folks to stop working when they want to.

Economists Joseph Quinn and Kevin E. Cahill demonstrated the cold hard truth that saving for retirement in individual accounts during a prolonged period of low interest rates can be a disaster that a worker might never recover from. And for many years since the late

1970s, when the do-it-yourself retirement savings system was put in place, rates of return on safe assets like government bonds were low. The do-it-yourself pension system divided people into those with access to sophisticated investment portfolios and managers and those who stuck their savings in ultrasafe assets.[6] The former were the winners and got much higher risk-adjusted returns than the latter, who played it safe. And this divide is not about personal preference; it is mostly about luck and structural advantages. Allow me to explain. Ordinary workers who have a retirement plan at work—which is just half of the workforce at any point in time—likely have do-it-yourself 401(k)-type plans, not the traditional defined-benefit (DB) pensions, whose assets were pooled and managed by professionals. In the defined-benefit plan, interest rates and financial market volatility could be smoothed over and hedged through diversification. The DB professionals also used the sheer size of the pooled funds to pay lower investment fees. In self-directed 401(k)-type plans, portfolio holders pay higher fees and have less diversification. Lower-income workers and women are more likely to have their money invested in lower-return assets.

The differences in investment strategies mean that traditional DB plans earn much higher rates of return than individual accounts earn now. In DB plans, all workers get the same return because all workers have professional money managers who are legally required to earn the highest risk- and fee-adjusted return to their pension funds.[7] And DB plans mandate that all workers participate. If you are working for an employer with a defined-benefit plan, you are automatically enrolled, and the employer automatically saves for you. In contrast, the current defined-contribution (DC) or 401(k)-styled system is a voluntary, commercial, and individually directed system. Workers decide whether they participate in a 401(k)-type or Individual Retirement Account (IRA) plan. Therefore, saving for retirement is voluntary. And as you might expect, lower-income workers and workers with unsteady employment and circumstances tend to opt out and not save for retirement. More importantly, many employers also decide not to be bothered by sponsoring or contributing to a retirement plan for their employees. These DC plans are self-directed, so even if people do save, they don't invest as well as a professional would—individuals tend to buy financial assets when the values are rising and to panic sell when values fall. And the plans are commercial—the investment fees are retail and often quite high. The American voluntary, commercial, and individually directed retirement system has created the predictable disaster of inadequate retirement savings and massive inequality.

The current do-it-yourself savings system was based on the false hope that interest rates would always be much higher than they turned out to be.

The essential truth about older people having to work longer is that it helps employers. Employers are better off because the increase in labor supply drives down wages, working conditions, and business costs.[8] Working longer reduces retirement time and helps employers maximize their profits. People working longer may save costs for governments—but not as much as one would think. We are compelled to ask: Where is quality of life in this arithmetic?

Advising people to work longer when retirement-income security fails serves businesses' bottom lines, but the advice is profoundly problematic for the economy and workers. First, the work-longer push makes life harder for most workers, and it falls particularly heavily on low- and middle-income workers and on those without advanced degrees. Older workers, in general, face more difficulties keeping and finding a job relative to younger workers. Second, Americans already have fewer expected retirement years than workers in other rich countries.[9] Third, retirees, even if they are physically able to work, overwhelmingly enjoy having time for themselves and want to be healthy and autonomous before they die.[10] Having autonomy and dignity in old age depends largely on your finances when you retire. Even if you don't retire, having a comfortable and secure financial situation when you are older reduces stress levels at work and reduces subordination for employers because they know a worker has a solid fallback.

Mitigating that desperation to work at older ages was the very intent of government policies that created pensions in the first place. Federal policy moved away from seeking to help workers and retirees in the 1980s and moved toward encouraging elders to work more, create their own retirement plans, or live on less pension income. The US was the first among rich nations to ban mandatory retirement, to institute laws against age discrimination, and to develop job-training programs for older people (on paper at least, because the training programs don't work well for older people). It is a telling sign of conflict to come that the labor movement had always been ambivalent about lifting mandatory retirement ages because the move creates new supplies of labor—or in political economy terms, increases the reserve army of labor. The move toward older people working more weakens political pressure to expand Social Security and employer retirement plans. Therefore, it makes sense, in contrast to the US labor movement's high-profile stance in the women's and civil rights movements, labor was not at the vanguard of age antidiscrimination laws and ending mandatory retirement.[11]

US labor's ambivalent stance toward federal laws banning mandatory retirement also makes sense. The US labor movement always has had to contend with American employers' relentless search for cheaper sources of labor; the arc of American economic history rests on surpluses of capital and land and relative shortages of labor. The American employer was already ahead of other rich nations in employing women, immigrants, and children.[12] It is logical that employers' search for excess labor supply would extend to elders.[13] Before Social Security was passed in 1935, most men worked until they died, with no retirement to speak of. That dreary fact changed as workers wanted more of a life, pressured politicians for improvements, organized into unions, and sought cultural changes to make dignified old age expected and normalized.[14]

During this Recession-era reform, to help older workers retire, railroad workers secured pensions, and unions led the charge in pushing for early retirement and seniority rules that helped older employees transition to easier jobs. Social Security legitimized the concept of retirement for all workers. The American folk singer Joe Glazer wrote the song "Too Old to Work and Too Young to Die" for the autoworkers' 1959 strike against Chrysler, capturing the labor movement's push to make retirement a normal part of life for poor and middle-class workers, not just top earners: "Your boss gets a pension when he is too old, / You helped him retire—you're out in the cold."[15] Unions expanded occupational pensions that often allowed workers in particularly arduous jobs, such as coal mining and steelmaking, to retire before Social Security eligibility began at age 62. But retirement wasn't just for the blue-collar worker in a gritty job. Andrew Carnegie endowed pensions for college professors when he funded TIAA, and K–12 teachers, nurses, and insurance salespeople all constructed retirement plans and expectations.

So, in the post–World War II era, unions negotiated for (and many nonunion employers adopted) traditional defined-benefit pensions. As I have explained, DB plans encourage retirement at certain ages: they typically end benefit accrual at age 62 or 65, allowing workers to choose when to retire. The best feature of these plans is their goal of smoothing the path to retirement and minimizing uncertainty. For this reason, they were especially common in jobs requiring extreme mental, physical, and routine labor, where workers might age out earlier, like firefighting, nursing, auto assembly, and construction. Likewise, some defined-benefit plans provided a larger benefit before the Social Security claim age to pave the transition from work to retirement. Still, most retirement decisions are a product of circumstance, not of employees carefully weighing costs and benefits. As numerous studies make clear, most older workers and recent retirees are bullied or gently pushed out of work through early retirement offers, layoffs, demotions, and outright firings. These postwar policies pro-retirement plans and policies were electric. Workers of all incomes started planning to retire before they died. These plans were a huge breakthrough in legitimating retirement and equalizing retirement time.

At the same time, by the 1960s, Americans were beginning to acknowledge age discrimination as a civil rights violation. But the Age Discrimination in Employment Act, passed in 1967, protected workers aged 40–65. Court cases challenged the justification for not protecting those 65 and older, citing a lack of evidence that age 65 was any meaningful indication of work capability. The advocates argued that employers were mistaken in factoring in a worker's age when deciding who to hire, train, promote, and pay well because age was an unreliable signal of quality at best, and it perpetuated bigotry at worst. But as I argue later, just because employers can't legally use an arbitrary age to decide who can work or not does not mean that work capability or the desire to work does not change as we age.

In legally banning age discrimination, policy makers were laying the groundwork for a political and pro-business consensus that working longer was good economic policy. Working longer became a convenient off-the-shelf and off-the-cuff catchall concept solving the nation's inadequate funding of retirement. Not all advocates for ending age discrimination viewed work as a substitute for pensions. The AARP, the Gray Panthers, and labor-union-affiliated retiree groups advocated for an end to age bigotry and a dignified old age with secure income and decent opportunities, including work. To these advocates, demands for better jobs, access to jobs, good pensions, and well-funded Social Security were complements, not substitutes. But in 1982, an influential official in the Republican Reagan administration person pushed forward a one-sided future that work would substitute for good pensions.

The Reagan administration's active measures to cut taxes and shrink government came with glowing views of older workers. Malcolm Lovell, President Reagan's deputy labor secretary, warned Congress that smoothing the way for elders to work made practical budgetary sense. With employers backing away from workplace pensions and Congress scheduling cuts in Social Security, the elderly would have to work longer.[16] Congress soon complied by passing aggressive laws prohibiting age discrimination and phasing out mandatory retirement at a certain age, though this was slower for key executives, pilots, and university professors. Evidence for what workers needed or wanted was not relevant; older workers saved Congress from funding pensions.

The Reagan-era policy shift and other trends conspired to lengthen work ages and expand the elderly labor pool. Economists reasoned along with employers and lawmakers that cutting Social Security benefits by raising the retirement age would gently nudge people to work longer. And the nudge, or push, seemed to have worked: since

1983, employment rates of older workers have risen substantially. Further study has shown the stick of financial hardship, increasing levels of educational attainment, and women's economic emergence all contributed to the elderly working more.[17] Older women in particular were more educated, faced better opportunities, and filed for more divorces. And the rise of pushing, prodding, and sometimes welcoming older people into the labor force coincided with the rise of finance, the decline of unions, and the shift toward more market-driven, do-it-yourself retirement systems.

Redefining Pensions: The Shift to Market-Driven Defined-Contribution Plans

In the 1980s, defined-benefit plans began to morph into a defined-contribution model as market-driven 401(k)-type plans emerged—and this alongside other pension-eroding trends. Defined-contribution plans are not insurance like Social Security and DB plans are. The 401(k) model requires workers to self-finance their risk of old age. As part of this deal, in 1979, Americans were offered tax incentives for individuals—mainly higher-paid management—to put part of their paycheck into a 401(k) to prepare for future risk rather than relying on Social Security insurance. The idea was that a person would accumulate enough assets in voluntary, do-it-yourself market-based individual funds, but these were not well regulated. It was akin to eliminating health insurance and giving people tax breaks to save for possible kidney transplants or difficult births.

So by the early 1980s, politics and policies had changed. In 1983, retirement was on the block when Congress cut Social Security benefits by raising the so-called full retirement age from 65 to 67. This age increase may not seem big on its face, but it represents a cut in benefits of between 10 percent and 13 percent for people collecting at all ages. In 2022, people born in 1960 were 62 and facing a 30 percent lower Social Security benefit than people born after 1930. I know 60-year-olds barely hanging on to their consultant jobs or who are bound to be laid off in the next recession, and I know they won't have enough at retirement.

Cutting benefits by raising the retirement age is especially hard for people forced to claim benefits before age 70.[18] The average benefit for new Social Security beneficiaries claiming at age 62 is about $13,000 per year, which was about the poverty line for individuals in 2020.[19] The Urban Institute warned that the future cuts in benefits would put more 62-year-olds at risk of poverty because replacement rates at age 62 would fall to about 25 percent of pre-retirement earnings rather than over 30 percent. This means that someone making the average wage and claiming Social Security benefits at age 62 would live below the poverty line. If the Reagan-era cuts hadn't happened, the average benefit at age 62 would be $15,600 per year, 20 percent higher—a substantial increase in benefits for a household with so little income.

Ted Benna is the famous employer consultant who was key to spreading the do-it-yourself retirement plan, showing employers how to use the tax code to phase out traditional DB pensions and use the cheaper 401(k) model. His blueprint spread among the pension-providing universe of employers. But the anointed "father" of the 401(k), a thoughtful man, has since called the tax loophole a "monster." The 401(k)—note it is named after a section of the tax code and is not called, for example, the American Retirement Plan—Benna said, is "a plan for the wealthy and one that leaves behind most Americans."[20] Indeed Benna saw what we all saw. Larger private employers who sponsored a retirement plan—and most medium-sized and small firms do not—gradually replaced defined-benefit plans with cheaper defined-contribution, 401(k)-type plans. And new employers either instituted a 401(k) or nothing at all. The 401(k) did not expand coverage; it only replaced more generous plans.

And in contrast to DB plans that max out benefits at age 65, defined-contribution accounts accrue benefits indefinitely. Vast research has concluded that the waning of defined-benefit plans and the waxing of defined-contribution plans has also induced people to work longer. Autoworkers with DB pensions retire without shame or defensiveness after thirty years of work. If they had only a 401(k), they might feel pressure to continue working to accumulate more and more.[21] The nation's weak workplace retirement system, shrinking Social Security, and anti-age-discrimination laws expanded employer access to older workers.

In short, using carrots and sticks, the US government since the Reagan administration has sought to encourage—and prod—work at older ages in five ways. First, the US leads the OECD member countries in laws against age discrimination, well-intended policies that have also promoted more elderly work. Second, the 1983 Social Security reform gradually increased the Social Security full retirement age from 65 to 67 for people born between 1933 and 1945—equivalent to an across-the-board 13 percent cut. Third, the Social Security earnings test—$1 of benefits was withheld for every $2 of earnings over a certain amount—was relaxed in 2000, so people could work and keep more of their Social Security benefits.[22] Fourth, Social Security increased benefits for a those who can postpone collecting Social Security benefits. These so-called delayed retirement credits increase benefits by a whopping 8 percent a year after full retirement (which is age 67 for people born in 1960). This means that by waiting, that is, by delaying collecting by one year, the monthly benefit goes up by a guaranteed 5 percent–8 percent per year between age 62, the earliest age to collect, and age 70, the age at which monthly benefits don't increase. To lawmakers, this present for waiting was supposed to serve as an incentive to keep working! It's the best deal on the planet for those who can work and wait. And it is a great deal for wealthy retirees who have other income to live on. But the reality is that people who work past 62 and on to age 70 rarely get the benefit of the generous delayed retirement credit. Only 6.3 percent of retired workers claimed benefits at age 70.[23]

Fifth, Congress incentivized defined-contribution plans that eventually displaced defined-benefit plans, which had promoted retirement. The shift to defined-contribution plans likely hinders retirement because people can accumulate more assets while they are working. It is a difficult choice for people to draw down their nest egg, so working longer delays drawdowns.

Fast-forward to 2000, and we find more dramatic changes reversing retirement progress. That year, Congress passed the Freedom to Work Act, penalizing retirement before age 70—the new age at which Americans could begin collecting full benefits under Social Security. With these major shifts, the United States stands apart from the European Union and OECD members in its treatment of retirement age and benefits.

Also in 2000, Congress gave even more generous incentives to prod workers to delay claiming Social Security until age 70—a lifetime benefits increase of 76 percent for people who delay claiming for eight years between age 62 and 70. But only 8 percent of Americans get this reward because most people can't wait to collect their Social Security benefits. The reality is they need the money sooner. The 8 percent of claimants who can afford to wait are more fortunate. They are more likely to be the well-heeled, who have reason to believe they will live longer than most.

As of 2020, workers still in defined-benefit plans—which included public-sector employees, pharmaceutical companies, contracted defense sectors, and other unionized workplaces—are not experiencing significant improvements in their plans. Most employers have mixed feelings about defined-benefit plans. They are useful tools to encourage older workers to retire because they allow employers to phase out older workers in a less clumsy, controversial, or anxiety-provoking manner. Workers stay longer in jobs that have only 401(k)-type defined-contribution plans. Workers can accumulate more benefits, and because defined-contribution plans are not paid out in the form of annuities, the fear of running out of money keeps people in their jobs longer than those who have defined-benefit plans.[24] If more businesses and employers followed this path back to traditional defined-benefit plans, many more elderly Americans would be far more economically secure. If more businesses and employers followed this path back to traditional defined-benefit plans, many more employers could more easily transition out older workers.

How Did the Working-Longer Consensus Replace Good Pensions?

It should be no surprise that the roots of the working-longer consensus can be traced to the 1980s, when policy makers, pundits, and politicians promoted working longer as a solution to the harsh reality of Congress cutting Social Security benefits and employers eroding pensions throughout that decade.[25] At the time, patching together paid work at older ages seemed a prudent response to these broad rollbacks.

But four myths seeped into the culture that served employers' and politicians' desires for more labor supply and less opposition to pension cuts, obscuring critical thinking about the approach. The first myth is that people choose when they retire—in truth, older workers are usually pushed out before they are ready. The second myth advertises that work is good for older people—but the reality is that older workers are more likely to find themselves stuck in low-paid jobs without benefits. The third myth purports that because we all are living longer, we should work more. But those longevity improvements are not spread evenly across race, class, and gender. Longevity gains in recent decades have all gone to the top half of the income distribution, a predominantly white and male cohort. The fourth myth insists that working longer makes people substantially more financially prepared for retirement; this sounds logical enough, but it's just not true, the evidence shows. Because older workers are usually low paid, often have mentally and physically taxing jobs, get no pension benefits, and collect Social Security while they are working, work in old age not only does not add to a person's wealth; work can hasten ill health because it reduces time for exercise, sleep, and other forms of self-care. People who work until 70 are not much richer, their monthly Social Security benefits are not larger, and working might have even made them sicker.

These four myths conspire to manufacture the working-longer consensus, and the next four chapters tackle them in depth. First, however, let's better understand the origins and growth of the consensus.

The working-longer consensus, a term I coined, is an homage to the pro-market Washington Consensus of the late 1980s, which emerged from institutions with DC headquarters—including the International Monetary Fund, the World Bank, the US Treasury—and was supported by American academics. The Washington Consensus rolled up the disease, the cause, and the cure into one big techno-cratic market-based set of economic policies that would cure sluggish economies that were supposedly stymied by "excessive" government regulation.[26]

Like the Washington Consensus, the working-longer consensus involves the promotion of neoliberal and technocratic ways to prod older people to work, to cure what is diagnosed as a "sluggish econ-omy," caused by aging populations and too-generous pensions. This consensus promises that persuading elders to work more will help a nation's poor retirees while also solving labor shortages and cut-ting government spending. The working-longer consensus promises healthier elders and richer economies, as well as improved economic performance. Making older people work longer is billed as the ulti-mate free lunch—all winners, no losers. But there is no such thing as a free lunch. Making older people work longer creates very real, specific losers, especially among older people who have a harder time meeting employers' physical, mental, and time demands. Meanwhile, according to the evidence, these elderly workers end up treading in the financial waters. Working-longer consensus policies have the same key ingredients—reduced pensions and longer work-ing lives.

Powerfully augmenting these messages and myths, the influen-tial 1999 book *Social Security and Retirement around the World* blamed generous pensions for elders' early departures from the labor force. The authors based their claim on a correlation between nations with low elder labor-force participation rates and nations that allowed people to collect Social Security at younger ages. Cutting pensions, they concluded, would get older people to work more. This book is a major source of the myth that pensions can be cut without losses.[27]

In 2019, the World Economic Forum and the consulting firm Mer-cer were still promoting the working-longer consensus by recom-mending that most nations cut benefits by raising the age at which workers can claim pensions. The *Melbourne Mercer Report*, as it be-came known, even recommended that workers in Japan and the US work longer, even though workers in those countries already work longer than others in OECD member countries. Yet the report neglected a key fact: Japanese and American elders also have the highest elder poverty rates, suggesting that working-longer policies correlate with weaker national commitments to decreasing elder poverty.[28]

But there is also growing resistance to the working-longer push. In September 2019, the Bank of Japan pushed back on the working-longer consensus. At a central bank meeting, a Bank of Japan official argued that Japan's economy in fact suffers from too many elderly people working in low-productivity, part-time jobs—and that meager pensions have driven Japan's elderly into austerity because workers saved way too much in fear of old age, and workers and senior alike do not consume enough to fuel the economy. What the Japanese economy needed instead, the bank official argued, was higher pensions and better jobs for the elderly.[29]

Workers and labor movements have fought the working-longer push, too. In January 2020, the French General Federation of Labor led a nationwide strike opposing President Macron's bid to reform French pensions. Macron clung to his plan for two years before finally caving and backing down in June 2021. But in 2023, more than a year after Macron won a tough election battle for president, he was bracing for more protests as he put through the pension reform. In spring 2023, protest trash fires and work-stop actions popped up in France to protest the government's raising of the retirement age.[30]

In Italy, pension reform attempts have frequently inspired strenuous resistance. The Italian populist Five Star and Northern League movements gained strength from resisting the Italian government's raising of the retirement age in 2011.[31] Edoardo Campanella, an Italian economist and Harvard fellow, pushed back against this populist resistance, arguing that underfunded Italian pensions were overly generous and that the only solution was for older Italians to work more—instead of making retirement work, his real focus is making retirees work.[32] This particular economist may not have been famous, but the view is mainstream among technocrats. Italian voters must not have squared the work-longer message with the Italian economy's failure to fully employ prime-aged adults.[33] The Italian far-right, populist government has not advocated cutting pensions.

Prime Minister Giorgia Meloni has not gone anywhere near the rising Italian cost of pensions, although Italy has the oldest population in the OECD.

The point I am making is this consensus among elites, technocrats, and lawmakers that working longer is a comprehensive, costless fix is political dynamite among ordinary people. The working-longer consensus aims to "fix" inadequate retirement funding by eliminating retirement. That's like "fixing" the car by junking it.

Unintended Consequences of the Active Aging Movement

Seniors and older workers may be experiencing the unintended consequences of what some might consider "progress" in aging. Policies in the US that promote more work for seniors are bolstered by thirty years of well-intentioned "active aging" or "forever young" movements—the rash of advice that exercise and well-chosen hobbies can stave off decline. In her book *Never Say Die*, Susan Jacoby challenges the comforting myth that aging doesn't have negative consequences on health or mental acuity. The chance of experiencing cognitive decline is related almost entirely to age. Believing that we can stay forever young has helped justify cutting benefits by raising the retirement age. As I have argued, what appeared to be a good thing on the surface—prohibiting mandatory retirement ages in most occupations—was the opposite when there was no corresponding move to guarantee pensions or improve the jobs that older people have. The freedom to work has come to mean having no other choice but to work.

The American approach of prodding older workers has not made US elders better off than their counterparts abroad. In fact, the differences are striking. About 23 percent of American elders are in poverty, while the rate in France is half that. Leaving aside developing countries, only Japan's elders work more than seniors in the US. As it happens, Japan and the US also have comparable elder poverty rates and startlingly similar elder labor-force participation rates. The evidence bears out a disturbing and surprising reality: elder poverty is positively correlated with working longer, despite the myths

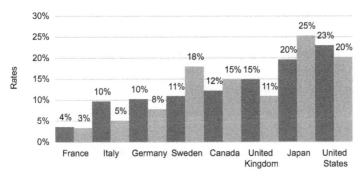

FIGURE 2.1 Working More Is Associated with Higher Elder Poverty

Note: The OECD uses a relative standard and the US an absolute, which is much lower than the national standard. OECD (2020), Poverty rate (indicator), https://data.oecd.org/emp/labour-force -participation-rate.htm. The poverty rate is the ratio of the number of people (in a given age group) whose income falls below the poverty line; taken as half the median household income of the total population.

propagated by the working-longer movement that laboring into your old age reduces hardship (fig. 2.1). Creating a reserve army of gray labor goes hand in hand with tolerating poverty among the elderly. A reserve army is often made up of desperate people.

Beyond the differences in elder poverty in OECD countries lie some commonalities. One is that the average work life is about thirty-five to forty years for men and about thirty years for women—but there is a great deal of variation by class or socioeconomic status. Pensions are typically funded at three tiers: by the state; by work-related retirement plans that are often heavily subsidized indirectly by government; and at a smaller scale by charity, family donations, and personal wealth. The US pioneered the ironic notion of earnings as a source of "retirement" income; since the 1980s, "retirement" has been work.

Another commonality among people is what economists call the income effect—as people get more income and after they have met basic needs, they want more of everything they like: better health, more years of life, more paid time off, more flexibility. But how countries have responded to growing income and wealth is quite different, with the US, again, being an outlier. Following World War II, as almost every demographic group in America began living longer, the US enacted policies so that children and older men worked less. But since the 1980s and the working-longer consensus, retirement—the ultimate paid time off—has been contested and eroded. Other nations used their riches to expand leisure time to its citizen—the US fell behind and opted to expand the labor force instead.

Why Focus on Older Workers?

It is quite stunning how much older workers matter to the economy. Older workers over age 65 are projected to grow by more than 4.8 million, which accounts for most (58 percent!) of the 8.3 million jobs predicted to be created between 2021 and 2031.[34] And older workers, and how they are treated, are gaining influence in the labor market. From 1995 to 2020, the share of workers older than 55 has more than doubled, to nearly 24 percent from 12 percent.[35]

If we as a country don't do something about creating better pensions, most older people will work or will seek work under circumstances that guarantee them to have weak bargaining power. The result, because of spillovers, is less bargaining power for everyone.

In other words, the sheer size of the baby boomer cohort, coupled with their insecure pensions, means that the quality and balance of power in the American labor market depend on the circumstances of older workers. When those 5 million older adults enter the labor market, bargaining power will shift to employers because those adults won't have enough retirement income to meet basic needs. Older workers' lack of retirement readiness will shape employment patterns, the direction of public policy, and the strength of workers' bargaining power for all American workers, old and young.

The Working-Longer Consensus Is Not a Plan

As we've seen throughout this chapter, the working-longer consensus has etched itself into our nation's retirement policy for forty years. But despite its ubiquity, it is not well thought out, and its myths are causing harm to older workers and society. The working-longer consensus is also a major front in social welfare debates. Since the early 1980s, the consensus has steadily eroded the long-standing social compact that, after a lifetime of work, a person deserves some years toward the end of their life without work. The working-longer consensus makes some accommodations for a small minority of people who cannot work (e.g., because of disability), but proponents insist that most elders must either have private wealth or work. As we've seen, this seismic shift in American retirement policy rests on dangerous myths about working through old age—that work is good for older folks and good for society. The evidence demonstrates otherwise, pointing to an urgent need for sweeping change.

In the following pages, I challenge the idea that people should work longer to make up for inadequate pensions. All adults should be able to work if they want to, but the conditions and terms of that work matter. Working because you must leads to quite different results in pay, conditions, and dignity than does working with a good fallback position.

The following chapters examine the false presumption that seniors choose whether to work or not. The reality is that some people have more free choice than others. We will find out who works and who doesn't, who must work, and who has a real choice to work because they have good pensions. In short, we find those who can work for "love" and who must work for "money."

PART II

The Hidden Costs of
Working Longer

3

Working Longer Is Often
Not a Choice

Jeff Goethelf is an enterprising 47-year-old software engineer and author of *Forever Employable*. The self-published book advises older people to post instructional videos to YouTube and hire themselves out as experts.[1] In this engineer's view, every older person has a choice to work for pay. But the truth is, only a small fortunate portion of people aged 62–70 (very few people work beyond age 70) can choose whether to retire or keep working. The share of older people who seem to genuinely love to work because they can afford not to is surprisingly small. In this chapter, I show the numbers that reveal the truth of what is really happening to people who say that they want to work and to retire in a sentence whose contradictions can take your breath away: "I want to work full-time in retirement."

Who Gets to Retire and Who Has to Work?

Imagine you walk into a party with a hundred people between the ages of 62 and 70. You mix and mingle and find out who is working and learn about their finances. I assembled such a get-together but with a big government data set. My coauthors and I "met" thousands of people in a computer database of the University of Michigan's Health and Retirement Survey.

We did this data analysis because we wanted to understand why older people were working and how they were doing in retirement. What we found was disconcerting. Only eleven out of one hundred partygoers were financially ready to retire but were still working. By "financially ready," I mean that they would have enough income and assets to maintain their pre-retirement living standards or stay out of de facto poverty even if they stopped working. Because those fortunate few have a good fallback position, I categorize them as working voluntarily—some positive aspect of work motivates them to stay on the job. That is, they probably like their jobs. As a group, these eleven older people among the hundred partygoers are the most educated of the group. They have well-paying jobs and likely control the pace and content of their work. This is not to say the money does not matter to them, that they would work for free, but because they could retire with enough money to maintain their living standard, their primary motive to work is engagement, status, or some other positive thing.

Another ten people at my virtual party are also financially secure and retired. They resemble the archetypical retirees from advertisements on sailboats, vacation cruises, golf courses, or buying apples at small-town farmers' markets.[2] The bottom line here is that only 21 percent of Americans aged 62–70 have enough money to maintain their standard of living in retirement; ten of them are retired, and eleven are working. That bears repeating: Only 10 percent of people aged 62–70 are retired and financially stable. Eleven percent could retire and financially maintain their living standards, but they are still working.

Back to our pretend party representing Americans aged 62–70. The rest of the seventy-nine seniors—all who had worked for pay sometime in their lives—in the room, or 79 percent of Americans aged 62–70, are not faring well. The majority, 51 percent, are retired but can't maintain their pre-retirement standard of living. And the rest, 28 percent, are working and cannot afford to retire. I worry a lot about this ignored 79 percent. Much too much has been said about the 11 percent of seniors who love their jobs and keep on working. Over twice as many older workers are working because they have to, and the majority of elders aren't working and are living on income living below their pre-retirement standard of living, even after accounting for reduced transportation and other work-related expenses. And the research shows that a lower standard of living after retirement is correlated with having the lowest levels of mental well-being, even if one's health is stable. These seniors are in worse shape if they are forced to give up work because of layoffs, age discrimination, or something else. The financially unstable retiree has low levels of well-being because of financial uncertainty.[3]

Older people are financially unprepared for retirement, and I have established that most older people are surviving on Social Security. Even if some people in their household work, older people still cannot afford to maintain the standard of living they had achieved in their late 50s. Many of these people are living with incomes up to 200 percent of the federal poverty level. If 200 percent of the poverty line sounds like a lot, think again. The official federal poverty level is so low—about $12,000 for an individual in 2020. Twice that is $24,000 per year, or $2,000 per month. To review: At our party of a hundred people representing all Americans aged 62–70, ten are retired with enough money; eleven are working even though they could retire with enough money; fifty-one are retired without enough money; and twenty-eight are working because they presumably don't have enough money to retire on. Seventy-nine people—the vast majority—do not have more than $24,000 a year to retire on. Scary stuff.

Americans over 50 or so are very worried and tense about their work and financial future. Most people won't have enough money to retire, and most people are forced into retirement before they are ready.[4] The gut-felt reality comes up against the cultural fantasy created by the working-longer consensus that no one needs to worry; if you don't have enough money at retirement age, you can just work longer. But most people cannot work longer. When norms and expectations clash with reality, it induces anxiety.[5]

Even more revealing, 19 percent of respondents in their 50s answered yes to an oxymoronic survey question during the pandemic: "Will you work in retirement?" That response was more than double the 8 percent reported in May 2020. You read that right—"work in retirement." I am guessing neither the respondent nor the questioner blinked at the contradictory phrase. Working is not retirement. But the doublespeak lives on in America.

The Contested Ages of 62–70

The Upjohn Institute's Beth Truesdale and Harvard's Lisa Berkman come to similar conclusions in their 2022 book focusing on a younger group, workers in their 50s, and find what people who age know viscerally. Many people in the age group—ten years younger than the group I focused on earlier—already face unstable and unfriendly labor markets.[6] My research shows that many people between ages 62 and 70 cobble together paid work and retirement leisure (table 3.1). In this contested and confusing age zone, older people are still able to be employed for pay, yet know that many of their best salaries, promotions, and chances for career growth are behind them.

For the rest of this chapter, we take a closer look at one of the four groups of elderly Americans. Who works for love or money, and who has adequate retirement income? Here is the summary of the four groups again.

- The first group (11 percent) can afford to retire but *choose* to keep working because they want to. They may be taking advantage of outplacement organizations like Encore and Career Pivot that link older workers—mostly white-collar professionals—to interesting jobs.
- The second group (10 percent) has retired and can afford to stop working altogether. They are enjoying their retirement, economic security, and well-being.

TABLE 3.1 Most people aged 62–70 do not have enough retirement income, and many work because they must

People aged 62–70	Retired (61%)	Working (39%)
Can afford to retire (21%)	10% (happy and free from work)	11% (enjoying their job)
Cannot afford to retire (79%)	51% (scraping by in retirement)	28% (working for money)

Source: Ghilarducci, Papadopoulos, and Webb, "The Illusory Benefit of Working Longer."

- The third group (51 percent) cannot afford to stop working but were pushed into retirement, typically through layoffs or early buyouts.
- The fourth group (28 percent) cannot afford to retire and must keep working. They have no real choice.

These working seniors in the first and fourth groups, but especially the fourth group, are the focus of this chapter. These 28 people at our fictional party are working because they can't afford to retire—because without a job, they would be below 200 percent of the poverty level, living off just $24,000 a year. This group, their economic precarity—and how that fragile status affects bargaining power for all workers—represents a huge opportunity for better public policy.

Working for Love versus Money

Some older workers love their jobs. I mentioned President Biden and Senator McConnell before. In the pandemic we relied on Dr. Anthony Fauci, who is now the former director of the National Institute of Allergy and Infectious Diseases and was the chief medical adviser to the president during COVID-19. He announced his retirement at the age of 80. Some financially well-off people might be driven to keep working. And then there is someone I admire, but bristle at the attention given to, the 100-year-old yoga teacher who wondrously declared, "I start every day an optimist," featured in a 2016 AARP magazine story.[7]

And then there are the amazing seniors featured in the wildly popular 2019 book *Successful Aging*, by Daniel J. Levitin. He describes a 90-year-old scientist happily researching brain chemistry.[8] To some, it might seem that we live in an age of senior glory, a "golden age," so to speak. Many seniors might find meaning in their work and joy in the engagement. However, older people who genuinely choose to work—those who work for pay when they can afford to retire—have vastly different circumstances from those who are working because they cannot afford to retire.

Beyond the famous few, most older workers do not control the pace or content of their jobs. Even after a lifetime of paying their dues, they are not in the driver's seat. There is some evidence compounding this: under certain conditions of job stress, hierarchy, microaggressions, and prejudice, working longer can shorten people's lives and make them sick. Very few people are working in their late 60s and 70s for sheer pleasure; more are working because their retirement income is low and unstable. Because of this, policies must be aimed at that majority. And the temperature of excitement about working-senior wonders should be dialed down.

There are hundreds of economic studies on what encourages an older person to keep working. Most presume that older workers "drive the bus" and are the masters of their own universes. In this typical conception, economists suppose that people make decisions to "maximize" their lifetime wealth, health, and enjoyment of leisure and work. Using these "free choice" frameworks, most economists downplay older people's lack of choices and the looming uncertainties about being fired or becoming injured or sick.[9]

Instead, the labor market is a dynamic set of bargaining relationships defined by power. That is why my research team posed the question: Which older people are working because they have little to no fallback? Having a weak fallback means they have little bargaining power and are employed on the employer's terms, not theirs. Older people with good pensions and high Social Security benefits can walk away from a bad job and bargain for the terms they want. Those with low and insufficient retirement income must work even if they want to retire, don't enjoy their work, or if their work makes them sick. Through this power analysis, we see the people who are working between the ages of 62 and 70 who don't have enough money to retire.

This regrettable reality has labor-market repercussions beyond this sizable group of older workers. More older workers toiling in poverty means less leverage for seniors in the larger labor market. And these dynamics of precarity and leverage in turn deepen the divide between those who can work for love and those who must labor on for survival. When older workers can walk away from their job, employers need to lure them to stay with higher pay and improved working conditions. Workers who have good pensions are in a better position to get employers (including shareholders and consumers) to pay more for their work. Thus, the social and political question of who among the elderly can retire and who must keep working, and under which terms, is driven by the existence of healthy pensions and retirement income. And retirement security is not doing well. When retirement security erodes, older middle-class workers can become downwardly mobile and part of the working poor.

Remarkably, given the extent of senior economic precarity and inability to retire, there has been scant research on what motivates elderly workers. When my research team began studying this in 2008, as the Great Recession was poised to take a mean toll on the oldest boomers, we were stunned to find that nobody had investigated why so many older people are still working or whether they stay on the job out of financial necessity.

Since then, a few influential studies have cropped up, but they make some problematic assumptions. Two studies—a 2020 article in a prominent academic journal and a 2016 Boston College study—advocate that people work longer and collect higher Social Security monthly benefits by postponing claiming benefits until an older age, up to 70 if they can hold out.[10] Both studies made a crucial assumption that turned out to be wrong. They assumed that people collect Social Security after they retire, which is simply untrue. The reality is that many seniors are working and collecting Social Security. Why don't they work and then collect to get a higher monthly benefit? From their wages and their other income, my coauthors and I conclude that, because of low wages and high expenses, they collect Social Security benefits while they are working to cobble together a living.

In the Boston College study, people with lower levels of education were more likely to choose to retire too early. The study emphasized individual choice over systemic analysis, conveying the idea that people had to make better decisions, including to work longer and claim their Social Security later, so that all would be fine in retirement. But the study assumed that only retired people claim Social Security and that when older people work, they continue to pile up savings in their

401(k)s rather than spend down retirement assets. Both assumptions are wrong.

On the first count, many academics, and even the Social Security Administration, in the way they communicate material to the public, conflate claiming Social Security with retiring. The reality of the labor market is that almost all workers over age 66 are collecting Social Security. Because many of them make low wages, they are likely collecting Social Security to supplement their low pay.[11] In fact, Social Security effectively subsidizes low-wage employers. The implications of low-wage older workers collecting Social Security means that cutting Social Security for people who claim benefits before age 70 would create perverse inequality. How so? Higher-income elderly folks, who can expect a longer life, can wait until age 70 to get a much higher monthly benefit. Lower-income people cannot wait.

Readers at this point might wonder why I go to the trouble to use data to find out how much retirement income people have to infer why they are working or how they are living. Why don't I just survey people and ask how they are doing? We economists don't trust surveys of feelings. We know it is dignified to tell a journalist, a surveyor, your friends, or family that you "love" your job, that it interests you, that you have a desire to "keep busy." We all feel better if we project control over our lives. Admitting that you are working in your late 60s because you got pushed out of your career job, or your divorce depleted your assets, or that you mortgaged your house to pay for your kid's education could cause shame and depression.[12] So we infer that people are happy to be working if they are working beyond Social Security age despite having access to enough money to maintain their standard of living without working.

But if people are working because they would be poor or near poor if they did not, we assume they are working to stay out of poverty and may not have a genuine choice to retire. About 10 percent of older workers are part of the working poor.[13]

All poverty is brutal, and being poor while old compounds other challenges of elderly life. For example, housing is becoming an uncertain expense for elderly renters and homeowners faced with rising utility, taxes, and maintenance costs, and transportation and medical expenses take up money and time. Having about $7 to $13 a day for food—about what people living at the poverty standard and twice the poverty standard, respectively have—is difficult when you have failing capacities and are at risk of isolation. The older working poor may have Medicare or Medicaid but no time to take care of their health, or they may have uncertain social support to get to the doctor or comply with complicated pharmacy regimes. At all ages, the working poor do not have the money or time to socialize or buy gifts for friends and family. Now, imagine struggling with this after working hard for a lifetime, losing your elderly friends, and experiencing chronic ailments (if you're lucky) and social isolation. This is a predicament nobody should have to experience at any age. Further entrenching this elderly poverty, older workers generally don't qualify for the major federal subsidy to low-wage workers—the Earned Income Tax Credit—because they don't have dependent children and are over 65.[14]

Questions of Class and Education

Older workers' economic class affects their options, decisions, and conditions. To understand how class affects older workers, we can take educational attainment as a proxy for socioeconomic status. This can be a crude measure, but education levels are generally fixed and thus can more reliably determine a person's purchasing power and economic security than a snapshot of their income in time can.

Education is an important determinant of how much people work in old age, but not in the ways one might expect. It is no surprise that older people with more education work more than older people with fewer formal degrees. Educated people are more likely to be sought out by employers and offered more interesting jobs. They also started in the paid workforce later than workers with a high school education or less. I was in graduate school until age 26; my childhood friend started full-time work when she was 18. Yet at the same time, rising labor-force participation by older workers is not driven solely by education—older adults at all education levels are working longer. Across education levels, workforce participation for

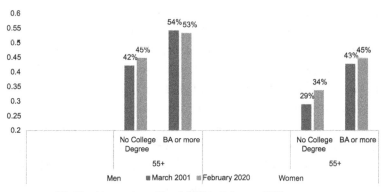

FIGURE 3.1 Working More or Less, March 2001 to February 2020

Source: Current Population Survey Monthly Data, Integrated Public Use Microdata Series (CPS Monthly Data IPUMS).

those aged 65–74 is projected to be 30 percent in 2026, compared with 18 percent in 1996.[15]

But factor in gender and the impact of education tells a more interesting story. The increase in work among older workers with a college degree or more is driven by women. Between 2001 and 2020, workforce participation among older male workers with a high school education increased, but labor-force participation among men with college degrees or more fell between 2001 and 2020.

For women, whose workforce participation continues to rise, older women with a four-year college degree or higher worked as much as older male high school graduates, both labor-force participation rates were 45 percent in 2020 (fig. 3.1).

These generational work shifts have paralleled (and propelled) longer-term slippage in wages and bargaining power. Since 1991, older men's wages have fallen relative to younger workers' wages.[16] For older workers with less education, the wage slippage has been even worse. Among workers aged 55 and over, those with a high school degree earned 12 percent less in 2017 than in 1990, while older college-educated workers lost 8 percent in that time. In contrast, during this same period, wages for workers aged 35–54 grew by over 10 percent.[17]

Looking ahead, we can expect similar trends to continue. The two jobs that the Bureau of Labor Statistics projects to grow fastest by 2026—personal-care aides and home health aides—are low-paying jobs (24 percent earn less than $15 per hour) that disproportionately hire older women (37 percent of workers in this field are women over 55). Unless we make some changes, these multilayered inequities are likely to deepen.

Probing further, we see more layers of age-related pay inequity. At all education levels, older workers have experienced less than 1 percent real wage growth since 2007, while weekly earnings for prime-age workers (aged 35–54) grew 5 percent.[18] In prior business cycles, older workers' earnings grew at similar or higher rates than prime-age workers' earnings. Now, that relationship has been reversed. From 1990 to 2019, older college-educated men working full-time saw their real median weekly earnings shrink by almost 3 percent, even as wages increased by almost 9 percent for prime-age male workers with bachelor's degrees. Here, again, older workers' fortunes have fallen.

Older Workers Are Not Worth What They Once Were

As I write this, I am reminded of Toby Keith's 2006 hit song "Good as I Once Was" in which an older cowboy laments the loss of his youthful talent for dating and fighting. Keith could have added the loss of his employer's regard.

Once upon a time, experience mattered. Employers paid decent money for it. Economists found that workers' accumulated job experience provided an "experience premium."[19] One's years of working were rewarded by pay increases based on experience, which helped explain the difference in pay between younger and older workers. This seniority boost was especially evident when skills and knowledge were connected to a particular occupation, like teaching or tool and die making.[20] There was a time when older workers earned higher wages and enjoyed faster wage growth than younger workers. But today, being loyal to one employer does not boost earnings like it once did.[21]

Since the early 1990s, real wages for older workers have declined relative to younger workers' wages; the experience premium is waning.[22] Older workers' bargaining power is declining, and many older workers find themselves in on-call and temporary jobs. Anemic pay and permanent layoffs among older workers indicate that decades of ladder climbing and loyalty have become less meaningful for workers nearing retirement age.

For the past twenty years, older workers have experienced falling returns for their years on the job, even after considering other factors that would explain wage losses, such as race, gender, union membership, and changes in occupation. Between 1992 (the first year the research started collecting all the necessary data) and 2002, each additional year of job tenure garnered about a 1.5 percent increase in wages per year. By the 2010s, the average returns to experience fell by almost half, to about 0.8 percent.

A 2019 Bankrate survey provides further evidence of the waning power of older workers. Half of workers aged 55–64 reported not getting a pay increase over the previous 12 months. Workers aged 65–73 fared even worse—nearly three in five did not receive a pay increase, the worst experience of all age groups in the survey. Back in 2009, Urban Institute economist Richard Johnson and colleagues found that having more work experience no longer protected older adults from job loss as it once did.[23] It's time to move that research forward. When the COVID-19 recession ended, older workers became more replaceable than anyone ever thought they would be.

For seniors who still need to work to pay the bills, the upshot of all this is that expecting a payoff for your years of experience and loyalty may cause you to overestimate your chances of working in your 60s and beyond. Returns to experience might fall even more because of the COVID-19 recession. Congress needs to get a grip and realize that people's market power falls when they get older. Knowing that the risk of job loss increases with age and that pay raises and promotions practically stop after 45 are essential facts for lawmakers, who wrongly think that a lacking of financial literacy or tax breaks are the key barriers to saving.

The Key to Happiness Is Choice and Agency

To be sure, retirement without income is harmful, but retirement itself, under the right circumstances, promotes satisfaction, heightened control over one's time, and less depression. Retirement can boost feelings of well-being. The economist Kevin Bender found that, while income boosts well-being in retirement, its effect is small; instead, a major factor in happiness during retirement is whether one chooses to retire or is pushed out of work.[24] Money isn't everything, but financial security is the broth to the soup.

Beyond whether one is compelled to work or pushed out of a job, senior happiness and security may also depend on the form of one's retirement income. Researchers have found that among retired people with the same wealth and income, earning from an annuity (a guaranteed stream of income), compared to an equivalent lump sum that one must manage to last a lifetime, is associated with higher levels of well-being. A million dollars converted to a stream of steady income for the rest of one's life makes older people less anxious (and therefore happier) than having to manage a lump sum of a million dollars.

Here I feel compelled to add an example repeated in every elementary research methods class in college: it is important to be aware of "spurious correlations," which conflate causes with outcomes. For instance, we might notice that more babies are born in the spring; at the same time, we see migratory storks roost in spring. And so storks bring babies (many think this is how that childish story arose). In like manner, happy old people may be working, but working doesn't necessarily make them happy.

Most People Can't Retire

As we have seen, the past few decades have not been kind to older people, whether they are "retiring" in poverty or working to survive. Declining bargaining power for older workers has become a huge issue as seniors have become a more prominent part of the labor force and as their economic fallback—and thus their labor-market leverage—continues to weaken. Conditions for this bargaining power and retirement security are deeply intertwined.

The working-longer consensus may sound good, but it has failed older working Americans, with grave consequences for the rest of us. The inescapable reality is that, after age 62, older people have constrained choices about work and retirement. While one small subset of older people aged 62–70—just 10 percent—can retire with enough money to maintain their standard of living, most seniors (51 percent) are retired but don't have enough money to maintain their standard of living or meet poverty-level income targets. Another 28 percent are still on the job because they don't have access to retirement income that would keep them above a de facto poverty level.

BOX 3.1 How Much Do You Need to Retire?

William Sharpe, a winner of the Nobel Prize in economics, once said that retirement planning is one of the nastiest and most difficult of all calculations. It is always a struggle to make it simple for people because, in doing so, you have to wave away all the contingencies and choices that happen in people's lives. But I will provide a few rules of thumb. Save, invest, and work so that you have 10-11 times your target spending in retirement (usually the spending you did right before retirement) to fund about 23 years of retirement. I refer to standard advice that workers who begin saving 15 percent of their salary at age 25 will have ten times their annual salary in their sixties and be on track to retire. If you are fortunate enough to achieve that, you are likely also in a good position to aggressively bargain for better pay and working conditions at your job. It is rare that people can save 15 percent of their paycheck for over forty consecutive years. (My colleagues and I found that even people at the top of the income distribution have saved only five times their salary when they hit retirement age.)

Given the difficulty of meeting these targets, in a 2019 study, Mike Papadopoulos, Anthony Webb, and I shifted our definition of *need* to gauge how many Americans between the ages of 62 and 70 had retirement wealth equal to a very low poverty standard. Stunningly, retirement savings are so low that half of Americans between the ages of 62 and 74 don't have an income of at least $24,000 a year per person, which is 200 percent of the federal poverty level. There are two rough ways to plan for retirement—plan to maintain your current living standards in retirement and plan to keep above the de facto poverty level.

Target Number 1: Maintaining Current Living Standards

The amount of income one needs to maintain a pre-retirement standard of living varies by income level, given different tax rates and work-related expenses. Lower-income workers need about the same amount of annual income in retirement as they earned while working, whereas higher-income workers need less, about 78 percent of earnings in retirement. Most researchers and financial planners use the replacement rate targets developed by the Georgia State RETIRE project, which uses information from the Bureau of Labor Statistics Consumer Expenditure Survey. It's not surprising that many people aged 62–70 can't meet these income levels to retire. At age 62, a troubling 76 percent of married men and 86 percent of married women do not have enough money to retire. At age 70, 31 percent of married men and women do not reach the target, and 43 percent of single women fall short. Single men fall in between.

Target Number 2: Live Modestly in Retirement

Another option is to go low; set the target to double the official poverty line. Yet even at this lower target, 37 percent of married men and 86 percent of single women do not have enough to meet these humble standards. If these folks waited to retire at age 70 (less than 7 percent work until they are 70), 37 percent of married men would fall short of basic anti-poverty standards ($42,000 or more per year for a couple), while 61 percent of single women would fall short of $31,200 per year, which is near the expanded poverty level for elders.

Let's remember that we're talking about the poverty level here. I don't use the poverty standard as an absolute because having enough income to be just above the poverty level is still not a decent standard of living. The official poverty level is tied to the cheapest cost of 2000 calories a day, multiplied by three to cover basic shelter and clothing. The poverty level is meant to maintain life for a short period of time, not a desired or sustainable existence. In 2019 the federal poverty level was $12,140 for a single individual and $16,460 for a couple. As anyone who has lived on that can attest, it's tough to survive on this at any time of life, never mind old age, when health becomes more fragile and health-care and other costs only go up.

The perhaps well-intentioned advice from policy makers and financial planners to work longer is simply not relevant for 51 percent of the senior population and is cruel to the 28 percent who are desperate to work to maintain a standard of living that is still hovering around the poverty level. As we'll explore in the next chapter, for many older folks, work grinds them down and takes time away from leisure, self-care, and control of their time—something that becomes increasingly precious as people get older. So far, the working-longer consensus has treated this loss of time as cost-free. But there's a big price to pay.

4

Working Longer
Can Harm Your Health

A cheerful headline in 2018 in *Harvard Health News* reported working longer provides mental stimulation and staves off chronic disease.[1] Who doesn't want to stave off chronic disease? The supposed pathway between these better outcomes and working longer is that people who work at older ages can solve many of the problems of old age. It is believed, wrongly, that because an older person with a job reports being connected and socially engaged and feels useful that it is the job causing these good feelings.

It is common for the professor and the lawmaker to embrace this "work is healthy" view. In their comfortable positions, the narrative that working in old age is healthy is a convenient untruth. Indeed, it's convenient for lawmakers intent on cutting government spending and avoiding solving the retirement-income crisis to believe that people working longer will solve budget, social, and economic problems. Believing that working longer is good is a shortcut for avoiding difficult choices about Social Security and pension policies.

And I have another hunch. Because professors and lawmakers look forward to a healthy and engaged job in old age, they are not naturally motivated to research the beneficial effects of retirement on health. Instead, professors and lawmakers are oriented toward documenting the joys of working longer. But professors and lawmakers are oddballs: most people, and most older people, don't have high-paying jobs like theirs that allow autonomy and confer high recognition.

This chapter weighs the evidence on the health effects of working longer. Briefly, the effects are complicated, but on balance, retirement is associated with greater health, control, and well-being. The belief that working longer is good for our health conflicts with a growing body of scholarship showing that older people experience work and retirement in a range of ways and that, for many people, working for pay in old age can bring illness and despair. Even the Harvard article noted that work in old age can be unhealthy for those with jobs characterized by stress, injury risks, and burnout. The question of how much work in old age degrades health is a matter of degree.

This chapter tempers the strong temptation to promote policies based on false hopes. People who want to retire and could benefit from a promise of adequate retirement income are not listened to and are shamed into working longer. The deep inequalities caused by the belief that work is good for old people are unfair. Society needs to hear from people who want, need, and deserve to retire.

Conflicting Narratives about Retirement

The Nobel Prize winner Robert Shiller warns that narratives in economics are powerful stories that spread and infect policy and greatly affect behavior. Misguided working-longer narratives have and will make many older people miserable.[2]

To counter the idea that retirement is bad for you, consider this story about one person's retirement plan gone wrong. I met this person when I testified in Congress in 2002 about the role of 401(k) investments in the Enron scandal, which eventually brought about the Sarbanes-Oxley financial reforms but not the retirement policy reforms I was hoping for. The illegality and self-dealing surrounding Enron executives' manipulation of state legislatures and energy prices often obscured the damage they caused to their employees and their 401(k) plans.

I will never forget the witness beside me who was a laid-off Enron lab analyst who lost his job during the company's bankruptcy.[3] The value of his 401(k) pension, which the company stuffed with what became worthless Enron stock, had tanked. He told Congress that Enron's bankruptcy and the collapse of his pension meant he had to postpone his long-awaited retirement. He planned to run a respite day camp for caregivers of disabled children. He held up a bandaged hand showing the effects of surgery for carpel tunnel caused by his return to work. I met his wife in the bathroom as she was trying to pull herself together. She told me he also wanted to retire to be able to take care of her; she had recently been diagnosed with a serious medical condition. Retirement and a secure pension would have been a good trajectory for this family. The man's shame that he couldn't retire and support his family was palpable.

The opposite narrative about retirement—that work in old age is good—is likely shaped by the lived experiences of the lawmakers and professors who shape retirement policy and like their jobs very much. In 2021, the average age of the US Senate leadership was 74; the president was 78 years old. In the same year, among professors, 37 percent were over age 55, compared to 23 percent of the US labor force. Doing research, making laws, and listening to testimony can be enjoyable into one's 70s and 80s. There is no heavy lifting or standing on one's feet all day. People in these jobs control the pace and content of their work and, crucially, are not subordinate to a boss.

In his popular 2019 book *Successful Aging*, Professor Daniel Levitan wholeheartedly recommends work—and broccoli, as you could probably guess—in old age.[4] The book features stories like that of the remarkable 94-year-old psychology professor at Stanford who found that the greater a person's sense of efficacy—that is, the sense they have that they can control their lives—the lower their stress is and the happier they are.

Levitan also cites evidence that retiring well might be the ticket to well-being, but he doesn't profile retirees. His bestseller tells stories about older workers. He emphasizes noncontroversial evidence that people are happier when they are involved with meaningful activities—this doesn't mean necessarily learning a new language at age 80—just that being engaged can have meaning. And here is where the faulty connection lies between what is obvious and the assumption work is good.

Much of the literature wrongly equates paid work with engagement. But this might be a major misstep. Assuming that paid work is synonymous with meaningful engagement helps strengthen the belief that work makes us happy and supports the working-longer consensus.

Sometimes it seems people think retirees are unhappy. A 2019 personal finance article on the twelve reasons work is good in old age listed "leisure is boring."[5] But retirement can be a great period of renewal. Unfortunately, this view is not so common in popular culture (except in ads featuring people in their 50s meeting with money managers). People want to retire. Years ago, while on a bus at the end of a long workday, I heard words I will never forget. A passenger said, "I have 380 days and 3 hours until I can retire." His friend chuckled, "I hear you." Lawmakers and executives don't generally take buses.

Retirement Can Be Good for You

In 2008, three young economists researching health concluded that retirement could make things worse for people—this coincided with a mountain of research, some showing the opposite and some confirming the results.[6] The study showed that retired people had more difficulties with mobility and daily activities, more illness, and more erosion of mental health over a six-year retirement period than workers of the same age. Retirees in the sample reported less physical activity and social interactions than people who were working at their same age.

This finding looked bad for the pro-retirement case. But it was their conclusions and policy recommendations that stretched too far. The study argued that public policy should structure public and private pension plans to discourage retirement by reducing benefits, because working longer made people healthier. That leap in thinking is a big part of the misguided working-longer consensus.

Over the years, we have gathered more detailed data from larger samples. We can control for health status before retirement and distinguish voluntary planned retirement from being pushed out of the labor market for life, which makes all the difference in studies. Some older studies concluded that retiring is bad for health because the methodology did not distinguish who was sick before retirement, what their jobs were like, and whether their retirement was involuntary.[7] Being miserable because you were pushed out of your job, laid off, or in poor health does not mean that retirement makes you miserable.

In 2019, PBS broadcasted a story on forced retirement about Gary, age 63, who was forced to retire at age 61 because the media industry didn't need as many photojournalists; they get photos from internet-based services. Also, the print news business had begun to contract, so Gary "lost his full-time position and began freelance work. Over time, he was getting fewer assignments and was required to work terrible hours for less pay. Gary found the work demoralizing and felt rejected. He hadn't wanted to retire—rather, Gary felt the industry retired him."[8] It is important to compare older people who are working under various conditions to retired people who retired in various circumstances. Selection bias—in this case, that means that people who retire early are more likely to have bad health than others—was finally fixed.

....

BOX 4.1 Don't Confuse Sick Retirees with Workers Who Retired Sick

Imagine a researcher who is comparing a group of retirees with a group similar in every way, except the group members are still in the paid workforce. The researcher might find that the retired group is sicker and dies sooner.

Researchers can show that a 68-year-old who is working is healthier than someone of the same age who is not working, but it is wrong to conclude that it is the work that has made the person healthier. The reason is that people who experience declines in their health and mental capacity retire earlier than people who do not experience these. Therefore, the healthiest segment of the older population is employed. Would they be even healthier if they weren't working?

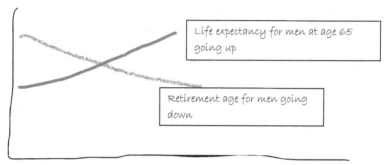

FIGURE 4.1 Napkin Graph of Retirement Ages and Life Expectancy

Better evidence turned on its head the commonplace notion that older people are living longer so they can work longer. A truer statement might be that older people are living longer *because* they are retiring more. Think about it like a graph. On the horizontal axis, place a hundred years of US history. On the vertical axis, chart men's life expectancy and retirement age (for decades women didn't retire because they didn't generally work for pay). Now draw the happy line going upward to indicate that men's life expectancy has increased over time. Next, draw the line indicating that men's age of retirement has fallen. Step back and realize the two trends could be independent phenomena or causal (fig. 4.1). I read the evidence as suggesting they are causal: being able to retire improved health and lengthened life expectancy.

Figure 4.1 is a classic Rorschach test. On the one hand, we see a yawning gap between retirement age and life expectancy, which begs the question: What are those people doing? Shouldn't they be working? Look at that! People are dying in their late 70s and retiring in their mid-60s.[9] Are older people enjoying too much retirement? The political question is this: are life expectancy and retirement misaligned because back in the day a 50-year-old man was expected to die just a few years after retiring?

Now, look at this with a different eye. Is life expectancy increasing because people can retire? Has older people's life expectancy increased because they can retire from the stresses and pressures of working for someone else?[10] Is the growing gap between retirement age and life expectancy related and causal rather than two independent trends? A 2021 review of nineteen studies found no evidence that working longer enhanced health, but it did find evidence that raising the statutory retirement age—the same thing as cutting pension benefits—did make people work longer.[11] The cuts in benefits were pro-work and not pro-health.

HAVING A GOOD JOB AFFECTS YOUR HEALTH

A 2008 study suggesting retirement could make people worse off spurred a mountain of research, some showing the opposite and some confirming the results.[12] The study's data consisted of people who are as alike in as many ways as possible, except one group was retired and the other working. Compared to workers, retired people experienced more difficulties with mobility and daily activities, more illness, and more erosion of mental health over a six-year retirement period. Retired people had decreased physical activity and fewer social interactions than workers. This finding looks bad for the retirement case. And it boosts the case for the working-longer consensus. And I maintain that the study's policy recommendations to cut benefits in public and private pension plans were a stretch. In contrast, more recent data from Europe—where voluntary retirement is much more common than in the United States—shows that retiring from jobs with heavy physical demands improves health, while retiring from psychologically demanding jobs reduces depressive symptoms.[13]

Increasingly, evidence, mostly from Europe—where voluntary retirement is much more common than in the United States—reveals that retiring can be good. For example, in 2018, the social scientists Levi van den Bogaard and Kène Henkens found that "escaping" work and retiring has a beneficial effect on health and well-being, especially but not exclusively for those whose jobs have high physical demands.[14] And a person who retires from a psychologically demanding job is associated with fewer depressive symptoms.[15] A 2019 study on Swedish workers and retirees teased out the effects of working longer on a range of outcomes, including well-being, and found that working longer was not an important independent factor, meaning that other factors had a greater effect in determining health and well-being in old age.[16]

Other studies explain that retirement's effect on health depends on not just a person's last job but also their whole job history. A 2009 European study found that people who hold poorer-quality jobs (those with a low reward-to-effort ratio, such as low-paid jobs that require physical labor or mental tedium) throughout their lives want to retire earlier than do those with better-quality jobs. The United States has one of the highest shares of all jobs that are low paying, and Norway has one of the lowest shares of low-paying jobs. Because the abundance of low-paying jobs differs widely by nation, the cross-national differences in the desirability of retirement may help explain differences in retirement health outcomes.[17] This research helps explain why workers in the United States, with its high proportion of low-paid jobs, are likely to have ill health in old age. The upshot of the research is that if the job you had before you retired was poor quality and you retired "on time," then retirement is beneficial to health.[18] Being forced to wait until you can retire is bad for well-being.

A 2013 follow-up study confirmed that not having control at work, not having effort rewarded, and not receiving significant recognition for one's work create a stressful psychosocial work environment. Retiring from that psychosocial situation improves health. But the timing of the job stress mattered. Being disadvantaged in one's work role or having suffered job insecurity and involuntary job loss in midlife meant that the negative effects of low-quality jobs were more likely to follow a person into old age. Also, retiring might help older people get healthy, especially those who have a higher propensity for depression because they experienced psychosocial stress at work or had low-status jobs. For them, working in old age is not good for them, and retirement is a relief. Men who had unstable working careers and involuntary job loss were at especially greater risk of depression in old age.[19] But note that doesn't mean that retirement causes depression; rather, depression follows certain kinds of workers into retirement.

Another 2018 paper overcame the healthy-worker-survivor effect using the retirement researchers' all-time favorite data set—the University of Michigan Study—the Health and Retirement Study. Using this gold standard enabled controlling for a person's pre-retirement health status. Compelling evidence emerged that retirement—compared to working—improves health, mental health, and life satisfaction, and eventually, retirement reduces functional limitations. Life satisfaction improves within the first four years of retirement, while health improvements show up four or more years later. This study found no evidence that retirees improve their health because they use more health care; in fact, results indicate that retirees may use fewer medical services.[20] Somewhat related, the economist Michael Insler found in 2014 that retirement boosts health significantly because retirees are more likely to stop smoking and exercise more. It seems that maybe habits are harder to break and form while working.[21]

A study published in the aptly named *Journal of Happiness Studies* surveyed the connection between happiness, "subjective well-being," and retirement in sixteen Western European nations and the US. It concluded that retirement had a large, independent positive effect on happiness. As people aged, the effect of retirement on happiness tapered off, so that in their early 70s, workers and retirees had about the same level of happiness. But the overall effect of retirement was more lifetime happiness. People who retired had more years feeling good than their counterparts who were working. In short, the study found that working longer reduces the well-being of 60- to 70-year-olds.[22]

A final health indicator—often studied and much admired—is resilience. Resilience is the ability to bounce back from adversity or "go with the flow," or "flourish despite adversity." So, does work in old age help an older person be resilient? The answer derived from psychological studies is a flat-out no.[23] Although resilient elderly people have good-quality relationships and are integrated into the community, work in and of itself is not connected to those good social and psychological outcomes in old age.

CLASS, GENDER, AND HEALTH IN RETIREMENT

Studies of retirement's effects on health show that they vary by class and gender (studies on how those effects vary by race are underdeveloped because researchers had not focused on those populations, and surveys did not survey enough people in these categories to make statistically reliable conclusions). Women are less likely to be bosses and more likely to have bosses at work, more likely to experience sex discrimination, and more likely be paid less for the same work as men. For women, working in old age is more likely to have low reward-to-effort ratio.[24] And low reward for high-effort jobs is a classic definition of a bad job.

Pension policy has made gender and class disparities worse. So not only do women have worse jobs than men; women with lower incomes and fewer college degrees are more likely to have even worse jobs. It used to be that in many European Union countries, women could retire earlier than men at full or slightly reduced pensions. But in a move toward gender neutrality—a laudable goal, to be sure— the modern European Union closed the gender gap in retirement ages. Unfortunately, and ironically—for the measure was supposed to promote worker well-being—instead of lowering the age for retirement for men, the nations raised the retirement age for women. For example, in Germany, women born after 1957 had to work three additional years before collecting a pension. The result was that women at the higher end of the income distribution continued to work at older ages, but women with less education became nonemployed and found themselves without pensions. The upshot is that aspiration for equality did not match reality. Women were penalized for leaving work, but little was done to help women, especially those with lower socioeconomic status, stay working. In Germany, the socioeconomic gap in wealth and well-being among older women increased.[25] Another study found insignificant effects of paid work on older women's happiness (after the state of their financial security was controlled for).[26] A similar study has not been conducted for US workers, but I have a good hunch the results would be the same.

And paid work in old age can make health worse. In a study called "Quit Your Job to Get Healthier," the American economist Kevin Neuman found that older women workers suffer accelerated declines in health if they work longer.[27] Economist Lauren Schmitz found that older women in service jobs would become healthier if they retired.[28] Schmitz also found that older workers who have less control over their jobs suffer worse health outcomes. Continuing to work in jobs that lack the basic characteristics of good jobs—high degrees of reward to effort and the ability to control the pace and content of one's time and work—shortens life spans and hastens illness. Work can kill.

For many people, the only way to get the control they need and to get away from stress is to retire with a decent pension so they can control the pace and content of their time.

Retirement is particularly healthful for Americans. A comprehensive study of workers and retirees aged 55–75 in Japan, the US, Denmark, Germany, Switzerland, France, and England found that, on average, retirees and workers aren't much different from workers, except in the US, where the well-being gap between workers and retirees is large! For example, non-US retirees have as many bad habits as workers in those nations. Retirees smoke, drink, and exercise as little as workers do.[29] But American retirees have fewer bad habits than European retirees. Retirees in the US smoke less and exercise more than workers of the same age. And the healthful effect of retirement is stronger for male retirees. Take 68-year-old retired Max from Ohio and his friend Tom, who still works in the same plant. According to the study's findings, Max is likely to drink less alcohol, smoke less, and exercise more than Tom. American female retirees, however, drink more alcohol than their working counterparts. The study also found, to no surprise, that Americans engage in less physical exercise, likely because of car dependency and suburban living, than their counterparts in Japan, the UK, Denmark, Germany, Switzerland, France, and England.[30] German female retirees were a little like American female retirees in terms of bad habits: German female retirees and low-income retirees exercised less than they did while working.[31] And another study piles on the evidence that retirement is good for your health. Among eleven European nations found retirement (at about age 65) was good for a person's health. Retirement any later, the researchers noted, could make men especially sicker and more depressed than they would be had they retired earlier.[32]

Retirement is especially helpful for people who have the worst jobs, are in worse health, and have the lowest status in society and the labor market. A Norwegian study found that when individuals retired, they experienced a boost in physical health and fewer hospital stays and that the effect was much larger for people with low socioeconomic status. The main reason for the extra positive effects of retirement on those with lower socioeconomic status is that retiring reduces pain. And relief from pain gives a person more capacity to engage in daily activities of living.[33] This finding on pain was a bit of a gut punch. Pain is a big part of an older worker's life.

The disparities persist in part because people with higher socioeconomic status make retirement policy and study retirement realities. I gainsay that elites with good jobs and health advocate working longer because work has been very good to them; however, raising the retirement age is a very unpopular issue among the public.

The thing I worry most about is the relentless increase in inequality caused by policies that force people to work longer. It is true that, on average, people are living longer. But if lawmakers and analysts focus on only the average experience, too many people are hidden from view. On average, Americans are living longer and healthier, but there are such large crucial differences by class, race, and gender that policies guided by the average will certainly hurt the least advantaged the most.

For example, let's say the US Congress cuts Social Security benefits by raising the retirement age based on the conviction that, on average, everyone lives longer so they can work longer. But the evidence shows that the 67-year-old nursing home worker's physical and mental state is worse and failing faster because she works more than her retired counterparts do. The 67-year-old retiree controls the pace and content of her own time; she can avoid heavy lifting, crushing work schedules, arbitrary changes in work duties, and the fear of being laid off.

Consider the disparity in working conditions another way. Over half of college-educated men aged 66–69 work, compared to 27 percent of those with a high school education. The more educated you are, the more likely your job is high quality, meaning it has a high reward-to-effort ratio. That means older workers, workers over the age of 65, for instance, may show up in the data as healthier than retirees, but the mediating force behind these workers' good health is class, not work. People in higher socioeconomic classes work longer and are in better health. But the work did not make them healthier. They might be even happier if they stopped working.[34]

Moreover, many people retire to escape bad jobs. Studies show retiring from highly physical jobs improves health, and retiring from mentally demanding jobs reduces depressive symptoms.[35] So, paid work for people with bad jobs makes them sick and causes pain. Retirement is their way to protect themselves against pain and wear and tear on the body and mind. If people in lower socioeconomic classes are forced to work, the disparity in health and well-being will only increase.

This recalls the credibility of the bon mot "where you were determines where you are going." If older people's jobs are getting worse, then retirement is becoming more beneficial. And if retirement is shrinking, then it is those in subaltern, lower-status groups who will be hurt the most. Unfortunately, job quality for older people is getting worse in some places and has stopped improving altogether in others.[36]

The physical demands placed on older workers today are no different from what they were in the 1990s. In 1992, 17 percent of older workers said their jobs required lifting heavy loads. That rate remained high, at 15 percent in 2014. Older Black men were more likely to do physical labor in 2010 than they were in the 1990s. Moreover, the share of workers reporting frequent stooping, kneeling, and crouching in 2014 was equal to that in 1992, at 27 percent. One in three older workers said their job required "lots of physical effort" in 2014.[37] And if you think computers save people from toil on the job, it is the opposite. Because of the computer, more older people have jobs demanding keen eyesight and intense concentration.

Older workers are increasingly employed in low-wage traditional jobs and in alternative work arrangements. For example, by 2035, the occupation with the most job growth will be personal and home health-care aides, with more than 1 million jobs. Government data projects that three-fourths of those new jobs will go to women older than age 55—older women will be taking care of even older women (and men). Just 7 percent of personal and home health-care aides are union members, and 24 percent earn less than $15 per hour. More than 85 percent of them are women. All signs point to the largest source of jobs for older workers being important jobs for society that require high levels of physical, mental, and emotional effort for low levels of monetary reward.

Older people working longer could reverse previous gains in longevity and worsen the class and race gaps in longevity. Employers are part of that story.[38] Next time you get an Amazon package from a fulfillment center, thank a granny. The writer Jessica Bruder embedded herself with older people living in their cars and traveling the nation working various jobs. Amazon recruited these people, hiring them from their vans in Walmart parking lots. These recruits were "workampers" who commuted to rural warehouses.[39] Bruder's book went on to win the Academy Award for Best Picture in 2020.

A NOTE ABOUT SHAME AND RETIREMENT

A key negative aspect of the working-longer consensus needs attention: shame. When I congratulated a successful colleague in her early 60s on her retirement, she averted her eyes and insisted that she wouldn't be idle: "I'm not going to do nothing!" I heard about her travel, planting, reading, and consulting plans. She added evidence about why she deserved it: "If you must know, I saved for retirement and worked fifteen-hour days as a lawyer." Every time I congratulate someone on retirement, I hear this bundle of shame-tinged explanations.

Due in part to the working-longer consensus, there is widespread shame about retiring in America and not having enough money to do so. In America's do-it-yourself retirement system, people are expected to be prepared for retirement from their own grit, long-term plan making, and investment acumen. They are expected to control their own destiny. Not being financially prepared for retirement can induce a sense of personal failure. If someone is working in old age to make up for a perceived character deficit for not saving for retirement, shame is a shadow on their work.

Our system of retirement savings requires people to do something people can't do well, manage their money to earn a return on their investments over their lifetime that is great enough to allow them to generate income in retirement. If they fail, it is their fault, which leads to shame and depression. The system sets them up.

Elders are especially sensitive about the state of their wealth (or lack thereof), and that feeling corresponds with their feelings about their own mortality. Recent research supports this idea. The economist Hannes Schwandt found that losses of wealth cause mental and physical health to deteriorate.[40] Also, poor people are more likely to be depressed and richer people to be happier, all other things held equal.[41] People who go into debt have sharp increases in mortality. Debt has an independent negative effect on life span.[42] Participants with the same wealth differed in health depending on the trajectory of their wealth. Those with negative wealth shocks during a twenty-year period had a significantly increased risk of mortality compared to those with steady increases in wealth.

I look forward to more research with better data to ferret out the hunch that older workers who don't have enough retirement income to retire (i.e., about two-thirds of all older workers) are more depressed, are more frustrated they can't spend more time doing what they like to do, and feel more shame because they were not able to save enough to retire.

Policy makers aiming to cut Social Security and not make any moves to improve pensions are warned that hoping people work longer to make up for the inadequacy of our retirement systems may not work. Evidence is mounting that work makes older workers sick and that retirement is good for almost everyone.

The Opposing View

So, despite ample evidence of voluntary retirement's salutary effects, why does retirement get such a bad rap among economists? There is some older evidence that suggests retirement is bad for health and working in old age is good for health. In 2011, Coe and Zamarro examined broad measures of health and found retirement has a significant negative effect on health for retired construction workers who stopped exercising but kept up a high calorie intake.[43]

And popular media has an opposing view that retirement is good for health. The media message that "70 is the new 50" supposedly sells financial products, cruise vacations, and vitamins. This message, though, promotes the wrongheaded belief that everyone can work longer because, on average, people are living longer. But life expectancy isn't health expectancy. A longer life does not mean better health at every age. A 2017 study compared the health and vitality of older people in the twenty-first century, say 70-year-olds, to 50-year-olds in the 1970s and found similarities.[44] Comparing the health and workability of today's 70-year-old with yesteryear's 50-year-old is typical of studies arguing for working longer. The methodology is the front line for advocates of working longer and raising the retirement age. They are wrong.

Hear me out. This study concluded if Americans today worked as much as those with the same mortality worked in the past, the retirement age would be much higher than today's average retirement age of 63. For instance, the article argued that because in 2017 a 69-year-old had the same expected life span as a 62-year-old in 1977, that person should work five more years to get as sick as their counterpart 62-year-old was in 1977. I put up my red flag here and reject the authors' blithe assumption that how long people in their 60s worked in 1977 is the appropriate benchmark for an economy that is forty years older and richer. The study assumes that all life expectancy gains should be translated into additional years of work and that leisure or retirement time has no value. If back in 1950 people got to retire for twelve years, that does not mean that twelve years of retirement is today's target. No other aspect of living standards is benchmarked to 1950. Today Americans expect indoor plumbing, paid vacations, clear air, auto safety, and civil rights. These were not widespread reality in 1950.

As I mentioned earlier, the 70-year-olds in 2022 may be as healthy as the 50-year-olds in 1960 because the 70-year-olds retired when they were 60. Today's older American may be healthier than a younger American in the past *because* more people were able to retire. Turning causation on its head and backward means that many of the cheerleader studies for working longer neglected a significant factor that improved population health: retirement. From the 1940s through the 1980s, older people were working less and retiring more. And as we have seen, mounting evidence suggests that working less causes health to improve. Making older people with the same expected number of years to live work as much as their counterparts did decades ago could reverse health gains. The working-longer consensus also challenges the social legitimacy of workplace victories. As the nation got richer, workers gained rest, recreation, self-growth, and control over the content of their time, which comes about in many forms of paid time off—paid holidays, vacations, sick leave, and retirement.

KEEPING BRAINS SHARP

Another area of vibrant research is scholarship on the effect of paid work at older ages and brain health. Any conversation about brain health and aging is electric. People panic about losing their cognition. So many of us were moved by the book or movie based on John Bayley's *Elegy for Iris* about his wife Iris Murdoch's failing brain, or Julianne Moore's Academy Award–winning performance in *Still Alice*. Many of us bristle or laugh nervously, or do both, at the endless self-deprecating and ageist jokes about "senior moments."

A 2014 French study concluded that elevated levels of cognitive and social stimulation boost brain health. Dementia risk was lower among more than 400,000 French people who became self-employed after age 60 or who had been self-employed their entire career, compared to those who stopped working at 60.[45] This brain-health effect of work was explained through "coherence theory." Coherence theory holds that controlling what you do and how fast you do it supports cognitive health and that independent, self-controlled work can help older people age successfully. However, another French study of work among the elderly failed to find retirement from paid work had any negative effect on brain health. (In fact, having a job requiring extreme physical and mental effort damaged health, confirming the evidence presented earlier and also common sense.) The workers, the researchers concluded, would likely be healthier had they retired sooner from their arduous job.[46]

A leading study in the pro-retirement case was a well-circulated and somewhat sensational 2010 study called "Mental Retirement," which compared Americans with Europeans. It concluded that working longer improves mental acuity (after careful accounting for acuity before working longer).[47] The supposed causal pathway from work to greater brain health was inferred because the researchers presumed that paid work keeps people mentally sharp through physical activity and social connection. And how the authors arrived at that conclusion may have explained the paper's popularity! They speculated that American elders' memory test scores were higher than Europeans' because in the US a greater share of older adults works than in Europe. They concluded that the pathway to a better memory is mental stimulation from work. They further presumed retirement from work causes "mental retirement," and therefore that retirement contributes to cognitive decline. However, cognitive decline in Europe could be caused by shrinking social networks or the despair caused by being pushed out of a job into retirement—many European nations allow mandatory retirement.[48] Subsequent studies find its involuntary retirement that hurts mental health in old age, rather than paid work helping people be healthier. Evidence from a 2016 study of older British men is consistent with the "use it or lose it" argument.[49] The results were not as strong for women who retired from rote jobs. No wonder people are afraid of retirement. But the jury is out on this cognitive effect on retirement, and more research is needed that examines the class aspects.

As we might imagine, the conclusion that Europeans experience more mental decline than Americans produced an immense amount of backlash research. One European study cautioned that the fact blue-collar, manual labor workers in Europe can retire earlier than Americans and have less education and score lower on cognitive tests may have led to the spurious conclusion that Americans are smarter because they don't retire as much as Europeans do.[50] In any event, the more we probe the link between paid work and cognitive health, the more nuanced and complex it looks. A 2019 study found that women's cognition (not men's) improves with working compared to their re-tired counterparts.[51] Another study reported that having a part-time job can alleviate some symptoms of depression but part-time jobs erode physical health.[52] A 2020 study concluded that UK pension reforms that equalized retirement ages between men and women by cutting women's pensions led to substantial increases in women's probability of depression, especially among women in poorer-quality jobs with lower socioeconomic status, what the study called "lower occupational grades."[53] Being in a high-strain job characterized by high demands and low control is a pathway from working longer to bad health.

Beyond all these variations, the research shows a pattern: retirees who are married, engaged in physical activity, and who voluntarily re-tired generally do well in retirement. People in unstable, controlling, and insecure jobs also benefited from retirement. People who retire and don't exercise and stop seeing people are likely to deteriorate quickly. And even if work is good for many people and retirement can be problematic, the leap between evidence that retirees do less exercise and have fewer human interactions to the policy recommen-dations retirement ages should be raised and pension benefits cut is illogical and a ridiculous lack of attention to what pension systems are built for.

ANTICIPATED PSYCHOLOGICAL
LOSSES FROM RETIREMENT

Only a few people have the privilege to decide to retire or not. Some of these fortunate people may not retire for a compelling reason, but a compelling reason doesn't mean it is a good, noble, or particularly salubrious one. People may work longer when they have the means not to purely to avoid the fear of the unknown. Staying in paid work is the status quo, it is known. Work, without our conscious thought or intention, provides many psychosocial benefits: easy time boundaries; ritual use of time; self-identification; meaning; and emotional support. However, staying on the job to avoid losing these benefits achieved with no effort means forfeiting a personal growth opportunity to create one's own structure and meaning. Avoiding psychosocial losses is something "to work through," say therapists. The few people who have the choice to retire or not, therapists say, need to intentionally consider how to manage what is lost when they stop paid work.

Therapist Kate Schroeder describes the emotional side of retirement in terms of people losing valuable emotional supports that the workplace provides: claims on your time, structure, and identity.[54] In this light, the feared psychological losses from retirement can make working longer more attractive. This therapist points to a choice. One can avoid these losses by keeping the status quo and working longer. The second choice is to embrace personal growth and take on the emotional tasks and benefits of retirement.

The "tasks" of retirement involve finding ways to make up for what's lost by no longer working. I use a mnemonic device for emotional retirement losses—PRIME, for *protection, routine, identity, meaning*, and *emotional regulation*. Each of these is a loss that must be replaced or mourned before people are ready for retirement, assuming, of course, that they have the financial means to retire.

The first thing we lose at retirement is protection, in the sense of protecting time from others' needs. When you are on the job, you always have the excuse that you can't do something because you are working. You may use work to protect yourself against being overwhelmed by an elderly relative or spouse's needs. People sometimes use work to protect themselves from their real selves. Work's demands, Schroeder argues, help us avoid setting our own boundaries.[55] Thus, the task of retirement is to protect yourself and create boundaries—to create time for yourself that your paid work once filled up.

When I took a friend to lunch to celebrate his retirement, I asked which loss troubled him most. By the time our meal arrived, he had confessed that his main loss was protection. Saying "I can't, I have to work" saved him from many family chores. He spent the first week of his retirement taking a relative to four medical appointments. He later told that relative a trivial lie that he went back to part-time work. That's protection.

The second thing we lose in retirement is routine. Ever since kindergarten our days have been highly structured. First, we go to school, then we go to work. Our psychological task in retirement is to give ourselves some structure.

The third thing we lose in retirement is identity. Many professionals are reluctant to say they are retired. One day an article appeared in my daily news feed that argued that we shouldn't even say the word *retirement*.[56] Euphemisms for retirement include things like "third act" and "consulting"; the best thing this article came up with is the Spanish word *jubilación*, which means retirement but to English-speaking eyes looks like *jubilation*.

The next loss is meaning. Many workers, particularly in white-collar professions and skilled blue-collar trades and crafts, derive meaning from their work; the completion of tasks, projects, and products was valued by their peers and sometimes by their employer or society. The work may have been challenging, and conquering it produced added meaning.

The last loss is emotional regulation. In a good job, one can get daily (or many times a day) microdoses of dopamine when someone says, "Good job." Even with lousy supervisors, the satisfaction and accomplishment of analyzing and complaining about those supervisors is an important social experience at lunch. Retirees' task is to find that same kind of emotional regulation and social connection on their own.

There are powerful reasons to keep working beyond money. How much one loses at retirement depends very much on the job and employer. These psychological factors make involuntary retirement so devastating.

Over decades of studying workers and retirees, I've learned that to know the mental health outcome of a retired person, the first thing

I want to know is not whether they're rich or poor, Black or white, female or male, but if they were pushed out, involuntarily retired. Mental health instability, including depression and anxiety, can come from suddenly losing protection, routine, identity, meaning, and emotional regulation.

If money is not an issue, a person contemplating retirement needs to weigh the psychological benefits against the psychological costs of leaving paid work. This is difficult when the known costs of leaving work are felt in the moment and the benefits of retirement are in the future and unknown. This asymmetry of certainty and time helps explain why someone who is financially able to retire would decide to keep working. People need time to assess who they are and how to replace the boundaries, structure, meaning, identity, and socializing they lost in retirement. People who must retire involuntarily or work out of financial necessity don't have this privilege of self-paced introspection and deliberation. The monetary losses when a person is forced to retire are difficult to manage and compounded by psychosocial losses. These psychosocial losses are relevant for everyone and need replacing. But just because paid work provides some of them, it doesn't mean that boundaries, structure, meaning, identity, and emotional support can't be found outside of paid work.

Remember from an earlier chapter that only 11 percent of seniors aged 62–70 are working even though they can afford to retire. Twenty-eight percent of seniors (aged 62–70) are working and can't afford to retire. These eleven out of one hundred are the small group with special positive factors on their side: they have enough money to retire on—so they can walk away from a bad boss and bad job whenever they want—and they are still wanted in the labor market. It's safe to conclude that these folks are apt to get meaning, identity, emotional satisfaction, and other benefits from working for pay.

THE WORK-HEALTH CONNECTION IS COMPLICATED

You might have an uncle who had a heart attack as soon as he retired. Or you have some friends who retired and feel depressed and lost without structure to their day. Change is hard, and these stories might loom large when you contemplate your own retirement, worrying that retirement will be boring and may cause mental decline and isolation. You might avoid retiring. And if you do not have a steady pension or do not have access to sophisticated financial knowledge, you may continue to work just to make ends meet. Take heart, the research on health and working longer is ongoing and, in general, shows that voluntary retirement yields superior results at all income levels. But working because you need to, under the conditions your employer dictates, may be bad for your health. In effect, the research indicates controlling the pace and content of one's own time is beneficial.

The impression that retirement is bad for health might loom large over lawmakers as they restructure pension systems in hopes that longer work lives will save the government budget. If you are a policy maker trying to balance the budget by cutting pensions, then stories and research about unhealthy retirement may make you feel better about not attending to the retirement-income crisis and pursuing pro-older-worker policies. This chapter has reviewed the literature on how retirement and work in old age affect health and well-being. Scholars agree that older studies tended to wrongly conclude (because of selection bias) that retirement was bad for health because older workers were healthier than people of the same age who were retired. The research that controls for the fact that people in poor health tend to retire sooner than healthy people shows that retirement has a neutral to positive effect on health. The big exceptions to those who benefit from retirement are those who retired because they were forced out of their jobs. Involuntary retirees tend to have more physical and mental problems and would be better off if they retired when they planned to retire.

This chapter also draws out the equity implications of pushing older people to work longer. If more people are working longer or are forced to work longer, older workers who are in subordinated groups—those with lower socioeconomic status, women, and nonwhites—will more likely be in lower-paid, lower-status jobs. I have established that being in those kinds of bad jobs when you are old has a measurable negative effect on health and longevity. Working longer could reverse historical longevity gains among subaltern groups and those in jobs with low ratios of reward to effort.

Elders forced to work longer will likely experience a deterioration in their health and well-being. At the same time, those with good retirement income will continue in enjoyable jobs or enjoy their income-secure retirements. The consequences are bad for equity. The longevity for the underdog group falls as it improves for older well-off individuals who can structure their time to their liking.

Public policy aimed at lengthening work lives and not improving pensions has two effects: it widens socioeconomic gaps in longevity and morbidity, and it creates an even more unequal distribution of healthy retirement time. Retiring before age 65 is a way some people can make their retirement time longer and more equal than people with higher incomes and status.

5

Working Longer Creates Unequal Retirement Time

Time away from work is like water or the sun—a vital resource for human beings. As societies grow wealthier, their residents typically clamor for more time for leisure, more family and friends, sometimes education, and more self-care. In advanced market economies, government policy, trade union demands, and employers' human resource management practices all play a role in permitting most workers to retire.

Retirement is conceptually akin to any kind of paid time off, such as paid vacation, sick leave, and, for salaried workers, the conventional weekend and an evening off. If we want an equitable society, we need to know if everyone gets this paid time off equally—presently, they don't. To understand these inequities, we need to measure the amount and distribution of time off work. Who gets to retire and for how long? Only by measuring can we assess our nation's progress toward equality of this important little-heralded resource, paid time off for life.[1]

Wealth is associated with more time off. Nations and households consume more time away from sweat and yoke as they grow richer. The postwar growth in pensions and the expansion of Social Security, Medicare, and Medicaid diminished gaps between rich and poor. Stark differences in wealth, access to health care, and time off shrunk. The rich and the poor were confirmed social entitlement to a special kind of time—time that grows in value as it becomes scarcer when people approach their death.

I fear that American workers are approaching the end of their lives with more inequality than when they were working. For the first time in modern American history, gains in retirement time are concentrated at the economic top. Let's set aside for now the political and philosophical questions of who deserves a healthy retirement, and what does it matter if only the rich can have it?[2] This chapter measures the distribution of healthy retirement years—who gets how much paid time off in their final years.

People Have Very Different Retirement Lengths

There is considerable research on working time, but I've yet to see any on the duration of people's retirement time.[3] Few scholars even try. Luckily, Alicia Munnell, director of the Center for Retirement Research at Boston College, is trying. I am highlighting her work because I trust her numbers and her compassion for the human side of retirement and work.

But Munnell stresses the financial benefits of working past age 65. I get it: I didn't protest when my mother stayed in her job selling classified ads until age 72. But now, I cringe when I think of her getting up so early to beat a grueling commute and the several car accidents she had. Her pay was less than $32,000 per year (in 2007), and she collected Social Security as soon as she could. As I first wrote this chapter, my mother was 83 and a bit sick; I hoped she would get twenty years of retirement life. She died at 84, with just twelve years of it. Was that too much?

In Alicia's eagerness to sell the idea of working a few more years, she insists that today's normal life cycle is to work forty years and retire for twenty. She hints that one retired year for every two working years is unacceptably generous given historical ratios of three years to one. If people were to push back their retirement age by four years, Munnell argues, they would work forty-four years and retire for sixteen, presumably more acceptable because this mirrors historical ratios.[4] Put that way, it may sound logical to trim the ratio, meaning work longer. On its own, this assertion about the ratios may seem obvious. After all, many of us know people who worked for thirty years and lived another thirty years in retirement. But new data just don't bear this out as common—in fact, quite the contrary.

Munnell, in making her moral argument, proposes that in the name of moving forward, we go back to the past, when we all worked for a greater proportion of our adult years. Back in the 1940s, Munnell implies, the US achieved the "right" ratio of work to retirement years, four to one. As the US and other developed nations grew, richer workers demanded and received more paid time off: vacations, holidays, sick leave, family care, and retirement. But there is no precedent in social policy making to argue for conditions that were in place when a nation was poorer, so why go back to that era's retirement levels. Munnell's assertion overlooks inequalities set in place by working-longer policies: better-off folks who live longer may not lose retirement time, but lower-income people who did not benefit from longevity gains most certainly do.

Facts about retirement length are hard to come by, inspiring me to open a new path of research, the results of which are in this chapter. I unfortunately have found much shorter averages than the twenty years Munnell found. It's also important to move beyond those averages and glean the distribution of retirement—this is the equity question of who gets the precious resource of time for their own actualization before they die and who does not.

The inequality of retirement time is caused by the crossing of two swords: growing inequality in retirement wealth and growing inequality in longevity. These inequalities are deeply connected. If people who died sooner had retired earlier than those with longer and healthier lives, then retirement time could be distributed more equally. Retirement trends depend on trends in retirement ages and length of life. But simply subtracting average longevity from average retirement age gives a distorted impression because both are unequally distributed, so we must go deeper and look at retirement ages and longevity by race, class, and gender.

As far as I can tell, my study of retirement time is the first of its kind, which is surprising: time is precious and universal. This is likely because no data was previously available on this. To really get at this question, researchers need to know a lot about people when they retire—jobs, health, wealth—and when people died and how sick they were when they retired. The state-of-the-art Health and Retirement Study (HRS) from the University of Michigan has that data, but collection started only in the 1990s. In the past few decades, there were not enough people who had retired and died (ghoulish but a research reality) to get a large enough sample to determine the characteristics of who and who did not get a healthy and fair amount of retirement time.

By 2018, enough people in the HRS database had died that we could begin exploring and learning. My coauthor Anthony Webb and I constructed a sample of people to figure out who had lived for how long and how healthy they were after they withdrew from the labor force.

Here are a few kernels from our findings: Men are more likely than women to die without retiring. Black women spend the most time in retirement sick. If men have a defined-benefit (DB) plan, they catch up with women in retirement time. Higher educational attainment helps women obtain more retirement, although men with higher socioeconomic status have more retirement time than do women with less education.

One significant reason men have less retirement time than women is straightforward: over time, private employers have replaced DB pensions—the usual ones we think of, the kind that pay out benefits for life—with 401(k)-type plans. Among men with low levels of formal education, not having a DB plan makes them more likely to delay retirement, especially while they are still healthy.

With so many different types of retirement plans out there, Social Security options, and flexible retirement dates, policy makers and academics hoped that people with shorter life spans could compensate by being able to retire earlier. Increasingly, they can't, because they lack secure DB pensions. Given current patterns and trends, access to retirement time (and healthy retirement time) is likely to become more unequal as pension wealth and longevity inequalities increase.

Retirement Ages Are Unequal

The story of Americans working longer at older ages is one of vastly divergent realities. Alongside the happy, healthy 75-year-old pediatrician who chooses to work is the 75-year-old janitor with ailing joints who must work for money to survive. The Black construction worker with a chronic sore back leaves work at age 61 and struggles until he can collect Social Security, while the college-educated white woman came late to accountancy at an auto parts firm, loves it, and retires happily at 75. The average retirement age—64.4 years for men and 64.2 years for women—doesn't give that rich detail. The real story of retirement and the quality of elder life lies in the distribution of retirement ages.

The economist Courtney Coile's effort and others to discover why Americans are, on average, retiring at later ages is a good place to start telling the story of American retirement behavior.[5] Coile analyzes all the imaginable push and pull factors that encourage older workers to work longer. Better health had a negligible impact on whether Americans work longer, which surprised most of us in the field. Being able to work longer did not pull people into longer work lives. One reason health does not appear in the data to be a crucial factor driving people to work is that healthy people like to retire—health makes retirement more fun. Push factors, such as workers having risky types of retirement accounts—more 401(k)s and fewer defined-benefit pensions—and many workers not even having a pension or 401(k) account, are significant factors in Americans' later retirements. Pull factors such as the elderly being more educated and having a spouse who works also helped explain the increasing average retirement age.

The problem is that attempts to reckon with why people retire at the age they do tend to assume that individuals have control over when they retire. The methodology of these studies is such that employers' priorities—their needs, habits, and power—are not considered by the model, although what employers want is germane to a person's retirement decision. This is a huge oversight. But many noneconomists are discovering something that may seem obvious: the quality of the job a person has when they decide to retire or when their employer decides they should retire is a key factor explaining the age at which that person retires. Employer actions, including outright age discrimination, workplace speed-ups—efforts to make workers work faster—and pressuring older workers to retire, must be part of the retirement picture. Most retirees tell researchers they are directly or indirectly pushed out of work because of a lack of training or microaggressions around age discrimination, or they are laid off.[6] This complex, contested terrain of employers' priorities is a major factor driving who retires, when, and how.

Let's shift our retirement lens away from averages to focus on inequalities by race, gender, and class. How do these inequalities shape who gets to retire and when? Analyzing who identifies as men and women separately (the existing data set requires people to identify as male or female, or the surveyor does it for them; these binary categories are clearly a limitation that must be rectified in modern research). To discern people's class status, we use their highest level of educational attainment.[7] We use non-Black and Black because there are too few people in the other categories who have retired and died for us to be able to make meaningful inferences about class and health impacts.

Since people retire at about age 64, gender on its own does not explain differences in retirement time. However, when we dig into some nuances, we find subtle yet significant differences. For instance, even though they live longer on average, women do not automatically get more retirement time. Many men retire early, and upper-class men have the same life expectancy as women. Don't ever be fooled that class can overcome many other differences.

People in the lowest third of educational attainment for their age group retire earlier, at about age 63. Men and women in the highest third of educational attainment retire later—close to 66 for men and 65 for women. As a rule of thumb, those in higher socioeconomic classes work longer. In other words, while gender affects some layers of the retirement picture, class makes a bigger difference.

The Health and Retirement Survey, with its extensive information

TABLE 5.1 Retirement ages for individuals who have survived to age 52

	Men	Women
Average	64.4	64.2
Lowest third of educational attainment	63.3	63.1
Middle third of educational attainment	64.1	64.6
Highest third of educational attainment	65.6	64.7
Black	62.5	63.5
Non-Black	64.7	64.3

Source: Health and Retirement Study (HRS), Institute for Social Research, University of Michigan, https://hrs.isr.umich.edu/about.

on life and work histories and age of death, allows me to limit my analysis to those who worked most of their adult life and lived until age 52. This older worker sample lets me examine the effects of class, race, and gender on retirement time.[8]

What did I find? Race, independent of class, significantly affects the age at which someone retires. Black men retire earlier. Non-Black people—controlling for education attainment—retire at older ages than Black people. The average retirement age for Black men is about 63, and for Black women it's a year older.[9] Non-Black men work more than two years longer than Black men; meanwhile, non-Black women retire at almost one year older than Black women (table 5.1). But I don't really care about retirement ages by themselves; I'm interested in retirement time. I hope to live in a nation where people who die earlier get to retire sooner.

Longevity Is Unequal

A central yet often ignored part of the retirement picture involves how long people get to live. Despite some other progress in racial disparities, race-based longevity gaps have grown over the past half century. In 1950, postretirement life expectancy for Black and white men at age 65 was equal, about thirteen years. Now there is a two-year difference in longevity for older men by race, and the probability of their even surviving to age 65 is widely disparate. While 81 percent of white men make it to age 65, just 70 percent of Black men do. Meantime, class-based longevity gaps have also widened. In the past twenty years, all our longevity gains as a society went to those in the upper half of the income distribution.[10]

The COVID-19 pandemic widened racial longevity gaps. Although US life expectancy is projected to fall by 1.13 years after 2021, declines for Black and Latino people are three to four times higher than for whites.[11] And nonwhites were much more likely to have had COVID—nonwhite people will suffer disproportionately from long COVID, making working longer even more difficult.

Life expectancy calculations by socioeconomic class are more complicated. Looking beyond the COVID-19 nightmare, the deeper we delve into the data, the more visible is the potent role of class in determining longevity. In looking at these numbers, we found that what everyone thinks is true is not true.

People think women live longer than men, but that's only in crude average terms. Bring in class-related factors, and the picture changes: men with the greatest educational attainment live longer than women with the least education and longer than Black women. That may sound sadly unsurprising, but what it shows us is that more than gender is at work, and class differences significantly sway longevity differences.

Once a person makes it to age 52, women in the highest education category live the longest at slightly older than 84 years, while men in the bottom education category live six years less just about 76 years. But as we might expect, high-income men live longer than low-income women. We shouldn't overestimate the role of gender in determining life expectancy—class matters greatly.

Class is a significant factor explaining an individual's predicted longevity. Brookings Institution economists Burtless, Bosworth, and Gianttasio found that women born in 1940 in the top 10 percent of household earnings who lived to age 50 were expected to live another 28.5 years.[12] Women in the bottom 10 percent who lived to age 50

TABLE 5.2 Longevity for individuals who survived to age 52 and worked for pay during their adult lives

	Death Age	
	MEN	WOMEN
Average	78.1	81.9
Lowest third of educational attainment	75.9	79.0
Middle third of educational attainment	78.4	82.1
Highest third of educational attainment	79.9	84.4
Black	75.3	79.4
Non-Black	78.6	82.5

Source: Health and Retirement Study (HRS), Institute for Social Research, University of Michigan, https://hrs.isr.umich.edu/about.

were expected to live only another 22.2 years. Rich people have more of everything, including life span.

But these are group statistics; none of us knows when we will die. As I have emphasized throughout the book, to behave optimally, American retirement policy requires that individuals play the longevity guessing game. And individuals will certainly get it wrong. I knew one couple, married for forty years, who worked skilled professional jobs longer than necessary to be sure they'd have enough. Two months after they left their cold Northern city to spend their golden years in the sunny Southwest, the wife was diagnosed with terminal cancer. Before her diagnosis, longevity tables predicted she would live another twenty years (table 5.2). Instead, she died three years later. They'd followed expert advice to a *T*. An early death was possible, just not probable or predictable.

Retirement Age + Death Age = Unequal Retirement Time

The longevity findings from the University of Michigan data corroborate previous research, including a 2015 study coauthored by Anthony Webb,[13] showing that for all those baby boomers born in 1946, the predicted retirement time for the highest educated man is 20 percent higher than for men with the least education (19.9 years compared to 16.6 years). Using more up-to-date data, we find the same pattern. In other words, the socioeconomic class divide in retirement has expanded for this prolific generation that's now older than 75 and well into what could be their retirement years.

Now that we have the two key ingredients that determine retirement time, we can put the inequality in longevity and differences in retirement ages together and estimate the unequal distribution of retirement time.[14] Here are our key findings:[15]

- Retirements are shorter than people might think—typically about fifteen years.
- Class matters more than gender. (High-socioeconomic-status men live longer than low-socioeconomic-status women.)
- Low-socioeconomic-status women have sixteen years of retirement time, but they spend a third of that time ill or disabled. Women with the most education get nineteen years of retirement and spend 20 percent of it sick and impaired.
- Black women have a 6 percent increased chance of being sick or impaired in retirement.
- Men with a traditional defined-benefit pension plan have a whopping advantage in retirement time—2.7 more years than people with a 401(k)-type plan. And men with DB plans are less likely to die while working or to be sick in retirement.

THE WELL-OFF LIVE LONGER IN RETIREMENT

The beauty of statistical analysis is that we can control other factors to isolate what independently affects people's retirement time. Controlling data in several ways can illuminate fascinating nuances that explain who gets to retire and when and how.

What the research tells us is that higher socioeconomic status helps people attain longer retirements.[16] But socioeconomic status matters more for women than for men, so gender does sway older workers' experiences in addition to class. As we've seen, educational attainment is not correlated with men's retirement time—but why? One reason is that people with higher levels of education retire and die at older ages. We find another class indicator: women with the highest levels of education secure the most retirement, at nearly twenty years on average.[17]

But when we controlled for what kind of pension plan men had, differences in socioeconomic status melted away. Men with no pension or retirement plan get the least retirement, just 10.4 years on average. Below, let's slice the data further to show the rich layers affecting retirement time, proving adages old and new: it's complicated, and intersectionality matters.

WOMEN LIVE LONGER BUT UNHEALTHIER

Because gender shapes the distribution of work and home responsibilities, it helps explain differences in retirement time. Paid work, compared to home responsibilities, remains a task highly delegated to men, so men may be more commonly discouraged from retiring and more likely to take on paid work as their responsibility, and thus they are more likely to die on the job.

The main reason women get more retirement time is because they live longer. On average, women get about eighteen years of retirement and men just under fourteen years; this is because women live almost 4 years longer and retire 0.2 years earlier than men. This idea of withdrawal from work is complicated by much of women's work being not paid.

Gender roles express themselves, of course, in heterosexual partnerships. Married and partnered women have about twenty years of retirement time compared to divorced or separated women, who have only a bit more than fifteen years. Partnered women probably have more support and are healthier. Married women live much longer than divorced or separated women—to about age 82 compared with 79. For men, the roles and retirement relationships are reversed. Married or partnered men work longer, perhaps because of pressure from their gendered role as workers—they have only slightly less than sixteen years of retirement time compared to divorced or separated men, who have more than sixteen years.

BLACK PEOPLE HAVE A SHORT RETIREMENT

Without isolating independent factors, we see stark differences in retirement time by race, especially among women. Black women get significantly less retirement time than non-Black women, about sixteen years compared to over eighteen. Black women retire nearly a year (0.8) sooner than non-Black women, but not soon enough to compensate for dying more than three years earlier. Non-Black men have about fourteen years of retirement, and Black men have under thirteen years of retirement time. Adding to the disparities, while Black men retire more than two years earlier than non-Black men, they die more than three years sooner. Earlier retirement does not make up for early death.

Isolating race as an independent factor in making retirement time short and unhealthy is difficult because race is intertwined with other factors, including access to health care, whether one resides in what public health experts call "healthy communities," and workplace protections from injury and illness. Although research shows that being Black is associated with many discriminatory and cumulative disadvantages over a lifetime—lower pay, having a greater chance of living in poverty and in poor neighborhoods, and experiencing racism and a lifetime of macro- and microaggressions—race on its own does not produce a statistically significant effect on retirement duration when we control for socioeconomic status and type of pension plan.[18]

Black Americans may be able to get as much retirement time as non-Black people of the same socioeconomic status and retirement plan type—but only if they are able to retire early to make up for shorter life expectancies. Union defined-benefit plans in industries with disproportionate shares of Black workers—auto and steel workers—had substantial effects on racial retirement time equity. The data show that Black workers may retire earlier than whites, but it is not a good retirement if it isn't voluntary. There would be little solace in having retirement time equity if you were pushed out of the labor market by family responsibilities, racial discrimination, or other industry and occupational factors, such as having a poor-quality job.[19] Bottom line, race affects the quality of retirement, not just the quantity: being Black is independently correlated with the amount of retirement time spent sick or impaired.

DEFINED-BENEFIT PLANS LEAD TO THE LONGEST RETIREMENT

The amount and quality of people's retirement time depend significantly on the kind of pension or retirement plan they have—if any at all. Workers with traditional, annuity-based, guaranteed-for-life pensions—DB plans—experience longer and healthier retirements (i.e., without major health issues) than do people with 401(k)-type plans or no plan.

To understand why DB plans allow people to get more retirement time, we need to know how they work compared to 401(k)-type plans. First, employers are not required to provide retirement plans, and most do not (far more did until the 1980s). Employers can provide a DB plan, a 401(k)-type plan (defined contribution, or DC), or nothing. The DB plan pays a pension for life based on salary and length of employment. The benefit is defined.

In contrast, DC plans pay a lump sum equal to all employee and employer contributions plus or minus investment returns; workers manage these plans, often with significant distress. DB plans are more secure than DC—they pay a lifetime annuity, do not allow people to withdraw money before retirement, earn higher risk- and fee-adjusted returns (because of more diversification and DBs have lower fees), and do not allow eligible employees to opt out, thus strengthening the plan's pooled funds.

Given the quite big differences between these offerings, it's not a surprise that DB participants retire about two years earlier than otherwise similar workers covered by DC plans or uncovered workers. Two key differences may help explain why. DB plans are more generous—people do not invest their own money or withdraw it. DC plans create incentives to keep working because people accrue more money.[20] Because DC plan values are tied to financial markets, people may try to minimize their considerable risk by working longer.

These plan disparities also may explain why people with DB plans tend to live longer than those with DC plans or nothing. Men with DB plans live a larger share of their retirement time free of limitations from illness and disability and are less likely to die on the job than men who have no retirement plan or who have only a DC plan. Men with DB plans live until 80 on average and retire at the relatively young average age of 63.6, for a retirement duration of 16.9 years—compared to 14.5 years for those with a DC or 401(k)-type plan and just 10.4 years for men with no plan. Following a similar pattern,

TABLE 5.3 Differences in retirement time for individuals who survived to age 52 and worked for pay during their adult lives

	Retirement duration (years)			
	MEN	WOMEN	SHARE OF RETIREMENT TIME SPENT SICK	SHARE WHO DIED WITHOUT RETIRING
Average	13.7	17.7	26%	9%
Lowest third of educational attainment	12.6	15.9	35%	10%
Middle third of educational attainment	14.3	17.5	26%	10%
Highest third of educational attainment	14.3	19.7	20%	7%
No retirement plan	10.4	16.9	29%	13%
Defined-benefit plan	16.9	19.4	23%	4%
Defined-contribution plan	14.5	17.8	25%	6%
Black	12.8	15.9	38%	10%
Non-Black	13.9	18.2	24%	9%

Note: The distribution of educational attainment is relative to one's birth cohort.

Source: Health and Retirement Study (HRS), Institute for Social Research, University of Michigan, https://hrs.isr.umich.edu/about.

female DB participants attain 19.4 retirement years, while women without retirement plans get only 16.9 years (table 5.3).

Having a secure pension for life—proxied here by a DB plan—significantly decreases the likelihood that men will die before retiring while increasing their retirement time. This is likely because DB plans are more prevalent among unionized workforces and are often designed to allow blue-collar, working-class men a way to retire before becoming eligible for Social Security.

The DB plan design enables some workers whose jobs are injurious to their health to retire earlier to compensate for their expected shorter life span, potentially equalizing retirement time. But that's just for union workers and some others who are fortunate enough to have such a plan. Equality of retirement should not be left to chance and luck. A nation's pension system should allow for disadvantaged groups to retire earlier than others to compensate for their shorter life expectancy and higher morbidity, as was often accomplished through union contracts in manufacturing, metalworking, and extractive industries. Disability insurance produces a similar equalizing effect.

Who Gets Healthy Retirement Time?

Although women have more retirement time than men, they spend a larger proportion of their retirement sick or impaired—26 percent of their time in retirement compared to 23 percent. Notably, Black women spend 38 percent of their retirement sick or impaired, while high-socioeconomic-status men and women spend only 20 percent that way. Working longer affects health differently depending on the type of work. Forcing elders to work to make up for eroding pensions could increase class- and race-based retirement quality gaps. The retirement health gap is particularly significant for women. Similarly, Black men and women have relatively less healthy retirement time than non-Black men and women do (when we don't control for other factors).

As with retirement time, the type of retirement plan has an

impact on health in retirement. Starkly put, DB participants are health-ier in retirement. Women with DB plans spend 23 percent of their retirement disabled, compared with 29 percent for women with no coverage and 25 percent for women with DC plans. Men with DBs and DCs each spend an average of 20 percent of their retirement disabled, compared with 28 percent of men without retirement plan coverage.

For all workers, lacking a workplace retirement plan causes a hefty 28 percent increase in length of retirement time spent with limita-tions on the activities of daily living (ADLs), a shortcut term used in health care and research to assess how well people can engage in their own daily care. ADLs are a big deal. Medical professionals and researchers often use a person's ability or inability to perform ADLs as a measurement of their functional status. The absolute number of ADLs someone needs assistance with reveals how functional they are: zero is the best, and ten means that one is, in practical terms, helpless. The type of pension or retirement plan (if any) makes a dif-ference not only in how much retirement income one gets but also in how healthy people are in retirement.

In a parallel reality to who gets to retire, we probed the data to ask, Who doesn't ever get to retire? Who works until they drop, "dying in their boots"? The answer to this morbid yet important question is multilayered.

Men work longer and live shorter lives, which gives them a higher risk of dying without any retirement. Strictly along gender lines, 14 percent of men die without ever retiring, whereas 9 percent of women meet this grim fate.

Among men, DB plan participants experience the least risk; 6 per-cent die before retiring. Having a DB plan decreases a man's prob-ability of dying in his boots by almost 8 percent. In contrast, having no retirement plan increases that likelihood by 10 percent.

Along class lines, 17 percent of men with the bottom third of edu-cational attainment die without retiring, compared to 14 percent for those in the top third. Men with less education die on average at age 76, while more highly educated men live an average of about 80 years. Interestingly, the risk of not being able to retire does not vary by race among men.

Among women, those who are widowed or lack a retirement plan face the highest risk of dying without retiring—15 percent and 13 percent, respectively. As with men, women with DB plans face the lowest risk of dying in their boots, at just 4 percent. High-socioeconomic-status women face a 7 percent chance of dying without retiring, whereas women with less education encounter a 10 percent risk.

....

BOX 5.1 Women and Precarity

Women study, earn, and work more than they did a hundred years ago—a sign of progress in the fight against sex discrimination—but women with equivalent skills and education still earn less than men, which adds up to much worse retirement security in old age.

The social construction of women's work and domestic life makes women dependent on the government or quixotic and unstable kin, charity, and the kindness of strangers, putting women in precarious situations as they grow older. Women are not paid for the domestic and generative care work they do at home, and that devaluation of women's labor carries over into the workplace. Since all retirement savings stem from deductions from a paycheck and Social Security credits stack up according to years in the paid labor force and earnings, women's subordinated earnings and uncompensated and uncredited care work suppresses retirement contributions and Social Security credits. In short, since a woman's labor is compensated less than a man's throughout her life cycle, her retirement is more fragile, and she faces a higher risk of poverty than men.

Here is what happens to women over the life cycle that makes women's retirement so precarious. Men and women take out similar college loans and pay the same tuition, but when they graduate and hit the labor market, women are paid less. In 2020, women only received a bit over 80 percent of men's median hourly earnings in the United States and were paid less in comparable jobs.

Adding injury to women's lower pay is that women in the US spend almost twice as much time as men doing unpaid domestic chores. And parenthood rewards men and penalizes women. Fathers increase their working hours, whereas mothers tend to reduce their time in paid work leading to a life with interrupted career paths, part-time work, or employment in more flexible low-wage occupations. Economists identify which relevant factors matter more to cause the gender pay gap—and the biggest ones are women's occupations pay less, women trim their hours to take care of family, and employers pay less to women because they think they are less valuable, and women will accept the lower pay.

The 401(k)-type plan design disadvantages women, who first drain their accounts for children's needs and to fund job transitions. Furthermore, because women retire earlier than men and their life expectancy is longer, women make do with their smaller savings over a longer period. The upshot is older women's poverty rates are higher than men's. The average old-age poverty rate for women in the OECD hovers around 16 percent (men's is about 11 percent). In the US, over one out of four women and one out of five men are poor in old age.

Retirement Time Is Bound to Become More Unequal

The equalization of healthy retirement times was an achievement Americans forgot to celebrate. The practical ability and social "right" to retire is becoming more contingent on whether a person is disabled or has saved enough money. Others, it seems, are not so deserving. A signature achievement of the postwar period—the democratization of who has control over the pace and content of their time after a lifetime of work—is being reversed.

This chapter has presented data never seen before.[21] I put together a unique data set from the Michigan survey and used a sophisticated methodology to reveal how retirement time goes to those at the top—to workers with higher socioeconomic status from their greater health and wealth. Another point to keep in mind: more highly educated workers are more likely to be appealing to employers. The top 20 percent have it both ways: they can retire, and they can work in jobs they like.

Making Americans work longer is especially harsh because people in the US already work more hours per day, more days per year, and more years per lifetime than their counterparts in any G7 nation—

a subset of large nations in the OECD. As the title of an op-ed by *Financial Times* reporter Sarah O'Connor indicates: "Living longer does not mean we should all work longer."[22] And in the working-longer bastion of the United States, there is layer upon layer of inequality in obtaining time to rest and recreate in one's later years.

The growing gaps by race and class of longevity and retirement wealth lead mainstream economists to conclude that cutting retirement benefits like Social Security will make socioeconomic inequality worse.[23] Likewise, if the racial and class inequalities in longevity, morbidity, and retirement wealth continue to grow along with do-it-yourself DC retirement plans, then healthy retirement time will become even more unequally distributed.

How many years do we have to work? How much healthy retirement time do we deserve? If people work for forty years, then is ten years too few and fifteen years too much? What is fair, and who gets to decide? The answer is not an economic number, even though political and social debaters want economists to provide an answer and conjure a magic ratio of work time to retirement time. We can't. Too many variables matter. For instance, in sheer economic terms, people who are highly productive in their working years—and in general, the nation's workers are quite productive—can afford longer retirement times.

As we'll see in the next chapter, the prevailing advice on working longer does not work for people's lives. Real-life factors make working longer a poor gamble for obtaining retirement security. Many jobs in old age are lower paid. With low pay, older workers claim their Social Security earlier and do not get the reward for waiting—the delayed retirement credit—that maximizes Social Security benefits at age 70. Few workers wait that long, and so they pay the price, which is a precarious old age.

6

Working Longer Does Little to Improve Retirement Security

A Morningstar personal finance column carried the fetching title, "Working Longer Can Be a Win-Win."[1] Typical of the genre, it contains seemingly good advice: work longer so you can "put off" that dreaded "dipping into savings" and delay Social Security to "improve your financial position once you do stop working." The advice is not altogether wrong—it's just irrelevant. Many older workers cannot and do not follow it, and for good reason: the advice parrots fifteen years of the working-longer consensus that's based on unreal assumptions.

Contrary to the column and to the reams of papers and pixels making a similar case, working longer does little to improve retirement security. But how can that be? Why does working longer not significantly help people become financially better off in retirement? Unfortunately, these are not easy questions to answer. Easier to find are advice columns and academic papers dispensing the sunny conclusion that there are many upsides and few downsides to working longer.

At a 2019 Brookings Institution conference on the benefits of working longer, Alicia Munnell again extolled the value of toiling a few extra years: "Many of today's workers face a serious income shortfall in retirement. . . . [A] few additional years in the labor force can make a significant difference. Extending our work life produces additional earnings; it can lead to a substantial increase in monthly Social Security benefits; it allows us to contribute more to our 401(k) and for our balances to earn additional investment income; and it shortens the length of retirement."[2]

Striking a sympathetic tone, Steven Sass, associate director of the Center for Retirement Research at Boston College, advises that many older workers "damaged by the recession" in 2007–2009 could "dramatically improve their retirement income by delaying retirement." The main reason these workers aren't doing this, he says, is it's "something they don't know."[3] But deeper inquiry reveals a more profound reason many elderly workers aren't dramatically improving their retirement security—because the advice just doesn't match up with people's realities.

To understand these realities better, my coauthor Anthony Webb and I analyzed a special survey that asks the same people questions over decades. This rich "panel" data set can tell us what people do over time. When people actually tell you what they are doing, you don't have to rely on spreadsheet simulations and guesses. Among other findings, our inquiry reveals that the key assumptions behind the advice—that older workers can save more and delay claiming Social Security benefits—are unrealistic. The only valid assumption is the grim one: working longer helps people afford retirement time precisely because it *reduces* the time one has in retirement. The logical policy extension of this bleak path is to "solve" the retirement funding problem by killing retirement altogether. That is a political choice—and one must wonder whether society will tolerate shrinking retirements in a wealthy nation full of hardworking people.

Again using the University of Michigan's HRS, my colleagues and I found that older workers work in jobs that often pay less than they earned in their "career" jobs. Also, older workers are much less likely to be actively participating in a retirement savings plan at work. In this reality, there is little chance that older workers will save more while working longer.

We found something surprising and unsettling for the working-longer policy architects and advocates. Our evidence makes the working-longer consensus case much weaker. Advocates for working longer stress that working longer enables older workers to delay claiming Social Security to get a higher benefit, to save more, and to not draw down any retirement savings so they will be better off in retirement. But examining how actual people live, we found that working longer barely improves people's retirement-income security when they do finally retire. Battling financial stresses, a sizable portion of workers over age 62 claim Social Security benefits while working and never get the large monthly benefit increases enjoyed by those who can afford to wait.[4] We found evidence that working longer did not improve financial preparedness for retirement as much as advocates said it would.[5]

Rethinking the Advice to Work Longer

The advice to work longer is meant to be practical and helpful. Working longer also has the magic of a free-lunch fix to inadequate retirement wealth and aging populations.

Back in the 1980s, when Reagan's deputy labor secretary Malcolm Lovell pushed policies coaxing older people to work longer, many hoped this extra labor would reduce the harm caused by Social Security benefit cuts and the increased risks from DC, or 401(k)-type plans, replacing traditional pensions. Lovell called for people to work more in old age to avoid falling short of retirement-income targets and plunging into poverty. Fifty years later, it's clear that Lovell's hope was not fulfilled. One major reason: the advice to work longer to boost retirement well-being is based on false information and assumptions.[6]

Despite the generous delayed retirement credit in Social Security, the pressure to supplement already-meager wages by collecting Social Security while working seems too great for low-paid older workers. One can imagine the relief of one such worker who can finally increase their pay with benefits. That allows them to work longer and collect Social Security in addition to wages![7] However, the penalty for claiming early is that the Social Security benefit is a lot smaller each month for the rest of one's life. That's a steep price to pay in old age.

Working longer was supposed to enable older workers to save more for retirement. But the added years of toil do not help as much as the consensus's architects wanted to believe. The data reveals that even if older working people refrain from collecting Social Security, they don't save money or stop withdrawing 401(k) money while they are working. In fact, when they finally do retire, they have less money saved up, not more, than before they were working longer, as our research shows. For example, at age 67, I knew someone who withdrew money from his 401(k) to buy a sturdier car to commute to work. Others undergo surgeries for chronic ailments such as carpel tunnel syndrome so they can keep working. When he was laid off at age 72, he was left with a nice three-year-old Honda that he barely drove and a much smaller 401(k).

The one way working longer makes retirement affordable is that it shrinks retirement time. Working longer means dying sooner after retiring; thus, a small amount of money covers a shorter retirement time. But this "reason" merely exposes the uncompromising and flawed vision of the working-longer consensus: solve the retirement crisis by killing retirement. As a rich nation, we can do better than that.

Most Workers Claim Social Security Benefits While Working

We tend to associate collecting Social Security with retirement, but it turns out that most people collect while they are working. Even college-educated older workers claim Social Security before age 70, when maximum benefits kick in. Over half (54 percent) of those claiming benefits while working do so to supplement low wages.[8] The other 46 percent are boosting their income, many times because their jobs pay less than what they once earned.[9] By age 66, not only do the 48 percent who claim Social Security earn less on the job than they would from benefits alone; they also have less than $20,000 in savings. For them, the decision to claim is both simple and reasonable—they need the money.

For other aging workers, multiple factors conspire to cause them to work longer and claim Social Security earlier. Foremost among these are cuts to Social Security benefits, the erosion of secure defined-benefit retirement plans, and most important, increased education levels of workers.

Between 1993 and 2000, 24 percent of workers and 59 percent of retirees claimed benefits at age 62. Reflecting the working-longer trend, between 2005 and 2009, a smaller share (17 percent of workers and 48 percent of retirees) claimed benefits at age 62. But after attaining the so-called full retirement age (this varies for those born between 1943 and 1959 and reaches 67 for those born after 1960—for example, it is 66 years and 2 months for those born in 1955), almost all workers combine work with benefits.

In 2018, more than half of 65-year-olds who worked claimed Social Security, and by age 66, 89 percent had claimed it.[10] But claiming while working can damage one's retirement finances. People who claim and continue to work at older ages do not benefit from the generous delayed retirement credit.[11] Compounding inequities, the well-off are more insulated from this harm than others because they can wait to get the credit.

The disparities in who needs to tap benefits early mirror broader inequities in retirement security. Full-time and college-educated workers are less likely than part-time and non-college-educated workers to collect Social Security while working to supplement their wages. Between 2008 and 2012, 73 percent of economically disadvantaged workers aged 65 claimed benefits, compared with 23 percent of better-off full-time workers. A smaller share of college-educated workers (36 percent) claimed while working, compared with 54 percent of non-college-educated workers (table 6.1).

What's particularly perverse about incentives like the delayed retirement credit is that part-time and non-college-educated workers are less likely than full-timers and the college educated to delay claiming, but these lower-income folks would benefit more by delaying because they are less likely to meet their replacement rate targets because they have more debt and lower levels of wealth.

To truly understand which workers supplement their pay with Social Security benefits and how they can be helped, we need to know more than their income and wealth levels, their education, and their work status. Where are they working? What are their jobs like? The system never intended for most older workers to claim Social Secu-

TABLE 6.1 Workers aged 60–64 who are receiving Social Security worker benefits

	Age					
	62	64	65	66	67	70
Full-time workers	9	15	23	85	91	100
Part-time workers	35	61	73	95	98	100
College-educated workers	15	22	36	84	98	100
Non-college-educated workers	23	40	54	93	95	100

Source: Ghilarducci, Papadopoulos, and Webb, "The Illusory Benefit of Working Longer on Retirement Financial Preparedness."

rity benefits while working. The grand design hatched in the Reagan era—which was based more on hope than on evidence—was that cutting benefits at earlier ages and raising them at older ages would mean that society, employers, and people would just behave differently and work more. But an entirely different economics took over. Employers benefited. Over half of older workers who claim Social Security while working, 3.8 million, earn less than $23,000 annually. Most older personal-care aides, cashiers, and office clerks, and half of all schoolteachers, collect Social Security while working (table 6.2). Workers' collection of Social Security surely helps employers because Social Security supplements their low wages, so employers don't have to. Incidentally, requiring older people to work to be eligible for food stamps also helps employers get access to an increased supply of workers willing to work for less.[12]

As we might expect, low-wage workers are three times more likely to claim benefits at age 62. However, by age 66, almost all members of both groups collect benefits (95 percent and 91 percent, respectively). Some higher-income workers also claim Social Security. Perhaps they want to be able to consume more. Of those higher-income workers, 6 percent claim at age 62, and 39 percent claim by age 66.

My coauthor, Anthony Webb, did this project with me to correct the mistake he made in his previous work. The old paper, using

TABLE 6.2 Older workers in select low-wage occupations who received Social Security benefits while working (surveyed in 2020)

	Share collecting Social Security benefits	Number
Personal-care aides	60%	150,658
Cashiers	60%	136,096
Office clerks	55%	145,925
Receptionists and information clerks	53%	106,213
Teaching assistants	53%	85,614
Elementary and middle school teachers	50%	195,451
Janitors and building cleaners	49%	168,417
Retail sales clerks	47%	165,092
Home health aides	43%	60,770
Drivers and sales workers and truck drivers	41%	240,860
Secretaries and administrative staff	39%	149,790

Source: Annual Social and Economic Supplement, Current Population Survey, 2020.

heroic assumptions, concluded working longer induced more older workers to delay claiming Social Security. But our project, using real human behavior, found that the incentive induced an increase in claiming age by only 3.7 percent, while Anthony's older, widely cited paper predicted an increase of 21.4 percent in the age of claiming.

Workers claim Social Security before they retire for many reasons. But I fear they also claim in part because of poor communication from the Social Security Administration.[13] Social Security pamphlets often talk about claiming and retiring as if they were the same thing. I suspect many people think they will die sooner than they probably will, or they want to claim what they have earned. (One of my co-commissioners on a high-level federal commission examining Social Security and pension policy told me he heard a janitor in the Social

Security waiting room tell an older woman not to claim too early—to no avail.) We need more research on communication, beliefs, and fears to understand why people claim Social Security when they do. But make no mistake, it is clear that most older workers claim Social Security before age 70 because they need the money.

Older Workers Likely Do Not Save
Additional Funds for Retirement

Another crack in the working-longer consensus is the assumption that older people who stay in the workforce continue to save in their retirement accounts. In my research, I have yet to come across any good data on how many folks in this age group withdraw from their accounts. It seems that people withdraw from their retirement accounts before retirement for many reasons.[14] The assumption that all older workers continue to save while they are working is an assumption that makes working longer look good on paper. But because most older workers don't save for retirement while working, working longer is not so helpful to their retirement security.

Why don't older workers save for retirement after age 62? First, only about 43 percent of older workers between the ages of 62 and 64 participate in a retirement plan. As older workers age, their retirement savings rates decline. Among 65- to 66-year-old workers, the savings rate falls to 42 percent; for workers between the ages of 67 and 70, retirement plan participation falls to 37 percent (table 6.3). And remember, these low rates are for workers who are fortunate enough to have a retirement plan; most don't even have the option to participate.

As we can see, the evidence is stacked heavily against the notion that working longer into old age boosts retirement security. Not having a retirement plan at work or not participating in one bodes poorly for any kind of wealth accumulation. The harsh reality is that most older workers do not have jobs with 401(k)s or pensions—so they must draw on Social Security and savings while working—then they either tread water or sink. Moreover, older people are taking on more debt than ever before.[15]

TABLE 6.3 Workers with retirement plans at work

	Age group	
	YOUNGER THAN AGE 62 (%)	AGE 62–70 (%)
Access to a plan at current job	46	49
Participating in a plan at current job	40	43

Source: Survey of Income and Program Participation, US Census Bureau, 2020.

Working after 62 Does Not Significantly Boost Retirement-Income Security

Basing our research on survey data instead of modeling activities, my colleagues and I found working longer, from age 62 to 70, increases monthly income during those work years, but crucially, that extra work does not boost retirement security nearly as much as overoptimistic financial models would have us believe.[16]

Work-longer advocates use models that predict people who act in certain ways and face favorable circumstances are better able to meet their retirement-income targets. These predictions are so favorable that one study says that the share of households able to meet retirement-income targets would increase from 23 percent at age 62 to an alluring 64 percent at age 70. If the circumstances these predictions assume were true, then financial retirement readiness could be solved simply by policy makers—through the clever design of Social Security benefits—coaxing people to work longer. We wish that were true. Even among those who work to age 70, households' preparedness for retirement grew from 23 percent to 41 percent—not even across the halfway mark. That means that more than half of folks who labored to age 70 still weren't financially ready to retire. Working longer does not solve the retirement crisis.[17] How do we explain this huge gap between models and real-life reports? Two-thirds of the disparity stems from the fact that most workers do not delay claiming Social Security.

Based on our statistical analysis, the big, shiny result is that working has no independent effect—positive or negative—on being financially prepared for retirement.[18] This turns conventional wisdom on its head. Working at older ages does little to improve financial readiness for retirement—and working does *nothing* to increase people's income-replacement rates.

We found no difference in changes in retirement readiness because of working longer among those with college degrees and those with less than a college education, those married or not, white or nonwhite, healthy or sick. In another surprising result, we found that, regardless of education, most workers claim Social Security benefits by age 65.

The only significant factor on retirement finances and working longer we found is when people were born (which is sheer luck), because that determined their age at the time recession struck.

Workers born between 1937–1941 and 1942–1947 were aged 62–70 during the Great Recession and stock market plunge of 2007–2009. These unlucky people just happened to be born in the years that would make them about age 64—cue the Beatles' "When I'm Sixty-Four"—when the big recession hit in 2008. These folks experienced smaller increases (between 3 percent and about 5 percent) in their retirement-income replacement rates, even if they worked as long as their older counterparts (born between 1931 and 1936), who had surpassed age 70 before the Great Recession. Another factor weakens the "work longer" case. Even for households where a college-educated spouse works past age 62, working longer can make things worse for retirement preparedness. Why? These spouses are unlikely to earn more Social Security credits—they will not have any of their top-thirty-five earning years after age 62—and the increased consumption during working years only steepens the income decline after retirement.

Being Financially Ready for Retirement

We further clarify the work-longer or retirement-readiness picture by asking more questions: Which factors help predict who is and isn't ready for retirement? Under which circumstances does working longer help make retirement more affordable? How do larger socioeconomic inequities shape the retirement picture? And what does "readiness" mean when older folks are so often in or near poverty? It bears reminding that by age 66, only 31 percent of men and 35 percent of women have enough income to maintain their pre-retirement living standards and stay above the poverty line. In such precarity, are these people ready to retire?

The usual suspects—those with high earnings and wealth—are more likely to be headed for a comfortable retirement. But there are still some surprises: some low-income workers have solid and secure finances (those with DB pensions), while some high-income workers and surviving spouses face cruel downward mobility in their living standards when they retire.

....

BOX 6.1 For a Vast Majority of People, Working Longer Does Not Make Up for Low Retirement Savings

What can and should older folks do if they're stuck without a decent pension and retirement security? Can working longer make a difference to a person's retirement well-being? The answer is a little bit, but not as much as you think. Using reasonable assumptions about jobs and pay for people aged 62–70, we found that a college-educated person working full-time in a job with retirement benefits and paying more than $15 an hour could increase their retirement-income replacement rate by about 15 percent over eight years. Sounds good in theory—but in real life, this kind of person is usually retired! In other words, the folks who could benefit from working longer are the ones most likely to retire and be well off. So, we're back where we started.

Others who are financially unprepared for retirement may take on part-time work. But paradoxically, working part-time can make one less prepared for retirement. The share of older male workers in part-time jobs increases with age, from a little over one-fifth of men who are working at age 62 to over 40 percent at age 70. Older women workers show the same pattern. As you might guess, people who work part-time are less likely to be prepared for retirement. The best advice: do whatever you can to delay collecting Social Security early. Delaying Social Security by even one year increases the income-replacement rate by 3 percent per year, and that adds up.

Keeping a job, taking on more work, and cutting spending are all good efforts to keep one's head above water. But these strategies won't do much to boost retirement security; individuals acting on their own have limited agency. What's needed is real federal assistance and policy leadership.

Using statistical techniques (and the best data) that isolate various independent effects on retirement readiness, we found no differences between two people who are statistically alike in every way except that one works between age 62 and age 70 and the other does not. Simply put, working longer does not help people be ready for retirement in any significant way. Except for one thing: Your economic situation at age 62 is the rare factor that can sway whether working longer affects your retirement preparedness. If you are a low-wage worker at 62, working longer can decrease your chances of reaching your target income-replacement rate. Although this does not guarantee you'll worsen your finances by working past age 62, it does mean that working for low wages beyond age 62 makes it more unlikely that you will be prepared for retirement. Equally worrisome, a whopping 53 percent of all 62-year-old workers earn less than $15 an hour.[19] This alone presents huge public policy and societal challenges that must be addressed. As we might expect, folks working past age 62 who earn more than $15 per hour have a better shot at retirement security.

Working for low wages hurts your chances of being financially prepared as much as being nonwhite and having lower educational attainment. At ages 66 and 70, workers making less than $15 an hour are 9 and 8 percentage points, respectively, less likely to be financially prepared for retirement than nonworkers.

The people most financially prepared for retirement are workers with the highest educational attainment. Among 66-year-olds who meet their retirement-income targets, 61 percent have a college degree.[20] At age 62, individuals with a college degree are 19 percentage points more likely to be financially prepared for retirement than those with high school education or less. Meanwhile, among the large group of retirees who are not ready, only 16 percent have a college degree. But a college degree does not give you immunity from financial disappointment in retirement. Among older workers who cannot meet their retirement-income targets, 30 percent have college degrees.

And it should be no surprise by now that the type of retirement plan one has is key to retirement financial readiness. The person with a DB plan, who is alike in every way to someone with no retirement plan or just a 401(k)-type plan, is much more likely to be ready for retirement.[21]

Beyond education and pay, the lifelong effect of structural racism also influences who is ready to retire. Black people are less likely to be prepared to maintain their living standards or stay out of poverty in retirement, as one might expect given racial discrimination and being treated with less regard in the labor market. At age 62, 13 percent of Black men are financially prepared to retire, compared to 25 percent of white men.

Working Longer Isn't Working

In conclusion, American workers financially unprepared for retirement are faced with the advice to work longer. This is not useful or relevant advice to most people approaching their early 60s. The reality is, working longer has a far smaller effect on retirement preparedness than predicted by numerical simulations, so-called spreadsheet models, and working-longer advocates. If seniors can find work, many must still supplement their low wages by claiming early reduced Social Security benefits and forgo the rewards for claiming Social Security at older ages.

Strengthening Social Security and expanding employer-sponsored retirement plan coverage would give those with poor labor-market options a real choice between work and retirement and would enable them to delay claiming Social Security. This would strengthen seniors' circumstances in their final years, allowing them to live in comfort and security.

Despite the significant rise in older workers, we still do not know enough about why they work, the jobs they have, and with whom they compete. In 2018, there were 43 million people over age 65 in the US labor market—and growing numbers of them cannot afford to retire. But there's a powerful labor-market dynamic at work here, too. Coaxing elders who do not have pensions to seek work and accept any job they're offered tilts bargaining power toward employers. The next chapter explores how this buyer's market affects older workers, examining how Social Security's implicit wage subsidy, which effectively raises employers' after-tax and transfer income, could be a boon for businesses.

....

BOX 6.2 Delayed Retirement Credit: A Gift to the Well-Off

The generous delayed retirement credit (DRC) increases benefits by 8 percent for each year a person waits to collect Security after full retirement age. The credit was intended as a modest inducement to work longer and delay claiming; the intention was not to penalize someone for working longer. But the reality is inequality.

In 2000, interest rates were a lot higher, so the 8 percent was set to mimic ordinary returns, and it assumed that everyone had the same chance to live a normal life span. But now returns on the typical retirement portfolio are between 3 percent and 5 percent, and the gap in morbidity by race and class is grotesque. The intention was that the 6 percent to 8 percent credit for delay claiming (and not taking an early retirement reduction) would be fair (actuarially speaking): the monthly benefit was only higher if one waited to claim because everyone had about the same longevity. Whether one collected sooner or later was not supposed to matter because the higher monthly benefit compensated for collecting for a shorter amount of time. But socioeconomic class and structural inequalities had their effect, and it turns out that people who have the money to wait are also the people who have jobs that induce health and who have better access to health care and healthy lifestyles—almost all the longevity gains are going to them.

The average claiming age rose, and some scholars believe the stick of Social Security benefit cuts and incentives of higher benefits by waiting are the main factors behind the rising labor-force participation among older people. Other scholars don't credit the incentives as much as the rise in work being a passive consequence of each cohort being more educated. The stick of eroding workplace retirement plans is another reason older people work longer.

My colleagues and I added more insight by finding retirement is not the worker-controlled event that policy makers and economists would have us think. Half of retirees say they retired because they were laid off or otherwise pushed out of their jobs—many seniors cannot work even if they want to. And we found many are working because they have no practical choice.

And the growing gap in longevity means that the juicy incentives to work longer are going to the well-off. People who can delay claiming Social Security until age 70—just under 9 percent—are in a swanky room all to themselves. Almost everyone else claims before age 65. The people who claim at 70 are those who not only can afford to wait and reap Social Security's generous delayed retirement credit (DRC) but also need the increased benefits the least. Quite an inequality paradox.

And that 9 percent is not timing retirement to the claim age of 70. Many have already retired; they just have enough money to wait to claim Social Security benefits and take advantage of the best financial deal on the planet—a guaranteed return between 6 percent and 8 percent for every year one waits to claim past 62. Waiting to claim from age 62 to 70 raises one's monthly lifetime benefits by more than 30 percent. The elite turned the claim decision into an investment decision rather than a work decision. The DRC is indeed a good deal for well-off people who can make optimal investment decisions. But there is no evidence that the DRC is doing what it was intended to do: incenting ordinary people to work longer and delay claiming to be better off when they retire.

7

When Older Workers Lose, All Workers Lose

In 2020, the movie industry served up a compelling illustration of how older workers are losing bargaining power when a film about real-life and fragile senior citizens won the Academy Award for Best Picture. *Nomadland* featured Amazon's CamperForce program and the road-weary older "nomads" who work there and in low-paid seasonal jobs. Frances McDormand's character in her early 60s, Fern, lives out of a van and takes on low-paying Amazon warehouse jobs.

Fern's story is based loosely on the real-life accounts in Jessica Bruder's nonfiction book, *Nomadland: Surviving America in the Twenty-First Century*.[1] Most of the homeless older workers Bruder interviewed took to the road after the Great Recession wiped out what little retirement savings they had and could no longer afford their rent or mortgage. Since the average Social Security benefit at age 62 is only $1,130 a month, or just $13,560 a year, it's clear they still had to work.

There is no romance in the *Nomadland* road life, although there is community and humor. Older worker nomads are certainly a tiny share of the tens of millions of older workers close to dire economic straits who are working in any job they can. As the situations of older workers like Fern become more precarious, the workers lose their bargaining power to command or demand better wages, conditions, or pensions.

Good pensions are fading fast from the American economic landscape. And bad pensions—or no pensions, for many—have helped make older workers sitting ducks in the labor market. When this happens, the wages, hours, and working conditions of all workers are imperiled. Making the crucial connection between inadequate retirement savings and pensions and older workers' weak bargaining power is the point of the following.

Older workers who have wobbly and inadequate retirement plans have less leverage when looking for jobs and accepting offers. Bad pensions lead to lower bargaining power. Less bargaining power means less pressure on employers to improve hours, wages, and working conditions. And less pressure on employers means worse jobs for seniors and everyone else. But there are winners: weak pensions create a built-in advantage for employers who want to raise profits by lowering labor costs. The working-longer consensus—buoyed by legions of researchers declaring that the average person's workability extends to age 73—is nothing but a win for employers.

The COVID-19 economic crisis, like the 2008 recession, pushed out older workers.[2] They may have told government surveyors they retired, but the truth is that millions of older workers were forced out of work earlier than planned. They had to stop contributing to their retirement plans earlier than they planned and to raid their retirement savings earlier than they planned. And for the older workers who kept their jobs, their retirement plan was still not safe. Many employers halted matching 401(k) contributions (including my own).[3] But 50- to 70-year-olds with inadequate savings have weak fallback positions to a current job or a lousy job offer. The upshot is that over 70 percent of workers aged 62 and older are working out of economic necessity.

Ten factors compel older people to accept terms favoring the employer:

1. Eroding pension income and more debt weaken older people's "fallback" position.
2. Fewer unions mean older workers have less workplace protection.
3. The decline in stable, long-term employment relationships means employers devalue older, experienced workers. Older

workers are the fastest group in contingent (i.e., part-time, contracted, and temporary) work.

4. Perennial age discrimination disadvantages older workers at work and in seeking work.

5. Older workers' tendency to not move as much as younger workers means that their lower geographical mobility increases employers' monopsony power.

6. The Earned Income Tax Credit is not available to older workers, which increases their desperation to work and causes income inequalities between workers with the same job and work effort.

7. The sheer size of the boomer cohort suppresses wages for everyone in the US labor market.

8. Older workers are more likely to work for low-profit, relatively lower-wage, small employers.

9. Industry business strategy models cultivate a dependency on low-paid and desperate older workers.

10. Low-paid older workers don't have employee benefits, easy work schedules, and other perks and rewards to compensate for their relatively lower wages.

These long-developing structural issues undercut older workers' bargaining power. And as we might imagine, the working-longer consensus leaps over these power issues, ignores the increasing inequality between workers and between workers and firms, and celebrates all forces increasing labor-force participation.

And because the labor market is one big market, when one especially large group loses bargaining power and becomes a ready and reserve source of labor, all workers lose. As a giant boomer cohort becomes a reserve army of labor—36 million out of 160 million US workers are over 55—wages, hours, and working conditions are suppressed for everyone.

Some older workers have held some ground, to be sure, because they are healthier and have more marketable skills, but on balance, power has shifted to employers.

Ten Reasons for Older Workers' Weaker Bargaining Power

Bargaining power is central to every worker-employer relationship. In nearly every treatise on the subject, the worker comes out worse. In 1942, unions were central—a strike could halt the war effort—yet Harvard economist John Dunlop warned the worker relative to an employer was weak and "lacked waiting power."[4] The worker did not have enough power to "withhold" from entering the relationship. Likewise, in the literature on domestic abuse, the spouse who faces the highest cost of leaving the marriage has the least bargaining power. Each party needs to assess their best alternative to a negotiated agreement to weigh whether it's worth giving in. Your best alternative to a negotiated agreement is your best fallback position if negotiations fail. Having a good fallback position can help anyone get the best deal in all types of negotiations, including the constant back-and-forth negotiations between employers and workers.

It's a commonsense concept that helps older workers know when they should accept a certain set of pay and working conditions, when they should fight for better pay and conditions, and when they should quit. A worker with pensions and wealth has a comfortable retirement as a fallback position, so the employer will likely raise pay and improve conditions to keep the older worker. A worker without a good fallback position is likely to settle for less. An employer has a great fallback position if the pool of willing workers is similar to their current workers.

People without good fallback positions do not have bargaining leverage. Insecure pensions keep older workers on the dip side of an unbalanced scale.

Before presenting the preponderance of evidence for declining bargaining power, I define power with a fascinating detour into the heart of labor economics theory—the reservation wage.

Worker vulnerability is measured by a simple concept that economists call the "reservation wage." The reservation wage is the lowest wage a person will accept to work (on a macro level, because clearly individual choices and contexts vary). This minimal reservation wage is what a person considers enough, influenced by how much money a person has without working. For example, having a working spouse, income from a trust fund, a universal basic income, or a pension allows a person to demand a higher wage and better working conditions. A personal fallback position is a personal bargaining position. With nonlabor income, a person has a better fallback position and more bargaining power.

The reservation wage explains why Brookings Institution economist Henry Aaron called older workers who do not have good pensions "the mugged."[5] These older people work because they have no practical choice. This group, the economically mugged or coerced, has had persistently lower reservation wages since 2008 and even earlier; it is these folks who populate *Nomadland*. Reservation wages and fallback positions—everyone has two!

The most potent sign of older workers' weaker bargaining power is their shrinking relative wages. Older men's wages started to fall dramatically relative to younger workers' wages in 1990 and have lagged ever since. Older women's wages have increased slightly, but due to the persistent gender gap, they still haven't caught up with men's. Take men with bachelor's degrees. In the twenty-nine years since 1990, their wages decreased by 3 percent, but wages for younger men aged 35–54 increased by 9 percent.[6] And male and female older workers have experienced almost no real wage growth since 2007.

1. PENSION INSECURITY

Topping our list of reasons older workers have lost bargaining power is the erosion of retirement-income security and rising elderly debt. Worsening economic fortunes suppress older folks' reservation wages, making them more likely to accept work under worse pay and conditions.

Yet over the past three decades, even as boomers have aged and have become more and more concerned about financing retirement, employers, Congress, and market forces did not serve up work-based retirement plans. Work-placed retirement plan coverage did not budge over 50 percent in forty years. In 2020, fewer than half of workers participated in a pension plan, about the same level as in the 1980s.[7] Folks are headed into old age without a fallback position, vulnerable to the labor market's worst offers.

Along with this pension erosion, the widening inequality of retirement wealth means that bargaining power among older workers is also more unequal. Of the 73 million boomers who reached retirement age right after the financial crash of 2008, the bottom 80 percent were not prepared for retirement. Sit with that for a moment: nearly an entire generation—and one vaunted for its labor successes—was not financially secure enough to retire. By 2019, the mean retirement account balance for people nearing retirement age was wholly inadequate at just $10,000, because 44.5 percent have nothing.[8] Sometimes the average account balance is reported as higher, at $222,000, but this is because a few households with large savings accounts push up the average. Worse, those in the bottom half have nothing but Social Security. Today, those with the top fifth in lifetime earnings hold half of all retirement wealth; the bottom quintile has just 1 percent. And these gaps are only deepening: the top fifth fared better in 2010 than in 1992, and those in the bottom fifth had less.[9]

Making inequalities, lower-income and middle-class Americans are likely to experience downward pressure on their reservation wage because their retirement assets have been hit the hardest. Yet we find that in the statistical midpoint, older workers at all income levels face some pressure on their reservation wage and working conditions. On average, middle-class households need $600,000 in financial assets to maintain their pre-retirement living standards in retirement, yet the median retirement account balance for families reaching retirement age is $0, and the average is just $15,000.[10] In other words, tons of older middle-income folks will need to either dramatically reduce their costs of living or take a job that may not pay or treat them very well. Many will have to do both. Eroding pensions and shriveling savings mean that 55 percent of older households must rely on Social Security for almost all their income in retirement.[11] That is, to put it bluntly, a recipe for disaster.

Declining nonlabor income for older workers—a primary feature of a weak fallback position and thus a low reservation wage—stems from the current system's failure to boost retirement plan coverage at work.

In 1980, 46 percent of workers over age 55 reported being covered by a workplace retirement plan. By 2013 that rate fell to just 41 percent, roughly what it was in 2020. That means that nearly six in ten workers nearing retirement age do not have a job-based pension of any sort. Another recipe for disaster. After the flashy 401(k) plan came on the scene in the 1980s, firms that offered pensions quickly switched away from providing defined-benefit to defined-contribution plans. But firms were less likely to offer any kind of pension at all. Employers' growing reluctance to offer good pension plans for their workers meant that while workers born from 1946 to 1950 could expect an average of $6,375 annually (in 2018 dollars) from pension benefits, people born between 1961 and 1965 would get only $3,750 a year. Although income from defined-contribution plans increased for the latter group, expected retirement income from sources other than Social Security is still $1,000 lower for late boomers.[12]

Unless we change current trends and policies, the combined effects of declining pension coverage, inadequate pension savings, and Social Security benefit cuts could well lead to large-scale downward mobility of middle-class near-retirement households into poverty.

2. FEWER UNIONS

Before we dive into the many ways that unions help older workers, we need a quick detour to economic theory. If the concepts of reservation wages and fallback positions help us better understand the labor market and our place in it, then consider the inelegant concept range of indeterminacy. Has quite a ring to it, eh? The phrase means that employers do not have just one predetermined compensation package they can pay workers before they must lay them off or go out of business. In fact, employers have a range of compensation levels they can offer, and what they eventually pay is not predictable merely from a perspective of supply and demand. Employers can still stay in business and earn profits at various levels of pay and benefits. That employers can pay within a range of compensation levels—according to what they decide they can spare, not only what they can "afford" to pay workers—is astonishing, as it changes the ways we consider what employers really can or can't do.

The textbook economist and business lobbyist would have you believe that the impersonal forces of supply and demand determine what employers can pay and that that's the end of the matter. But as labor economists have known for over a hundred years, many other factors, especially institutional and psychological aspects, determine what (and how much more) employers can pay workers before they go out of business or must lay anyone off. Pay is the outcome of a form of regulated or bargained prices.[13]

The union provides a structure for administered wages and a channel of give-and-take between employers and workers over productivity and pay. The bargaining process itself means that what they settle on will be indeterminate and exists within a range of possibilities. Unions are an effective force for raising wages when employers can pay higher wages but instead offer less. The John Deere strike settlement is a good example. In October and November 2021, the United Auto Workers went on strike at the company for over a month, the first strike at John Deere in thirty-five years, after union members rejected a wage contract proposal that offered a two-tier wage boost—5 percent raises to some workers and 6 percent to others. The final-year agreement included a 10 percent increase in wages in 2021 and a total increase of 20 percent over the life of the contract.

When employers have advantages of time (they don't need to hire immediately) or of having many applicants for one job (which is almost always true), they have monopsony power, which creates a "buyer's market," the opposite of worker power. As unions have waned, monopsony conditions have become especially acute in older workers' labor markets. According to Urban Institute economist Kate Bahn, "the decades-long decline in private-sector union membership presents . . . the strong possibility that more and more employers will be able to exercise monopsony power over the wages of their workers."[14] Union membership losses are especially acute for workers older than 55. In the sixteen years between 2004 and 2020, older workers suffered a sharper decline in their union membership (from 17 percent in 2004 to 13 percent in 2017) compared to prime-age workers.[15]

This ongoing union erosion spells weaker bargaining power for all workers. And as older workers' union membership sinks, they have even less ability to negotiate the pay and conditions they deserve. This dynamic further depresses older workers' fallback position and reservation wages.

3. INSECURE JOBS

When workers find themselves in "contingent" jobs—such as independent contracting, on-call positions, temporary agency, and gig work—they typically have less bargaining power. And it should be no surprise by now that older workers are the fastest-growing group in alternative employment arrangements. A 2017 study found that 15 percent of workers aged 55 to 75 worked in an alternative work arrangement, and a 2021 study found 24 percent of older workers did.[16]

Except for independent contractors, workers in alternative employment arrive at those jobs with much less bargaining power than their full-time employee colleagues. Whereas 6 percent of all older workers report losing their previous job involuntarily, 17 percent of older workers in on-call, temp agency, contract firm, or gig work were much more likely to experience involuntary job loss. The median older worker reported personal wealth of 171 percent of earnings, while older workers in alternative arrangements held assets that were just 77 percent of earnings. Less wealth means a much lower ability to retire, less fallback bargaining power, and thus a smaller reservation wage. Alternative arrangements also remove workers from a firm's job ladder, meaning little or no opportunity for promotion.

Economist Michael Papadopoulos found while some researchers assume older workers actively choose alternative work schedules—many workers in alternative arrangements would prefer traditional jobs. Nearly half (46 percent) of workers in temporary agency jobs and 40 percent in on-call positions in 2017 said they would prefer a traditional arrangement (12 percent and 10 percent, respectively, said "it depends"). And no wonder: that year, median earnings for full-time workers in traditional jobs was $32,500, while those in alternative work (excepting independent contractors) earned just $14,000.[17] Meanwhile, only 21 percent of workers in alternative arrangements believed that they could find an equivalent job if they lost their current one, compared to 35 percent for workers in traditional forms of employment.[18]

Labor economists love results from surveys that ask workers how easy it would be to find a comparable job if they lost their current one. The answer is a good measure of the fear factor in the labor market. Suppose the answer is high—"I have a 99 percent chance of finding an equivalent job if I lost the one I have now"—then the worker is not too afraid of losing that job. If the confidence number is low, it usually means a worker is stuck.[19] This confidence-fear dynamic factors into people's decision-making and influences the wages and conditions these workers will accept.

Another trend alongside the rise of alternative work demonstrating that employers are less committed to workers is the fall in job tenure, or the number of years and months a worker has been with their current employer. In the past three decades, average job tenure has fallen in the US. The proportion of workers who have been with their employer for more than ten years is down, and the share who have moved jobs in the last year is up. Interestingly, the group affected most by this erosion has been men with a lot of job market experience.[20]

The slippage in job tenure is significant. Back in 1987, the median US male aged 45–54 had been with his current employer for thirteen years; by 2018, he had been with his employer for just eight years. For older men, the erosion is less but notable. In 1987, the median older man ages 55–64 had been with his employer for seventeen years, and that dropped to fourteen years by 2018.[21] The less job tenure one has or can expect, the more they are at the precarious mercies of the labor market, with less fallback negotiating power.

The shortening of employment relationships has occurred predominantly at large firms, mostly because of declining unionization. There is little evidence that foreign competition or technological change causes people to leave their employers more frequently.[22] On a human level, declining job tenure means that people are with their employers for less time; there are fewer thirty-year anniversary watches and forty-years-with-the-company celebration dinners; shorter periods of employment at the end of a career to accumulate money for retirement; and more wealth-draining job changes.

Displaced older workers are more likely to job hop, to suffer further involuntary job losses, and to experience subsequent unemployment than are those who continue working for the same employer.[23] Older workers must confront this reemployment disadvantage even in good times. The growing turbulence of the labor market over many decades has hurt older workers.[24] After becoming unemployed, older workers face substantially longer periods of unemployment than younger workers. In 2015, the average duration of unemployment was thirty-five weeks for workers aged 45–54 years and twenty-seven weeks for prime-age workers 24–34.[25] We see the same aftereffects from the COVID-19 recession of 2020. In October 2021, the average duration of unemployment was thirty-two weeks for workers aged 45–54 and a long thirty-six weeks for those aged 55–64. That is in comparison to the shorter search times for younger workers—twenty-nine weeks for those aged 24–34.[26]

After a partial economic recovery, older workers' labor-force participation fell continuously, reaching its lowest point in January 2021. During this time, roughly 1.1 million older workers exited the workforce between August 2020 and January 2020—and past practices mean they may never come back.[27] The cost of job loss is higher for older workers, and the risk of never finding another job means older workers feel more pressure to keep their current job, even if it doesn't pay or treat them right—yet another way elderly workers are pushed to the labor market's margins, with meager fallback options.

This evidence punctuates the fear that every older worker feels when they're pushed out of a job at the tender ages beyond 55—the fear that they will never get back into the labor pool. OK, you might ask, what does this higher cost of unemployment have to do with bargaining power? When a worker's cost of job loss increases, the worker has less power to negotiate a good next job. The key factor here is that people in their 50s who separate from their employer—for whatever reason—risk missing their peak earning and savings years. Not saving in your 50s increases the risk of not being adequately prepared for retirement. Do you know what happens then? You have a weaker fallback position, which means you have less bargaining power.

4. AGE DISCRIMINATION

Another way older workers lose bargaining power in the workplace is through age discrimination. Note that the distinction between employers discerning and being discriminating because they want the best worker for a job is not illegal or untoward. Being discriminated against for factors unrelated to your productivity is the classic definition of market discrimination. *Discrimination* is a term used to refer to treating people according to factors not related to worker productivity. Sexism, racism, and ageism involve employers assessing and treating applicants and employees on the basis of their gender, skin color, or age and not on their talents, skills, and productivity.

BOX 7.1 Explaining Age Discrimination, Ageism, and Bigotry

Ageism is a set of beliefs—usually negative, but not always—attitudes, assumptions, and stereotypes about age and older people. The positive feelings associated with ageism are, for example, the assumption that older people are always wiser. The negative feelings, and many of them are implicit, aid and support legal and illegal discriminatory behaviors that marginalize older adults. In the labor market, ageism informs the false view that older workers are less trainable, flexible, and efficient and are weak and less technologically proficient. Older people can internalize ageism by viewing themselves with stereotypes that erode their confidence and impede their job search.

When employers treat—pay, promote, hire—employees differently on the basis of age, it is age discrimination, which is illegal. Age bigotry is strong attachment and devotion to one's own opinions and prejudgments about a person's value (in a variety of realms, such as sex and work) because of their age. When the term *age bigotry* is used, it is almost always negative.

Ageism, age discrimination, and age bigotry are complicated by the truth that as we age, human capacity diminishes.

If age discrimination is widespread, then older workers will have fewer job offers that pay appropriately for their productivity. Proving which factor an employer uses to decide hiring, firing, pay, and promotions is tricky. The preferred methodology to discover discrimination is "audit studies." In audit studies, employers are given résumés of fake candidates with equal qualifications. One résumé indicates the candidate is older. You probably guessed what the outcome is. Audit studies reveal that applicants perceived as older are less likely to be called for an interview.[28]

A Transamerica Center for Retirement Studies survey found a gap between what age employers and workers feel is too old to work. Employers perceived age 64 as too old to be considered for employment, and workers responding to the same study said age 75 was too old to work.[29] This gap suggests older people are looking for work in markets that aren't looking for elderly employees—a situation that favors employers and weakens senior workers' bargaining power.

Workforce rationalization can also disproportionately affect older workers, and age discrimination plays a part in that. The pioneering work of Pro Publica journalist Peter Gosselin estimated that, in its 2010 downsizing, IBM eliminated more than twenty thousand American employees age 40 and over, who accounted for about 60 percent of the company's estimated US job cuts during that period.[30] Reviewing internal company documents, legal filings, and public records, Gosselin concluded that IBM "flouted or outflanked US laws and regulations intended to protect later-career workers from age discrimination."

In another survey, 40 percent of employers said older workers were a positive asset to their firms, and 20 percent viewed older workers as a liability that may increase costs or reduce productivity.[31] That is sobering. One in five employers thought that older workers were a liability to their organization. This perception doesn't exactly put elderly workers in the employment driving seat.

5. LESS MOBILITY

As people get older, they are less likely to leave a job, less likely to move to a new job, and less likely to move somewhere new for a job.[32]

This shrinking mobility erodes older workers' bargaining power. In this sense, we might say the labor market discriminates against older folks who are less mobile.

Being able and willing to bounce from Toledo to San Jose is a crucial factor in securing higher pay and a better job.[33] Employees can pose a credible threat to leave as one way to pressure an employer to treat them better and provide a counteroffer. Even the impression of employees leaving can boost job position and negotiating power. I knew a fierce lawyer who told his law firm before he was partner that he was a renter: He wanted to make clear they couldn't exploit him. Moving from a rental would be a lot easier than having to sell a house. He wanted to signal that he was footloose and ready to run if he didn't get a promotion.

In America, being able and ready to move is the way workers leverage promotions and garner higher wages. In 2017, about half of interstate moves were for work.[34] But older workers face higher indirect costs of moving because they have family and roots in a community—positive stuff that shouldn't be an economic penalty. However, older workers are also more likely to be stranded in more economically stagnant regions with falling home values and low wages. Distressingly, the one way in which older workers experience "mobility" is downward: from 2008 to 2014, at least 52 percent of retirees over 55 had left their last job involuntarily, the result of job loss or deteriorating health.[35]

6. THE EARNED INCOME TAX CREDIT

The Earned Income Tax Credit (EITC) is a "work bonus" plan supported by Republicans and Democrats. The government supplements the wages of low-wage workers and, by extension, helps boost employer profits by allowing employers to keep wages low because their workers will get the EITC subsidy.

The EITC is highest for parents and lowest (or nonexistent) for those over age 65 or under age 25. Compare the maximum of $538 for childless workers with over $6,000 for low-income workers with three or more dependent children. The EITC has raised living standards for single mothers by supplementing low wages and has encouraged more single mothers to work for pay but at a cost.[36]

The low-priority, low-wage workers—those too young, too old, or too childless—are exposed to wage suppression in the sectors with high concentrations of low-wage EITC recipients but don't get the subsidy.[37]

Let me explain. Employers can pay EITC recipients lower wages for the same work because the government essentially pays for some of their wages; thus, the EITC lowers employers' wage offer for all low-wage workers, whether or not they are eligible for the EITC.[38] In this way, the EITC keeps wages low for older workers working with EITC recipients. More than one-third (34 percent) of personal and home health aides are over age 55, and many are not eligible for substantial (if any) EITC subsidies. They work alongside low-income younger women who are paid the same lower wage but have higher annual incomes because they get an EITC. The older worker, most likely a woman, is stuck with the low wage but gets no EITC tax refund to boost her income.

7. OVERCROWDED BOOMER COHORT

The forces of market supply and demand can also explain older workers' declining status. Older workers are in an overcrowded age group. Older workers are doing worse than in the past partly because there is such a large cohort of older workers. In fact, there is plenty of evidence that the sheer size of the boomer age cohort has suppressed their cohort's wages throughout their entire work lives. This unlucky demographic reason is not anyone's fault; it simply means that boomers compete with one another (I should know: I am a boomer).

The sheer scale of aging boomers exerts an outsized impact on labor markets. In 2017, 35 million older workers (boomers) constituted 24 percent of the labor force, up from 12 percent in 1990. By 2026, 40 million older workers will make up 25 percent of the workforce.[39] Seventeen million older workers have been newly employed since 2000, and the US economy's total net increase in jobs since then is also 17 million. In that period, older workers were predicted to account for all the employment growth. The estimates vary year to year, but older workers are always the largest share of predicted new jobs.

Because of their generation's size, boomers have "suppressed" their own wages since they were teenage workers. Of course, "they" didn't suppress their wages; their sheer scale did. As a late boomer myself, I recall overcrowded schools and fierce competition for jobs—my fourth-grade classroom was a temporary trailer, and in college I couldn't even get a job cleaning hotel rooms. My personal story is not evidence, to be sure, but the scholarly evidence tells me that my personal story was caused by a larger phenomenon I couldn't see. I remember things being extremely hard because I couldn't find work as a teenager, and now I know some of the reasons why. Past research confirms that birth cohort size affects wages throughout your working life. Between the years 1946 and 1964, 77 million baby boomers were born. In comparison, 65 million people were born into Generation X. People born into larger cohorts earn a significantly lower wage than do members of smaller cohorts at all stages of their careers (even when other significant things—like war and famine— are considered).[40]

The large boomer cohort slowed wage growth when they were young; it grew by just 4 percent a year before age 55 compared to 5 percent for the silent generation and 6 percent for Generation X. In their prime working age, boomers' wages grew only about 1 percent a year, less than any generation in the past seventy years.[41] These stark facts reveal common sense: the larger a group that is looking for work at the same time, the less bargaining power that group has.

8. LACK OF WORK IN LARGE FIRMS

Another reason for older workers' falling relative compensation is that large firms pay more, but older workers are more likely to work for smaller firms. Smaller firms have fewer economic rents and prof- its to share with employees.[42] Older workers are less likely to be em- ployed by highly productive and profitable firms, which is too bad for older workers, because so-called superstar firms capture greater market share and are in a better position to share rents and profits.[43]

Thirty-two percent of workers in large firms are over 50 years old; 35 percent of employees in very small firms (fewer than 100 employees) are over 50 years old. This amounts to a 3 percent negative likelihood of being over 50 and working for a large firm, which contributes to wage stagnation and lowers bargaining power for older workers.

9. FAST-GROWING, LOW-WAGE INDUSTRIES

Another reason for falling wage premiums paid for workers' experience is that older workers are in sectors and jobs that are in more demand. Indeed, if an industry shrinks, employers don't hire anyone new, including younger people, so the average age naturally increases—think bank tellers and watch repairers (readers under 40 might not even know what I am talking about). And while it is true that younger workers are relatively more desired in tech and finance—"hot" fields where pay is high—my research teams found not a speck of evidence that falling demand for older workers is an independent factor explaining wage declines for older workers. There is little evidence that older workers are disproportionately employed in high-unemployment occupations. In fact, you'll find older workers in the hottest fields of care work and janitorial services. And the firms in the fastest-growing and largest occupations—home health and personal care—seem to be using low-paid (desperate) older workers as part of their business strategy. Walmart, in rural labor markets, also sought older workers desperate to work—good at the time for older workers but bad for the broader public.

Care work offers a poignant illustration of this. From 2019 to 2029, jobs in nursing, psychiatric care, home health aides, and personal aides will increase by nearly 2 million (out of a projected increase of 6 million jobs for the entire US economy). These low-paid jobs—earnings average about $24,000 a year—are filled overwhelmingly (85 percent) by women. While the portion of the US labor force earning low wages is 12 percent, the share of low paid in these care occupations is a bit over 30 percent. A disproportionate share of workers in this massive occupation is older, and much of the most robust job growth is among low-wage jobs that employ older workers (table 7.1).

TABLE 7.1 Low-paid occupations with the most job growth

	Employment 2019 (in thousands)	Employment 2029 (projected)	Median annual wage (2019)	Workers older than 55	Share of workers receiving the EITC	Female workers
Total, all occupations	162,795	168,835	$39,810	24%	10%	47%
Low-wage occupations	21,715	24,447	$29,746	19%	19%	51%
Home health and personal-care aides	3,439	4,599	$25,280	34%	25%	86%
Fast-food and counter	4,047	4,509	$22,740	8%	14%	65%
Cooks	1,417	1,745	$27,790	15%	19%	36%
Medical assistants	725	864	$34,800	11%	17%	93%
Laborers and freight	2,986	3,112	$29,510	16%	15%	19%
Landscaping and groundskeeping	1,188	1,308	$30,440	23%	22%	6%
Nursing assistants	1,528	1,646	$29,660	19%	25%	89%
Janitors and cleaners	2,374	2,480	$27,430	34%	18%	40%
Waiters and waitresses	2,613	2,711	$22,890	8%	16%	70%
Construction laborers	1,398	1,473	$36,860	19%	15%	4%

Note: For total employment, 45% of workers are in low-wage jobs.

I looked for any smidgen of evidence that older workers are low paid because they happen to be caught in declining sectors by correlating the median age of workers by occupation ranked by their respective unemployment rate in 2017. Industries with shrinking employment have older median ages because employers in shrinking sectors are not hiring—especially not younger workers—so most remaining workers are older. Using the March 2017 supplement of the Current Population Survey, we found that older workers are not disproportionately employed in occupations with high relative unemployment rates.[44] In fact, some of the occupations adding the most job growth are disproportionately filled with older workers.

10. NO COMPENSATING BENEFITS OR PERKS

I am being persnickety about including this compensating wage factor in the already-extensive list of reasons older workers are losing bargaining power. I am anticipating someone saying, "Maybe older workers are taking lower wages because they have flexible schedules and great benefits." The answer is, unfortunately, that there is no evidence that older workers' pay is eroding because older workers are accepting lower wages as a trade-off for another desirable job characteristic like health insurance or scheduling flexibility or something ineffable like "meaning." An economist might raise the possibility that the bad jobs low-wage older workers have just "appear" to be bad. The idea is that a low-paying job may be better or just as good as a high-paying job if it has desirable job qualities. Economists have a wonky name for this—*compensating wage differentials*. If older workers are compensated for their work in some other desirable way, then it only seems like older workers are paid less when, in fact, their lower wages are compensated for by desirable fringe benefits and working conditions. Is it possible that older workers' low pay is offset by desirable job characteristics—like flexibility, high degrees of social engagement, and so on?

The answer is no. Older workers' nonmonetary benefits, schedules, and ease of work are not improving. In fact, older workers have increasingly dangerous jobs, less paid sick leave, and less pension security.

Let's zero in on retirement plans and health insurance—in case you still think most older workers are working for retirement benefits and health insurance. From 1990 to 2017, among full-time, non-self-employed workers over 55, the rate of employer-provided health insurance coverage fell from 90 percent to 87 percent, and retirement plan coverage decreased from 56 percent to 44 percent.[45]

To add injury to insult, older workers' jobs are not getting easier, despite the rise of computers and the decline of manufacturing, mining, and farming in the economy. Since 1992, the share of workers aged 55–62 reporting difficult physical demands at work decreased only slightly. In 1992, 40 percent of older workers reported that their jobs required "lots of physical effort." In 2014, this decreased to 34 percent. However, other dimensions of physical work, including "lifting heavy loads" and "stooping/kneeling/crouching," saw no improvement—so much for the working-longer consensus insisting we can work until our 70s.

Over 30 percent of workers near retirement (ages 55–64) and over 40 percent of non-college-educated workers in this age group had jobs that required "lots of physical effort" most or all the time. And jobs don't get that much easier with age. The share of non-college-educated workers aged 65 and older with physically demanding jobs is high, at 32 percent.[46]

Education and Banning Mandatory Retirement Boost Bargaining Power

Amid all this gloom, there are some glimmers of progress. Older workers, on average, are doing a bit better than their counterparts in the past because the cohort has more education, as each subsequent generation of Americans is going to college and graduating from high school. Typically, more education enables more job choice and thus bargaining power. One study shows the fact that older workers are more educated over time accounts for almost half of the increase in their labor-force participation. In 1985, fewer than 20 percent of workers between age 60 and 64 had college degrees; thirty-five years later, in 2013, over 36 percent did. (In a remarkable testament to aggressive public policy to improve K-12 education—including deseg-regation and keeping girls in high school—the share of older workers without high school degrees fell from over 26 percent in 1985 to about 7 percent in 2013.)[47]

More education is also associated with better health. Workers with college degrees are not only healthier than those with less education; they are more likely to say that their work is satisfying and to have some autonomy on the job.[48]

Legal Bans on Mandatory Retirement

The United States is among the few rich countries that ban manda-tory retirement as a form of age discrimination, so America's older workers can sue for age discrimination. With few exceptions, Ameri-cans cannot be banned from work—or from being paid, promoted, or trained less—because of their age. Despite these legal protections, worker advocates and labor unions were not at barricades demand-ing the end of mandatory retirement. Many workers want to retire, witness the more than two thousand readers pushing back in the comments to a 2023 *New York Times* article arguing that increased life expectancy should mean higher retirement ages. Instead, con-sider this; "Working until you pass away at your desk or assembly line is cruel. The goal of your life is to get back some time to express yourself, the way you want and when you decide so. Retirement should be considered the start of a new life not the graveyard waiting room."[49]

Worker advocates used the existence of mandatory retirement to justify higher Social Security benefits, better pensions, and retiree health care.

That older women workers are more enfranchised into main-stream economic life is progress. In 1980, the headlines screamed that over half of mothers with young children were working and more likely to work than women without young children. It's hard to balance work and family, but forty years later, those working mothers are still working. Labor income gives women some independence and more equal footing with men, and that's good news for men and women.

Telescoping Policy Recommendations

No single policy on its own will strengthen older workers' bargaining power. Boosting the minimum wage would help increase compensation for older workers in low-paying food service, retail, and care work. More unions would help improve service work where split shifts, job fissuring (branded companies outsource functions to small firms or independent contractors), and other erosions to job quality occur.[50] Aggressively tackling age discrimination would give older workers more bargaining power. If employers (and older workers themselves) falsely perceive older workers to have less value because of the prevalence of age discrimination, then employers would be less likely to promote and train older workers. Older workers' having a good fallback position will help them negotiate better pay and working conditions. A strong negotiator must have a suitable alternative to a negotiated agreement.

Older workers' bargaining power would be improved by policies such as higher Social Security benefits, expanded and improved pensions (e.g., a guaranteed retirement account), and the establishment of an Older Workers' Bureau at the Department of Labor.

Five key policy reforms will help older workers: (1) raising older workers' reservation wage by improving retirement security; (2) protecting workers' union rights, raising the minimum wage, and improving the conditions of alternative work schedules by enforcing labor laws against wage theft and employee misclassifications; (3) strictly enforcing age discrimination laws; (4) creating an Older Workers Bureau at the Department of Labor to formulate standards and policies that promote the welfare of older workers, to improve their working conditions and advance their opportunities for profitable employment; and (5) correcting the unintended consequences of the EITC that suppress wages for ineligible workers.

Older Workers Need More Bargaining Power

Work is good, and many Americans like it. Anyone who wants to work should be able to. But finding and keeping work that is satisfying is no simple task—particularly as an older worker. And much of what makes a job gratifying derives from workers' economic security and bargaining power in the labor market. Securing an adequate nest egg and having a small (or no) mortgage are among the best ways older people can help ensure that if they work, they will like the job. Having a good fallback position strengthens their hand in the labor market. As we've seen throughout this chapter, bad pensions are a big reason for bad jobs.

This power dynamic is a constant struggle. Older workers are in a weak position if public policies entice labor substitutes who will take a lower wage; everybody suffers, an injury to all. For instance, older workers and EITC-eligible workers work side by side in all industries, especially in nursing, and among psychiatric and home health aides and personal aides. Whenever older workers work alongside low-paid workers eligible for the EITC, they compete against younger mothers who are eligible for EITC income subsidies and will accept a lower wage than they otherwise would. This effect puts downward pressure on wages. Further research will help illuminate how these impacts vary among different workers. Older personal-care workers, for example, are more affected by EITC wage suppression, while older male workers in higher-paid jobs are hit harder by the loss of unions. Our nation has allowed (and enabled) older people's bargaining power to fall in ten distinct ways. Chief among these is the erosion of retirement-income security. But other factors loom large— fewer unions; more contingent and "alternative" work arrangements; fewer long-term employment relationships; more monopsony power by firms; persistent age discrimination; and EITC policies that suppress wages. We've also seen that the large size of the boomer generation cohort suppresses wages, as does older workers' tendency to work for small firms.

Without secure pensions, more older people must work, and more older people will accept wages, hours, and working conditions that prioritize employers' terms. If nothing else happens, an increase in the supply of labor invariably redistributes income away from workers' wages and toward employer profits. The working-longer consensus contributes to older workers' weakened bargaining power.

8

The High Cost of Bad Pensions

Economic security for elders is not free, but the high cost of bad pensions makes good pensions a necessary national expense. Bad pensions can turn around and bite the government if it is trying to save money.

....

BOX 8.1 Good and Bad Pensions

How do you know if you have a good or bad pension? Examine its size, composition, and control. First, if your 401(k) when you are 65 is less than, say, $600,000 (assuming you earn the median of $60,000 per year), and you don't have a traditional pension, you probably have a bad pension profile. For most older workers, household retirement savings fall far short of adequate.

Although experts disagree about what is adequate or what people need in retirement (see box 3.1), rule-of-thumb advising targets about ten to eleven times your annual salary by age 67, which can happen if you save roughly 15 percent to 20 percent of your gross pay for forty-two years in a diversified, balanced portfolio. So how far off are Americans?

Very.

The median older household has retirement savings of about $43,000. Say a household has two workers in it; the median retirement savings per member is $21,500. Based on standard advice, each member needs about ten times their pre-retirement spending to fund a twenty-three-year retirement. Median earnings are about $60,000, so they need about $600,000, but each worker only has $21,500. Woe to the single-person older household who can't share expenses.

Even if the median retirement savings were even close to $600,000, the composition is not good. (A $600,000 lump sum could be turned into a guaranteed stream of lifetime income of about $40,000 per year at age 67, in theory, but going out in the for-profit marketplace to buy an annuity from an insurance company is ill-advised, fees are too high, and you won't get that much.) Only people in defined-benefit plans, where the fees are low and the annuities are bought on a group basis, have a practical way to turn a lump sum into a guaranteed income flow for life. The second reason people have a bad pension is that they pay high retail fees for an amateurly constructed portfolio. (That is why I support legislation that helps people pool their lump sums in a professionally managed, low-fee annuity fund.)

The third reason most people have a bad pension is because the do-it-yourself pension system means you are on your own. You are responsible for investing and deciding how much to take out each year to ensure you don't outlive your assets. Most people would prefer less control and more guarantees. Managing hundreds of thousands of dollars to last your lifetime right at the age when cognitive decline and financial predation is at the highest risk is a bad structure that creates bad pensions. On balance, Americans have too little retirement savings, the savings are in the form of a lump sum, and an individual—an elderly person—has complete control of the investment and drawdown decisions. In short, most Americans have bad pensions. See box 10.2 for advice about how to handle your pension money.

Bad pensions can create high political costs as populations age and wealth gaps grow. Making Americans work longer and causing them to retire without enough income costs cities, states, and the federal government extra in Medicaid and social service expenses. Bad pensions can lower economic productivity and make it hard for employers to renew their labor force. Bad pensions can hurt children, but surveys of younger people signal that they would support increases in Social Security and mandatory pension savings.

Being stingy on retirement benefits seems like it would save the government money, but the cost of good pensions can easily outweigh the excessive costs of a bad pension system. Doubling the retirement wealth of the bottom half of the income distribution costs about 5 percent of the gross domestic product. Is another 5 percent of gross domestic product too much to equalize retirement wealth, raise productivity, stabilize a political system, make it easier for employers to promote younger workers, and help stabilize household finances? That is a political and social question, not math.

Bad Pensions Hurt National Unity and Political Stability

Far too few Americans have a direct stake in the rewards of national economic growth. Markets reached historic highs during the COVID-19 recovery, but many hardworking people have few reliable pathways to build wealth and achieve retirement security. And they noticed. Mildly worded surveys are finding that 82 percent of American voters are concerned that retirement security is a problem for the country.[1] An August 2020 poll of Americans between the ages of 50 and 75 with a net household income of at least $100,000 by Kiplinger–Alliance for Lifetime Income found a great deal of concern about retirement security, with older women more attuned to retirement insecurity.[2] Fifty-six percent of women are less confident about retirement income (compared with 43 percent of men).

Also, if we do nothing, elder poverty will skyrocket, and workers could find themselves in the labor market well into their 70s. Or if they are unable to work, they will try to survive on Social Security alone.

The political consequences of not paying attention to the growing retirement crisis are huge: 65 percent of voters are over 45, and 27 percent are over 65 years old. Older voters are more likely to sway elections, not just because older voters vote more but also because there are more of them. Near retirees, aged 45–64, were the largest segment of the voter population in 2018, at 38 percent. Voters over age 65 had the next-highest share, 27 percent. That means voters over age 45 are 65 percent of all voters. In contrast, only 7 percent of voters are the much-discussed youth vote—voters between the ages of 18 and 28. And older voters vote about twice as much as younger voters: Voter turnout for age 65 and over is 66 percent; for those aged 18–34, it is 34 percent.

What kinds of older voters are more likely to get out and vote? (The voter registration files from the US Census Department help identify the characteristics of states with the highest older-voter turnout, which infers what kinds of older people vote.[3]) More highly educated older workers with retirement plans offered at work are more likely to vote. It seems that economic engagement and security lead to voting. Voting behavior is complex and involves more than just age, but the stark fact that older people vote almost twice as much as younger people is vital to candidates.

In the nail-biter states in the 2000 presidential election—Arizona, Georgia, Pennsylvania, North Carolina, and Florida, only Georgia had a younger voter base than the national average. In contrast, consider Joe Manchin, from West Virginia, which has the oldest average age of voters in the nation. There, 36 percent of voters in West Virginia are over 65, compared to, say, 33 percent of voters in Florida. This analysis raises the question, Why aren't politicians more concerned about older workers and older people in financial trouble? I think I have the answer. Older-voter rates lag in states with high rates of elder poverty, where elder earnings are low, and where there are higher shares of nonwhite voters in the ranks of older voters. Older-voter turnout is also lower where workplace pensions are fewer. Where older voters face these precarious circumstances, they also exhibit less political power. 'Twas ever thus. Groups left behind are marginalized in the political arena.

Votes in these impoverished places could have significance. The fragility of older workers and impoverished elders in a community can bring down the entire community. As more older workers face downward economic mobility, more communities could feel the tug. Not attending to retirement security could hurt incumbent politicians, for example, if millennials start to vote in larger numbers or if their vote increases as they age. Millennials and Gen Xers are most pessimistic about their retirement. When asked by the National Institute for Retirement in July 2021, a whopping 72 percent of millennials said they were concerned they wouldn't be able to achieve a financially secure retirement; most baby boomers—46 percent—said they would not have adequate retirement (they are probably too optimistic).[4] I don't know when financial anxiety turns to resentment and backlash. But there are signs that the economic fallout from the pandemic and the long-standing erosion of retirement security has created substantial uncertainty about retirement that could trigger Americans to work longer or rethink retirement altogether.[5]

The National Institute for Retirement survey also reveals the endurance of hope and not reality. People say they will work longer because of their shaky faith in their retirement finances. Over half of boomers and Gen Xers say they will work past retirement age, and 76 percent of Generation Y say they'll have to work past retirement age because of their financial insecurity. But of course, what I call the plan B response does two things—it fuels the working-longer consensus, and it ignores the fact that most people don't choose when to retire: economic conditions, their employer, or a loved one's health makes the retirement decision.

Another sensible economic reason to have good pensions is to let older people, who may be in their waning years of productivity, leave the labor market. It is a simple mathematical fact that if the least productive leave a group, the average productivity increases. As the smallest strawberries in a bowl are eaten, the average size of the strawberries increases. The Brookings economist Gary Burtless found between 1985 and 2010 (and especially in the 1980s) that older workers came to retirement with defined-benefit plans and Social Security, which allowed the least productive workers to retire.[6] The higher-paid older workers delayed retirement.

Economist Owen Davis also found that in the COVID-19 recession, those with higher education levels stayed in the labor market, and those with less education retired from the labor market at higher rates. This pattern is good for the economy, he concluded. If the least able can't retire, that would be bad for the economy. But that result is good only from a productivity perspective. Most of these older workers without college degrees pushed out of the labor market were in their late 50s and will seek any kind of work because they will have next to nothing to live on except Social Security, which can be collected only starting at age 62. I fear that as pensions erode and the population ages, the failing retirement system could lead to less productivity as less productive workers stay attached to the labor market.

The math is easy: overall productivity will fall if a significant share of workers with waning productivity (relative to when they were younger and relative to younger workers) are clinging to their jobs because their pensions are inadequate. The point is pure math. If everyone retired right when their productivity started to decline, then the average productivity of a nation's economy would stay high and even increase. When productivity increases, every priority is more affordable, including longer retirements. It is sad to see people struggling because of their age to stay in a job because they can't afford to retire. The sadness partially explains the GoFundMe accounts created by charitable and helpful people for tired old workers. The trend isn't "feel good," though; it is sad for the person and sad for the nation. I reported on the GoFundMe for an 81-year-old retiree at the beginning of the book. One year later, in 2023, an even older GoFundMe-retiree, Betty Glover, a 91-year-old Oregon grocery store clerk, retired after an online campaign raised $80,000 for her.[7] The result is really not OK for Betty; all the evidence suggested that her well-being and health would have been higher and better if she shopped at rather than worked at the store. A GoFundMe retirement system indicates a severely broken national retirement system. The story also helps explain sluggish productivity. I don't have direct evidence, but it is safe to say that a 91-year-old cashier is likely not the highest producer in the store. A nation depending on desperate old workers does not have the "pep in its step" to raise national productivity numbers.

Further benefits from providing an adequate pension system are indirect economic and productivity knockoffs—a secure pension base ensures that those working at older ages find employer matches that add to national productivity rather than subtracting from it. There are two parts to that argument. National productivity is given a boost if workers with higher-than-average productivity work longer. The opposite is true.

Not having a convenient way to help workers retire after their "time" will raise some employers' costs. A considerable number of employers want a decent national retirement policy. Not all employers are able to use cheaper older workers profitably. Some employers have the opposite problem: they will face an aging work-force that won't leave after their "time" because they can't afford to retire. Most employers say a good retirement age is below 64.

Here is another big cost to working longer. Millions of elders stay-ing in or entering the labor market will lower wages for everyone. If older workers are used as substitutes for younger workers or com-pete with each other—as baby boomers have their entire lives—wages and productivity will fall, and profits will increase. Having workers compete with younger workers will lower pay and blunt job oppor-tunities. More hidden elderly unemployment will lower wages for all workers, too, because older workers often compete with prime-age workers. How does this work? An increased supply of desperate older workers may tempt employers to use part-time staffing—we al-ready see that older workers are the fastest-growing group among gig workers—and continue the erosion of full-time work for everyone.

If older workers lack bargaining power because they can't afford to retire, the ratio of capital to labor (physical capital and technology per worker) will remain high and productivity sluggish.

Taxpayers and the economy benefit from good pensions. If work-ers do not have good pensions, then aggregate demand can fall and pressing needs for spending on impoverished elders will increase. If workers who have lost skills have lower-than-average individual productivity and less ability to adjust to new demands at work, and are not up to date at work, then average national productivity could fall. Thus, national productivity will suffer as millions of elders stay in or enter the labor market.

Bottom line: four groups have a stake in retirement: workers, children, employers, and taxpayers. All of us need a robust national economy, and a robust pension system is necessary for an economy to keep productivity and aggregate demand high.

Bad Pensions Hurt Young Workers and Children

There are three reasons young workers have a stake in retirement security: first, they want a secure financial future; second, they want their aging parents to be financially independent; and third, older people working longer (especially those who are working because they cannot afford to retire) could "spoil" the labor market for younger workers. Evidence shows that older workers are substitutes for younger workers.

Why should a 33-year-old care about the Social Security system and whether elders have retirement-income security? Despite the romance about multigenerational households, most elders do not want to live with their adult children, and adult children with needy parents are not the ones likely to have an extra bedroom. Millennials and Generation X workers are quite concerned about their prospects for a secure retirement. Young people are concerned that the increased labor-force participation of older people—who either can or cannot afford to retire—may be spoiling the labor market.

This chapter drives home these dangers of large supplies of labor without bargaining power by comparing the entrance of older workers to other labor supply shocks in the US: the Mariel boatlift of tens of thousands of Cuban emigrants to Miami, the Great Migration, and the labor-market entrance of educated women in the 1970s. This is not a lump-of-labor argument that there is a fixed number of jobs, and if one group has jobs, the other won't. The argument is about job quality, not job quantity. Each of those events lowered the wages of other workers.

Similarly, older workers will spoil the labor market for younger workers and for the wages, hours, and working conditions of the elderly. The boomer generation has always put downward pressure on their own wages and the quality of working conditions because it is a large cohort. Therefore, it may be no surprise that, since 1990, older workers face more intense concentration; more lifting, kneeling, and stooping; and more tasks requiring keen eyesight than in the past twenty years. Older workers have difficult and demanding jobs.[8]

The standard case for reducing retirement benefits is that more older people will work, which would at first create a "migration" bonus: more output at lower prices as marginal employers—those who otherwise could not afford to pay the going rate—come to market and produce with the lower costs and charge lower prices. As

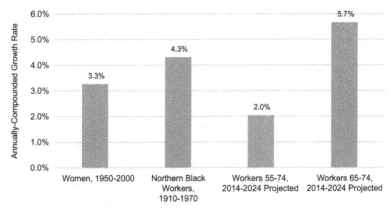

FIGURE 8.1 The Impact of Older Workers Entering the Labor Force

Source: Author's calculations using labor-force data from Bureau of Labor Statistics and Current Population Survey annual income and demographic supplement to the March Current Population Survey (CPS) for 2016; Burtless (2013); Census Bureau, Decennial Census, 1910, 1950, 1970, 2000.

labor supply increases, consumer and producer surplus increases, profits increase, and wages fall. Employers and consumers win, and younger and older workers lose. From the perspective of younger workers, wages and benefits are lower than what they would otherwise be if older workers had more bargaining power and left the labor market.

Let us now turn to the myth of the greedy geezer.

There is no evidence "the old eat the young." In 63 nations over forty years, nations with high education spending generosity—that is, GDP spent per child on education—also spend more per old person on pensions.

As nations become richer, the ability to retire becomes accepted by society. At the same time, economic prosperity causes aging populations. It might look like pension generosity is increasing because the old are getting politically stronger, but pension generosity is increasing because a nation is getting richer. When we control for aging populations, there is a 10 percent increase in education spending that accompanies a 7 percent increase in pension generosity.

Among the G-7, Canada has the highest spending per child on education and among the highest rates of spending per elderly. The US is the lowest in both. But the positive correlation between education and pension spending still holds up in the US.

American children receive a substantial amount of Social Security income. In 2017, over 8 percent of American children lived in families that received Social Security income. Social Security income lifted 1 million children out of poverty, which is about one-third of how many children received payments from the program aimed at poor children, Temporary Aid for Needy Families. In 2018, Social Security Survivors and Disability benefits paid $21 billion to children, compared to the Earned Income Tax Credit, which paid out $58 billion. Although old-age programs are not means tested, disability and early death are more common among lower-income groups, so Social Security disproportionately helps low-income children.[9]

Axel Börsch-Supan examined sixteen countries and concluded social expenditures for programs targeting the elderly do not reduce the share of total social expenditures for programs targeting youth. Bommier and colleagues' 2004 study of US education, Social Security, and Medicare concluded that people continually get higher returns on their taxes paid than do cohorts before them. There are detractors. Robert Novy-Marx and Josh Rauh argue that state and local government pension underfunding will increase debt burdens for future taxpayers. But in the late 1990s, New Jersey underfunded state pensions to increase education spending. Those future taxpayers had more human capital. In 2019 Charles Steindel in the New Jersey Department of the Treasury found that pension debt had no association with state economic growth.

There is little evidence in the labor market for a gerontocracy, a greedy geezer effect. Education and pension spending go together because of what political scientists John Williamson and Frank Pampel call the social democratic effect: "pensions are the outcome of a struggle between organizations and political parties representing the interests of capital and those representing the interests of labor."[10] Political coalitions to boost workers' pensions are political coalitions that boost public education.

The evidence points to solidarity among generations of working-class people, not strong-armed generational politics.

Bad Pensions Hurt Some Employers

Some employers have a stake in workers not delaying retirement. And some employers may have a stake in an orderly retirement process, as I wrote in the *Harvard Business Review*.[11] According to research by the University of Connecticut and Prudential Insurance, every year that an older worker delays retirement, the company bears an extra cost of $50,000 above the productivity of that older worker who stayed beyond his or her time. This is a bold assertion and serves in part as an advertisement to encourage companies to buy Prudential retirement plan services. After all, it's designed to scare companies into having workers whose pay doesn't match their productivity on the job but who can't afford to retire. This would induce an employer to create a generous pension plan, the assets in which might include some Prudential products.

The advertisement strategy is a little dubious. Plenty of research shows that older workers are sometimes quite productive. But employers that provide health insurance do face higher costs of employing older workers, everything else held constant. And sometimes older workers are the highest paid in an organization. Older workers must be even more productive than their younger counterparts just to pay for their higher pay and higher health insurance costs. That's hard for employers and for older workers. That older workers are both more expensive in some circumstances and represent a loss to employers does not conflict with the notion that desperate older workers cost less in other circumstances. Both can be true.

Out of concern for cutting spending in 2013, executives of the largest American corporations called on Congress to raise the eligibility age for Medicare and full Social Security to age 70. In 2017, some companies began second-guessing themselves. Because many older workers will have to be retrained, and jobs and workplaces would need to be adjusted to older workers' needs and abilities, raising the retirement age could get employers to reverse their erosion in training and start valuing older workers. Although employers (in surveys, at least) praise older workers' sagaciousness and experience, few employers accommodate older workers' preferences for phased retirement or improved conditions, training, and pay. Similarly, workers tell researchers they plan to work, but workers with more pension wealth retire sooner because they can.

Bad Pensions Create Poorly Functioning Labor Markets

Importantly, employers try to attract and retain the best workers and ease out those whose productivity has fallen. Additionally, each middle-class retiree at age 65 provides a potential $1.5 million in life-long spending and, because of their income security, becomes an anchor in a stable community. A community filled or sprinkled with stable retirees makes for a desirable neighborhood.

The large economic benefits of providing pensions are indirect but real. A solid, adequate pension system allows people to take risks, which aids society and helps employers and workers to find a good match. A secure pension base ensures that those older work-ers don't just work in any job they find because they are desperate—older workers with a pension work for employers that provide the best fit. That is a win-win for employers and workers.

Without adequate pensions, we do not have prosperity. Americans already work more hours per day, more days per week, more weeks per year, and more years per lifetime than their counterparts in other rich nations. So, Americans working more in old age may signal a basic problem in the US economy—it produces low-quality jobs. Add-ing millions more workers desperate for jobs into the labor force will make the economy less robust. There is likely a link between low pensions and elders desperate to work, which causes the US to be the OECD leader in the rates of elderly labor-force participation, elderly poverty, and share of jobs that pay less than two-thirds of the median wage.

Forcing older people without a safety net to seek paid work can create significant costs for all workers. Low-paid, low-status work de-teriorates health and well-being and will widen socioeconomic gaps in longevity and morbidity. Working longer has macro consequences, as well. Making people work because they would otherwise be poor in old age will cause average productivity to fall as employers face less pressure to make workers more productive. Productivity drives wage growth and government revenues. Last, a supply of precarious older labor may put downward pressure on job quality for all workers.

We Can Afford Good Pensions

The maximalist solution to the savings gap—the amount that would instantly make every household secure in retirement—estimates that every married couple facing retirement needs about $40,000, and single women about $76,000, for a total of $4 trillion or $14 trillion, respectively.

Doubling the retirement wealth of the bottom half of the income distribution costs a lot less and relieves the tension from wealth inequality. Social Security pays about 5 percent of GDP in benefits every year. Doubling the benefits for the bottom 80 percent would cost much less. Would we pay less than 2 percent, 3 percent, or 6 percent of GDP to equalize retirement wealth, raise productivity, stabilize the political system, make it easier for employers to promote younger workers, and help stabilize household finances?

DOES WORK IN OLD AGE REDUCE PENSION COSTS?

The case for older people working longer is founded on budget reasons, not human well-being. If both young workers and their employers, with assistance from a government-refundable tax credit, paid about 6.02 percent more of payroll—about 3 percent of payroll tax for Social Security to maintain current benefits, 0.02 percent for a boost in Social Security aimed at raising benefits for the lowest Social Security recipients to end elder poverty; and 3 percent in a well-managed and invested retirement account—they would be secure from poverty and near poverty in retirement. Workers approaching retirement without adequate savings would have to increase their savings by considerably more than 3 percent because they don't have a long work life to contribute and accumulate investment earnings. Still, these workers would be better off than they are today with universal access to a low-cost retirement savings program.

The case for pro-work policies comes from Gruber and Wise, who argue that generous pensions cause more retirements.[12] The availability of pensions at, say, age 62 enables retirement. But weak labor markets, which increase the risk of older workers being pushed out of employment into retirement, are significant drivers of early retirements. Chronic unemployment and volatility in the labor market could cause nations to implement, and employers and unions to demand, better pensions. The coincidence would cause a spurious interpretation of the correlations between high unemployment, expanded pension benefits, and low labor-force participation by older people. In other words, unlike the common interpretation of the data, generous pension benefits may not be driving people to retire. Instead, what is happening is that lower demand for older workers drives legislators to make pensions more generous. Gruber and Wise emphasize the supply side—older workers decrease their work effort when they get better pensions. I emphasize the demand side— nations with chronically high rates of unemployment may adopt early pension ages and generous pension benefits.

If Gruber and Wise were right, pension generosity would be correlated with more time in retirement. I found no such relationship. Among forty-two OECD nations, the correlation coefficient between pension generosity—the amount of money spent per old person and the average time a person spends in retirement—was a small and insignificant .12 in 2005 and .16 in 2015. That people with wealth in the form of generous benefits are more likely to retire does not explain macroeconomic dynamics.

High-unemployment nations that have the right soup of unions and political movements to increase social insurance spending bargain and push for generous pensions to alleviate the suffering caused by unemployment.[13] I find weak support for Gruber and Wise's supply-side argument.

A difficult direct but real calculation to make is that the morale and productivity of the workforce may drop if less educated older people work longer because of financial insecurity. The gerontologist Scott-Marshall found that work-related insecurity negatively affected the health of all groups, but the effects were greater at older ages and for those with visible minority status—those who are visibly distinct from those of the predominant ethnic or racial group in society.[14]

Policy options to promote an equitable distribution of secure healthy retirement time include expanding retirement plan coverage, which supplements Social Security, including a universal workplace pension system, and encouraging or mandating retirement plans to have some defined-benefit features: continual employer contributions and annuities.

OUR FAILED RETIREMENT SYSTEM IMPOSES COSTS ON SOCIETY

A national pension system works when workers can consistently over their working lives accumulate claims to income when they retire. But our national pension system has fallen short for most people because coverage is spotty and uneven; most workers in the bottom 80 percent of the income distribution do not have employers that contribute to or sponsor a plan.

Because of the poor design of our system, most workers don't voluntarily save for retirement because it is simply not feasible. Another source of inequality stems from the lavish government subsidies given to the very top earners by way of the tax favoritism for contributions to 401(k)s, IRAs, Roth IRAs, 403(b)s, employee stock ownership plans, and so on—all aimed to encourage at retirement contributions. The top earners receive at least 60 percent of the tax subsidies directed toward retirement savings. Different methodologies change the exact number but don't change the conclusion that the rich get most of the tax breaks for retirement savings.[15]

We have moved away from the vision that working in old age should be a genuine choice. The working-longer consensus may have started from good motives about active aging. But instead of giving people more opportunities, US old-age policy evolved to tell working people to construct a "do-it-yourself $600,000-plus pension account" or work longer. These policies have been widening the already-large gap in Americans' well-being.

We need the Gray New Deal: job and pension improvements for older Americans.

The shame of our system is that we think good retirement comes about because of decisions made around the kitchen table, but the fact is that most people cannot retire well without government co-ordination. Coordinating a public option for a universal supplement to Social Security will not harm the government financially, and the new system could raise wages and productivity. A public-option pension system will plug gaps in the voluntary, commercial, individually directed, do-it-yourself system we currently have.

PART III

The Gray New Deal

9

Good Jobs for Older Workers

We have a choice. We can flit, nick, and tuck around the edges of Social Security until it can't pay full benefits in 2035, keep hoping elders work longer, and nudge workers into commercial, market-driven inadequate retirement accounts to avoid making hard choices about the precariousness of our aging population. Or we can face reality and create policies to spur better jobs for older workers and good pensions. In short, we can choose to replace the working-longer consensus with the Gray New Deal.

There are two parts to the Gray New Deal: improving jobs for older workers and improving pensions. I can already hear the concerns: Can we afford it? What kind of public investment are we talking about? How big? As we saw in the previous chapter, we cannot afford not to make a big, bold reinvestment in older workers and retirement security. Creating conditions improving older workers' jobs and improving pensions does not cost as much as we might think. Creating better jobs and stronger pensions mutually reinforces the other.

First, let's look at policy opportunities to improve the labor market for older workers. The next chapter turns to pension reforms that can secure and stabilize people in their later years. Improving the labor market for older workers requires two sticks and carrots. First, firms need carrots to improve pay and conditions for older workers and to profit from using older people's skills, abilities, and experience. Profitable employers who treat their employees well need to be protected against those employers that bring down labor standards.

Enforcement sticks from unions and government, including wage and hour protections, occupational safety and health rules, and anti-discrimination policies, protect high-quality, high-road employers.

How do we get there? Here is an eight-step path to improve jobs for older workers. The eighth task, to improve pensions, will ensure we don't create an economy of desperate older workers and make someone's grandma your new barista:

1. Establish an Older Workers' Bureau in the US Department of Labor.
2. Lower the cost of employing older workers. Expand health insurance to help older workers pushed out of the labor market afford medical insurance and make it cheaper for employers to employ older workers before they reach Medicare age. Lower the Medicare qualifying age and make it first-payer insurance.
3. Push employers to create better jobs through federal and state policies to create jobs by eliminating barriers to labor unions, increasing minimum wages, and reforming the EITC to include older workers.
4. Revamp worker training and job programs to make them worker-friendly.
5. Ensure that volunteering is a dignified experience for older people.
6. Enforce antidiscrimination policies and campaign to end stereotypes of elderly people.
7. Remove any unintentional barriers that discourage older people from working if they want to.
8. Ensure better pensions.

1. Establish an Older Workers' Bureau

The entire labor force is expected to grow between 2021 and 2031 by 7.7 million workers, and over 3.6 million of them will be older than 55.[1] The aging of the workforce presents a challenge to the well-being of the nation and power struggles between workers and employers. National leaders must turn the spotlight on older workers and the quality, pay, and conditions of their jobs. Many college-educated older workers can command decent salaries, but many still face sudden involuntary retirement. The myth of the happy, healthy older worker obscures a glaring reality: millions of Americans must toil through their elder years just to stay afloat.

Despite older workers' increasingly central role—famously holding down jobs in the Oval Office, Congress, and the Supreme Court—millions of senior workers toil in dangerous conditions for meager pay, and there is little reality-based policy making to fix that.[2]

Akin to what the Women's Bureau has accomplished since its creation in 1920, an Older Workers' Bureau at the Department of Labor—charged with researching, coordinating, educating, and advocating for America's growing elderly workforce—can bring older workers' needs to light and spur reform.[3] Representative Don Beyer (whose economist grandmother Clara Beyer ran the Women's Bureau) introduced a bill in Congress to form this bureau in 2022.[4] What jobs do older workers have and need? Who among the elderly workforce is economically precarious? Which state and federal programs work against each other, and which complement efforts to provide high-quality jobs for older workers and secure, stable retirements for those ready to leave the world of work?

The need for older workers and better pension advocates is urgent, vast, and complex. That most retirements really aren't—most "retirees" say they are retired after being pushed out, laid off, or forced out by bad health—is one of the most outstanding findings in my career. Premature retirement is a problem, too. Millions more elderly workers are being pushed out of the labor force into an early retirement marked by economic insecurity. The COVID-19 pandemic and ensuing recession hit older workers hard. Amid the era of "essential workers," research at the New School's Retirement Equity Lab found nearly 2 million more older workers than expected had retired due to the pandemic recession.[5]

Contributing to this compelled early retirement (which is often not a retirement at all), older workers are less likely to have paid sick leave, which is hard anytime, as older people go to the doctor more, but the lack of paid leave proved especially harmful in pandemic times.[6] These trends are exacerbating inequality: at earlier ages, vulnerable older workers are being pushed to retire sooner while more privileged workers can delay retirement and pile up more savings.

2. Lower the Cost of Employing Older Workers

I am not against elders working. A functioning, human-centered economy should provide decent jobs to every adult who wants to work. By bringing down the Medicare qualifying age to below 65 and making it the primary insurance for employed older workers, we can simultaneously improve elder health and enable employers to provide older workers with decent pay and conditions. And that is the whole point of reform. Helping employers close the age-price gap in health insurance could help increase pay and save money. Making Medicare the first payer can put $10,000 a year on the table for every full-time older employee, some of which could increase pay.[7] Creating this cost advantage could help overcome employers' distaste and avoidance of older workers and help prevent forced early retirement for those who still want or need to work. (This is not to be confused with the working-longer agenda; these reforms are about enabling older workers to work if they need or want, with better preventive health-care coverage.)

There is some political momentum for lowering the Medicare age; President Biden has called for lowering the Medicare age to 60.[8] That's a good start, but 50 is even better. Think of it as economic and health insurance. Bringing down the Medicare age, especially to 50, protects older workers from being sidelined in the economy way before they planned and losing their health care along with their jobs.

These losses are harsh and cruel. Take the case of 52-year-old Suzie Davis, who until 2021 worked as a concierge supervisor at the Hampton Inn near the Pennsylvania Convention Center. She had given her whole life to the hotel, she told the *Philadelphia Inquirer*, working nearly every role during her twenty-three years for the company: housekeeper, bell clerk, front desk, breakfast bar. "We're losing our jobs," Davis said. "That's a big thing. And to turn around and you can't go to the clinic because you don't have health insurance? It's just like we're a piece of garbage. They just threw us to the curb."[9]

Congress has the power to prevent this suffering. Bringing in more people into the Medicare insurance pool increases public costs in the short term, but as younger people enter the pool, the average age of people in the Medicare insurance pool falls, so Medicare costs per person will fall. Overall costs may decline over time. Here is the logic: if people in their 50s and early 60s don't have health insurance, they cost more when they eventually join Medicare at age 65.[10] Among the most vulnerable are adults over 50 without health insurance, especially those with cardiovascular disease or diabetes. Going without medical care for years means that once they reach Medicare eligibility, they will use more health services than Medicare beneficiaries who were insured before they came in. Because chronic diseases are prevalent and insurance coverage is often unaffordable for older uninsured adults, the Medicare system is more costly per person than it would be if people were continually insured before age 65. Lowering the Medicare age will bring down the average cost of Medicare participants aged 50–64, evidence shows.[11]

There's nothing radical about Biden's call to make 60 the new Medicare qualifying age; many lawmakers had proposed this even before the COVID-19 recession created a greater urgency for this reform. In 2019, Senator Debbie Stabenow launched the "Medicare at 55 Act," which would enable those aged 55–64 to buy into Medicare. In many cases, Medicare premiums would be cheaper than what is offered through the Affordable Care Act. Decreasing the Medicare age is also good politics—bipartisan and popular. Polls tell us that 77 percent of Americans support the move, including 69 percent of Republicans.[12]

In 2019, New Jersey's representative Tom Malinowski, a Democrat who won a Republican district, introduced incremental legislation allowing retired first responders aged 50–65 to join Medicare.[13] This may not be a big group, but even extending Medicare to these much-celebrated workers was too much for the Republicans, and the bill never had a chance. Despite his pronouncements, Biden didn't propose this popular and vital reform in either the infrastructure or Build Back Better bills of 2021.

Despite nearly 2 million older workers being pushed out of the labor market due to the pandemic recession, there was just one paltry

168 · CHAPTER NINE

proposal to alleviate the situation—a meager effort to encourage hiring and retaining older employees during the pandemic by allowing employers not to pay their share of Federal Insurance Contributions Act, or FICA, taxes for older workers. It was like robbing Peter to pay Paul: those taxes fund Medicare and Social Security.[14] Depriving Social Security and Medicare of revenue in the name of helping older workers? Surely, we can do better.

3. Push Employers to Create Better Jobs

We regularly hear from workers from all walks of life that work is vital, meaningful, and fulfilling, that it provides more income and wealth.[15] And for some, it's true. But America's profound wealth gap only deepens as people grow older. Nearly 21.5 percent of 34 million Americans over 55 are in the working poor,[16] earning less than two-thirds of the US median hourly wage for all workers—just $15.96 an hour. Reflecting other gender inequities, an even higher share of older working women—26 percent—are working poor.

Older workers are commonly stuck in the kinds of jobs that break down their physical health, steal their free time, and provide little in the way of retirement or health benefits. Personal and home health-care jobs—among the occupations adding the most jobs in the next ten years—pay low wages, offer few benefits, are physically taxing, and are disproportionately performed by older workers (31 percent of home health and personal-care workers are over 55). Likewise, in an occupation filled largely by men, 34 percent of janitors are over 55. By comparison, workers over 55 make up 23 percent of the overall labor force.

As another measure of elder working poverty, in 2021, nearly 1.5 million low-income older workers would have benefited from an expansion of the popular Earned Income Tax Credit because they earn wages so low that they qualify for federal subsidy. This is a key policy lever to improve work and pay for older Americans. As it is now, the EITC functions as a partial subsidy that enables employers to continue paying low wages, as this extra income supplement to low-paid workers relieves pressure on employers to raise wages.

The popular EITC is lauded for raising the income of lower-wage workers, but it also lowers the wages paid by employers. Thus, childless and older workers who get reduced or no EITC benefit work alongside workers who are eligible for the subsidy, meaning they are doing the same jobs for lower pay. The older worker is paid a lower wage but is not eligible for the EITC subsidy.[17]

In the next decade, the share of older workers over age 65 will increase by a whopping 50 percent, translating to an additional 250,000 workers becoming eligible for the expanded EITC.[18] And here is a big warning—without proper reforms, the problem of low pay could be made worse by the EITC. Even if we expand the EITC, employers are still incentivized to create low-paying jobs because of the wage subsidy. The way to counteract the EITC's negative side effects is to raise minimum wages and reduce the barriers faced by workers to form unions. This key twin boost of raising the minimum wage and empowering unions is backed by some fellow scholars.[19]

4. Revamp Worker Training and Job Programs

Rising economic productivity and innovation pose significant challenges for workers. Industrial restructuring and downsizing propelled by technology and automation especially threaten older workers because workforce development and training programs are incentivized to avoid older workers.[20] Worker training programs are evaluated on how fast their trainees get work and whether the pay exceeds that of the previous job. But older workers take longer to find work, and the pay in their new job is usually lower, so having more older workers in a training program makes the program look like a failure.

At the same time, research shows that societies that provide secure and voluntary retirements boost their productivity. In a 2017 paper, Europe's leading retirement researcher, Axel Börsch-Supan, and his coauthors anticipated that employers would automate as populations age. When older people stop "commodifying" their time by selling it—employers will adopt more labor-saving technologies. And that is (or can be) a good thing. Employers will have to work more efficiently as wages increase because labor becomes scarcer than capital. And workers everywhere, even the ones who stay on the job, benefit from more retirements. I'll go back to this economic point over and over again: it is good for society when people retire.

What is their evidence? They found that three relatively "older" nations in demographic terms—Italy, France, and Germany—tended to boost education and training while they cut pension benefits (by increasing the retirement age). Training older workers was a significant factor in getting people to work a little longer, thereby increasing their economic growth.[21] But the US, at its economic peril, is not creating activist employment programs for older workers.

The US economy's success in producing good-paying jobs and increasing productivity will depend on how the country oversees the aging population and trains older workers. The federal-state workforce development system is the main vehicle for helping displaced and unemployed workers find new jobs. But while older workers face an elevated risk of displacement and unemployment, these training agencies famously avoid older clients. The US has a vigorous system in place for jobless young people, perhaps because youth unemployment is deemed especially wasteful and unemployed young men tend to scare societies. But no special programs exist to serve older job seekers in need of retraining. Meanwhile, the metrics the US Department of Labor uses to evaluate workforce agencies' performance penalize programs if they don't place workers in jobs that pay close to what the worker earned in their previous job. Yet older workers typically take longer to find a job and most often take a job that pays less. So, a workforce program with older workers is already disadvantaged in getting a good score from the evaluators.

In 2020, the economists Katherine Abraham and Susan Houseman proposed ways for workforce development services to help older workers: hiring specialists focused on older workers, promoting self-employment among older adults, and most importantly, avoiding placement incentives (like those penalties for not placing people in jobs that pay at least as much as their last one) that bias a program against serving older workers. Policy makers could also help by expanding the Senior Community Service Employment Program, which serves disadvantaged older adults. Currently, these meagerly funded programs serve only about 67,000 older workers, compared with the 35 million younger workers benefiting from job-training and workforce development programs.

5. Make Volunteering Dignified

While the psychological and social literature on aging and work is beyond the scope of this book, I've kept Erik Erikson's book *The Life Cycle Completed* in my sights while writing.[22] Erikson and other scholars teach us that, particularly in our older years, people seek and need meaningful work that fosters connection and generativity. We seek ways to create meaningful contributions that will outlive us. In old age, we are concerned with establishing and guiding the next generation and understanding the meaning of our lives. If paid work helps this function, we should seek it. But others may find the activity that enhances connection and generativity is volunteer work.

Recognizing the glorious supply of people freed from career and paid work, the nation's policy makers could help create structures to raise up the dignity and recognition of volunteer work. As one example, my mother was in a program funded by the Older Americans Act, the Senior Community Service Employment Program, which paid minimal stipends for low-income seniors volunteering in schools and a few other venues. Her stipend amounted to $1.50 per hour. Many have called for increasing the range of work options as well as the stipend. For my mother to qualify, a social worker came to her house to verify her income and then helped her deduct the cost of Band-Aids and aspirin so she would qualify as low income. I was grateful for the attention to my mother, but the process was time intensive and not dignified.

Many of the psychological and social benefits of work can be achieved through various volunteer, mentoring, and/or part-time paid work that retirees choose to do. The desire for workers to achieve a healthy balance between paid work, leisure, and volunteering could show up in union negotiations for part-time work or enlightened employers adding phased retirement to attract and retain the best workforce.

Without a policy to secure pensions, the working-longer consensus persists, and the pressure diminishes for government to create dignified volunteer opportunities for older people. Government policies can be a good place to create reinforcing mechanisms to lift up meaningful activities for older people. Social provision of goods and services to the elderly also produces jobs for the elderly. In my own life, I know an 87-year-old man who is healthy enough to work and wants to. He drives for Meals on Wheels for fellow seniors in his neighborhood. At 87, he could easily be receiving meals from the program himself.

6. Enforce Antidiscrimination Policies

Google "jokes about older people," and you'll find demeaning sentiment disguised as good humor. A website promises the jokes are provided because "getting old doesn't have to be sad. Make fun of those gray hairs with these old people jokes and jokes for seniors."[23] Some may privately chuckle at these jabs, but they're part of a broader ageism proliferating throughout our culture.

As those online "jokes" attest, ageism is one of the few types of bigotry still considered socially acceptable. Like all bigotries, ageism is based on falsehoods. My college students frequently forget their earbuds, appointments, and just about everything else and never attribute it to their age. And when society perpetuates ageism, this prevents full use of older people's potential, pervading every part of the labor market.

On the surface, the working-longer consensus seems to attack ageism and put forward a liberating view that older people can work forever because they are just as good as young people. Indeed, paid work has many noneconomic benefits for the elderly and for younger people, but working after a certain age should be a choice.

At a minimum, age discrimination laws, including protection against discrimination in training and retraining, should be stepped up. Comparing states with strong age discrimination laws and those with weaker or no protections, economists Song and Neumark found that stronger age discrimination laws help older people work longer.[24]

Neumark argues that Congress needs to strengthen enforcement of age discrimination in hiring because workers need "bridge" jobs because pensions aren't secure or adequate. Providing teeth to our age discrimination laws means making the penalties bigger. It means amending the Age Discrimination in Employment Act of 1967 to clarify that disparate-impact claims are allowed in cases of hiring discrimination. And it means encouraging federal contractors to hire and retain older workers.[25]

The economic literature is clear. Older workers face considerable obstacles to work in the form of ageism, age discrimination, lack of training, and contingent and fragile work status. Because the US does not have the activist, pro-older-workers systems of some European countries, such as incentives for phased retirement, older workers are often trapped and struggling in the labor market, with or without the skills employers are demanding, and doing their best to pretend they're not old. By the way, until Congress acts and you actually have to work when you are old, never make reference to your age or jokes about senior moments.

7. Remove Unintentional Barriers to Working Longer

A big part of the working-longer consensus is composed of "sticks" to prod people to work longer—such as eroding pensions and cutting Social Security. Sticks do work, but they also cause hardship. Most retirees say they retired sooner than planned because they were pushed out or could no longer work.[26] Carrots, another tool deployed by the working-longer consensus, include well-meaning policy recommendations to encourage older people to keep working, such as reducing taxes on older workers and eliminating the Social Security earnings test.

Some of this is perception; some is policy. Currently, if someone claims Social Security and continues working and earns above a certain amount, benefits and payment are delayed, and the worker gets credit for working. This really isn't a penalty, but some people think it discourages work. The earnings test is often fingered as a culprit in causing people to retire too early and to their detriment.

A 2016 economic study inferred that since older workers' earnings clustered around the level above which Social Security benefits are reduced, older workers hesitated to earn more.[27] The economists assume that workers both cluelessly misperceive the earnings test as a tax when it is not and are so sophisticated that they can calculate how tax rules, requirements for food stamps and housing assistance, and so on, interact to change their take-home pay. But that is illogical and contradictory. And the study assumes that employers want to hire older workers, and the only thing holding older people back from working is food stamps, housing assistance, and earnings tests (which, taken together, on paper create high marginal tax rates for working). Maybe that is what workers are deciding, but I don't believe it.

My takeaway? Sure, it can't hurt to better inform people about how the earnings test operates, and that might increase labor supply a bit. But the real problem with low-income elders not working is likely mental and physical limitations to work, bad job quality, and age discrimination.

8. Ensure Better Pensions

The idea that workers simply need food stamps and other assistance has a big effect on policy makers, who blame the worker and ignore structural inequalities and challenges. In 2000, following the logic that the earnings test was discouraging work, policy makers devised the carrot of eliminating the test past age 67 for those born after 1960. But this hasn't been shown to help; in fact, it may have hurt. I have noted repeatedly that raising the retirement age cuts benefits at every age a person collects Social Security, and most older workers collect Social Security while they are working, presumably to supplement low wages. The earning test is not a significant factor in a person's decision about work and claiming.

Another carrot to encourage older people to look for work is to engineer a way for workers to accumulate more Social Security credits beyond their highest-paid thirty-five years. But this would benefit only workers with more education, who get wage increases at older ages, helping the top more than those at the bottom.[28]

Some hoped that educating people about the rewards for delaying their Social Security claims, for not drawing down their financial assets, and for working longer would save the day. But being financially informed does not change the reality that when older workers are paid poorly, they will claim Social Security while working and draw down their assets rather than save for retirement.

Other carrots to induce working longer include shifting economic risks even more heavily onto workers by restructuring retirement plans. For instance, secure defined-benefit plans give confidence to retirees—the ability to accrue benefits after, say, age 65 is limited and the benefits are guaranteed—but 401(k)-type plans keep people uncertain and worried, compelling them to keep working for fear of not having enough.

Eliminating mandatory retirement may not have persuaded many Americans to work longer. It may have helped workers and employers view age discrimination more negatively, and that is good, but tight labor markets and more educated older workers have been the main drivers of longer lifetime careers. And women working at older ages has also boosted retirement ages. That trend has more to do with women's economic emergence over the past forty years—reproductive rights and more education—which has also boosted overall labor supply.

Why am I bothering to add up all the policy attempts to "encourage" working longer, including cutting Social Security benefits? Because I want to emphasize that large systemic issues pertaining to profit taking and policy making create labor-market challenges faced by workers over 50. The following list summarizes much of what is documented in most of the book: age discrimination, forced retirement, and bad jobs for older workers raise profits, and having health insurance at work ends up hurting older workers.

1. Employers' age biases and stereotypes lead employers to underappreciate older workers' skills and experience. The result? Pay

does not increase after about age 45, and there is a documented trend of older workers not getting the same compensation premium for their work experience and skills as they had in the past. And when older workers are displaced from sectors that are shrinking, their skills and experience are often not as valued in emerging new sectors. Take, for instance, the welder having to find work as a home health-care worker. This leads to downward mobility for older workers through no fault of their own.

2. Most retirement is involuntary. In surveys, most people over age 55 who say they are retired report being pushed out of their jobs or leaving the labor market earlier than planned due to health issues. We should substitute *forced retirement* for *retirement* because the first is closer to the truth; *retirement* implies that the worker had the choice and agency to decide to leave the labor force. Older workers are less likely to have paid sick leave than younger workers, even though they may need it more often, which forces them to retire. Once they are displaced or unemployed, older workers typically take much longer to find a new job. Policy makers may need to extend long-term unemployment insurance for these folks.

3. Bad jobs for older workers are profitable for many industries. Older workers are disproportionately represented in many low-wage jobs, like janitorial services, warehouse work, and personal home and health care—yet they do not qualify for income supports like the Earned Income Tax Credit. This leads them to collect Social Security while they are still working, permanently reducing their benefits.

4. The US system of having employers pay for health insurance is very disadvantageous for older workers. Older workers may cost more to their employers because medical insurance premiums are higher for an older workforce. The Medicare age should be lower—to age 50—and Medicare should be the first payer.

5. Better pensions and secure health insurance would give older workers a stronger fallback position. Better pensions are secure and adequate, and good health insurance is decoupled from employment.

Conclusion: Make Jobs and Pensions So Good That Elderly Workers Work by Choice

It is easy to see that having bad jobs in one's life leads to bad retirement financial readiness. What is less well-recognized is the reverse causality between bad retirement financial readiness and bad jobs for older workers. In the presence of widespread retirement insecurity, older workers' earnings are lower than if employers had to lure and entice experienced workers who could otherwise comfortably retire. Older workers with fewer options have less leverage to bargain for raises, benefits, or improved working conditions; their ability to negotiate higher pay depends partly on their options, whether it's other employment or retirement.

With far too much optimism, the Department of Labor noted in 2021 that "the economic downturn, shifting perceptions of retirement, increased workplace flexibility, and the aging of the 'baby boom' generation are all contributing to people working longer."[29] The list is overly upbeat and incomplete—eroding pensions are a major force compelling older folks to work longer. The department could well have added that "eroding pensions are a major force reducing older folks' ability to ask for better pay, hours, and working conditions."

The Gray New Deal aims to solve two problems at once: to strengthen pensions to raise the bargaining power of older workers and to create better jobs for older workers to improve the living standards of America's elders. It's simple—we do everything we can to improve the labor market for older workers, and we improve pensions and help people secure retirement and economic stability in their final years of life.

To fill these and other key gaps in policy and awareness, the last chapter focuses on how we can secure and afford better pensions as a society.

10

Creating Better Pensions

Fixing our broken retirement system is not that hard. The framework for reform is simple, but the entrenched interests of retail money managers stand in the way of change. A dollar saved for retirement must be saved consistently, invested early and well, and structured as a payout that lasts a lifetime.

Almost all experts agree that if we could start from scratch, we would have required universal advance-funded pensions in addition to Social Security. Some institutions did fund their pensions in advance, including state and local governments, large employers, and unionized companies. But because the US didn't require universal pension funding, huge gaps remain, leaving millions of older folks financially insecure.

A Better Pension System Is Doable

If I could wave a magic wand, I would set up a plan to require all employers to provide a platform for saving and investments with mandated employer and employee contributions; it would involve investments made by professionals with heavy federal oversight and most of it would be annuitized alongside Social Security. We would accumulate investment capital and have a hybrid system of advance-funded social insurance and that would be that. I could dedicate my life to something else besides producing policies to help workers have a dignified old age. But wand waving is not the way the world works.

Policy makers should have required every employer and worker covered by Social Security to also contribute to individual pensions. These accounts would be owned and controlled by each worker. Their accounts would be flexible and tailored to fit their lives and needs. After meeting the minimal contribution, workers and employers could add money to the account, further solidifying people's economic futures and retirements.

A MAXIMALIST PLAN FOR GUARANTEED RETIREMENT ACCOUNTS

In a different book, *Rescuing Retirement*, Tony James and I offer a detailed plan for Congress and the president to implement Guaranteed Retirement Accounts (GRAs), derived from a program I devised with the Economic Policy Institute in 2005.[1] This bold plan provides adequate and universal retirement-income security that would maintain older people's living standards into retirement.

In our plan, all workers and employers would contribute 3 percent of pay at the beginning of their career and for as long as they worked. (The self-employed would be required to have a GRA just like they must contribute to Social Security.) Over forty-five years, this money would accumulate to the point at which it replaces a worker's pre-retirement earnings, enabling people to retire and avoid poverty. The GRA would have to be invested well. This proposal for GRAs would pool investments to ensure that workers earn the highest risk-adjusted returns possible. The principal would be guaranteed, regardless of fluctuations in investments. Payouts would come in the form of annuities to ensure that retirees don't outlive their savings. The GRA also includes a tax credit—like the Earned Income Tax Credit but an earned wealth tax credit—so that the government pays the required contributions for low-income workers who don't have a dollar to spare for savings.

STATES IMPLEMENT AUTOMATIC INDIVIDUAL RETIREMENT PLANS

In the face of decades of minimalist and austerity-minded policies, the GRAs are a maximalist solution. Another important policy movement toward retirement security involves state and city initiatives to make pensions universal. This follows a long-standing pattern in American progress on social policy innovation: states and municipalities will move until the federal government acts. Famously, President Roosevelt enacted Social Security in 1935—but before that, in 1934, over twenty-five states had or were considering old-age income security legislation.

As of 2023, more than twenty-five states sponsored some version of an automatic IRA plan to help some workers save. There is talk of implementing a national automatic IRA plan. But IRA plans have structural problems that will always make them inferior to a national, universal retirement plan. IRAs are individual accounts, liquid, commercial, and self-directed plans.

In an automatic IRA plan, the employer automatically enrolls a worker into an individual retirement account. But after that, workers are on their own. The responsibility for contributing, managing, and maintaining the account lies with the worker. The worker decides how much to put in and where, the worker can withdraw the money whenever it is needed (even before retirement), and the worker doesn't have any negotiating power to lower fees on the investment vehicles offered in the account. Employers cannot contribute to the IRA with tax-favored accounts because IRA accounts are not protected by federal regulations. Savers in IRA plans pay retail fees and construct their own portfolios. Workers end up with an inferior, low-performing, and suboptimal account, paying high fees on amateur investment portfolios. In short, IRAs are inappropriate for long-term retirement savings.

A BIPARTISAN PLAN TO EXPAND THE THRIFT SAVINGS PLAN

When it became clear the state-by-state efforts for individual retirement plans weren't going to work, and neither would a national automatic IRA—and when protests, clamor, and political criticism of glaring national wealth disparities were mounting, I teamed up with an unusual partner for me. The economist Kevin Hassett—of Trump's Council of Economic Advisers—and I proposed a variation on the GRAs. Our plan—the Thrift Savings Plan (TSP) for Most Who Have None—invites Congress to give low- and moderate-income Americans access to a new retirement savings program modeled after the federal Thrift Savings Plan, a 401(k)-like program for federal employees. Key features of the TSP include automatic enrollment for eligible workers, low fees, simple plan options, and federal matching contributions to reward and encourage savings. Projections show that more wealth for half of workers, the lowest end of the wealth distribution—most have barely anything except debt—will make them more income secure at retirement.

Research shows that the right incentives can play a crucial role in helping people achieve their financial goals and attain self-sufficiency. The TSP is a proven program that draws from important findings in behavioral economics to deliver outstanding results for eligible workers, including those with low income and educational attainment.

These plans are close to what a good pension system looks like.

For most people, in a face-off between an automatic IRA and a GRA or TSP, the GRA plan wins hands down. Savers in a GRA-type plan pay wholesale fees, and professionals construct portfolios.

With help from a government-refundable tax credit, workers and employers would pay about 6 percent into a retirement account income. But wait, would those higher taxes hurt employment? No economic model has found that this payroll tax increase would significantly harm jobs by reducing workers' incentives to work or employers' incentives to hire people in robust economies. Higher labor costs often result in higher productivity.

Consider the treachery and damage of today's status quo. By not moving to bring more revenue to Social Security—for instance, by raising the cap on the amount of earnings taxed for Social Security—the system slips perilously closer to insolvency. If we do not change the Social Security status quo, 75 percent of benefits owed will be paid by around 2034; because the system is progressive, Social Security cuts will increase US elder poverty rates, which already are the highest among rich nations. Inaction in pumping new revenue into Social Security is a deadly action.

Promisingly, some political leaders are at least heeding and speaking about threats to Social Security and the need to act. During the 2020 presidential campaign, several Democratic candidates put forward plans to shore up and beef up the system.

When Pete Buttigieg, now transportation secretary, ran for president, his platform included plans to expand Social Security and create something similar to the GRAs.[2] Buttigieg would have made employers pay 3 percent into a workplace-portable pension (the GRA plan is a 1.5 percent shared cost between employers and employees, raising the same amount by different means).

Senator Elizabeth Warren proposed expanding Social Security and raising all benefits by $200 per month; Senator Bernie Sanders also campaigned on expanding Social Security; and on the campaign trail Joe Biden proposed expanding the employer pension system through a voluntary method.

Momentum is building to strengthen Social Security and other core elements of a Gray New Deal, which would expand the current system and layer on top of it an advance-funded retirement system like what workers have in public employment, unionized workplaces, and in large firms. Another sign the policy window for a Gray New Deal is opening is that—like the year before Social Security passed—over thirty-four states now require employers to offer (though, sadly, not to pay for) a retirement plan.

A Better Pension System Is Affordable

My vision constructs a politically sustainable and adequate pension system with fewer opportunities for financial predation, confusion, and self-dealing. I advocate a fully funded system of universal pensions, delivered through a GRA-like plan, which the TSP-for-All plan is. Similar to the Dutch system, the GRA supplements Social Security with advance-funded pensions, paid for by employee and employer contributions.

How would this ambitious program operate? Workers would be completely or partly subsidized by a tax credit, and these credits would be paid for by eliminating tax breaks for higher-income earners. Depending on the size of the tax credit and how much tax deduction money is kept for existing 401(k) plans, the net cost to the US Treasury could be zero and still raise everyone above twice the poverty line in old age. Imagine that for a moment: we have the opportunity and the policy know-how to eliminate elder poverty. We can stabilize life and retirement for millions of older Americans. This is an opportunity we cannot afford to miss.

Unlike Social Security, income from the GRA accounts will rely on the actual balances in each person's individually owned retirement savings account. People could add more to their accounts to get an even higher benefit. The GRA plans function as both pensions and accounts, arrangements by which individuals have some influence over the size of their eventual benefits. For instance, union workers will sometimes accept lower pay to have more money poured into their pension plans. In 401(k)-type plans, workers can vary their contributions to get higher benefits in retirement, but these plans are not as professionally managed as GRAs would be.

Indeed, superior management is a distinct advantage GRAs have over individually directed commercial accounts. When real capital is pooled in large GRA accounts, highly regulated plan managers—as they do for big pension plans, endowments, and the like—would choose a portfolio of long- and medium-term, high-performing investments that yield a much higher risk-adjusted rate of return than the current system of 401(k) plans and IRAs, which tend to be held in short-term liquid assets, whose assets can be marked to the market daily. Getting a higher return for a dollar of savings would help close the retirement wealth gap without adding costs for anyone. Everyone would have the advantage of returns from a professionally managed account, such as the Harvard endowment or the teachers' pension funds.

Still, some may ask, why do we need a GRA plan—why not just strengthen Social Security? The short answer: We absolutely must do both. Social Security could be even more progressive and insure elders against poverty. It would take relatively small increases in premiums—garnered by raising the tax rate or expanding the revenue base—to lift benefits for the very poorest Social Security recipients. But on the current policy landscape, no practical and proposed expansion of Social Security does enough to replace the 70 percent of middle-class wages needed to sustain a pre-retirement lifestyle for these workers. By combining GRAs and Social Security, we can create a system of fully advance-funded accounts that would replace about 70 percent of workers' pre-retirement income in retirement—enough in most cases to maintain people's pre-retirement living standards into old age.

The Low Cost of Good Pensions

The fact is, we can afford good pensions and better jobs—and we really can't afford bad pensions and bad jobs. Most people want (or at least are willing) to pay for adequate retirement security. With an average of about 6 percent of our pay, as a society we can secure middle-class retirement and prevent poverty.[3] In fact, some versions of the pension plans are revenue neutral, meaning that the government doesn't pay any more than it is paying now but there are much better pensions for people.

Meanwhile, we pay exceedingly inflated costs when older workers are stuck in bad jobs with a meager (if any) pension—additional higher costs for elderly health care, economic assistance for the elderly poor, and much more. Any upfront costs for protecting and training our elders—remembering we will all be "old" one day, if we're lucky—is more than worth it.

But how we create and structure this system matters. A well-functioning and sustainable pension system provides pensions to high-income, middle-class, and low-income workers alike. Including disabled and low-income workers with high-income workers helps stabilize such programs in political terms.

In contrast, a pension system funded entirely from general revenues is neither stable nor equitable: depending entirely on pay-as-you-go systems to fund a pension system could be foolhardy and harmful. Variations in demographics and in the productivity of unfortunate workers who are in cohorts that experience an unlucky share of severe recessions can make pay-as-you-go systems unstable and unsustainable; through no fault of their own, the unlucky cohort's payroll tax rates could double to pay for existing pensions.

Paying for pensions involves taking resources from current consumption to ensure later consumption. This can be accomplished through government promises, through private arrangements that depend on returns from private bonds and stocks, through a mixed public and private system, or, as the pension economist Nicholas Barr noted, by burying things you will need in old age—drugs, canned goods, adult diapers—in the garden.

But politically, how pensions are arranged matters—and stability and predictability are key. In 2020, if Social Security was funded from general revenue, tax rates would have had to double to over 30 percent of pay as a small cohort pays for a big one. The required rate may fall or spike year to year. Politically negotiating those allocations each year is not feasible. The two-tier model—a layer of pay-as-you-go beneath a layer of advance-funded pensions—is the most stable one for funding for old age.

As an economist, I argue that it's possible to fund both an expansion of Social Security and mandatory individual retirement accounts. Ensuring a secure retirement for all workers and the end of elderly poverty would require an additional $500 billion in retirement contributions from workers, employers, and the government. While that's less than 3 percent of GDP, $500 billion is not a trivial sum. For comparison, it is similar in magnitude to the annual cost of the 2017 GOP tax cut ($5.5 trillion over ten years).

How does this work? Every worker and their employer would pay a total of about 6 percent more out of payroll toward their retirement security—about eighty cents per hour. This breaks down into three parts.

First, about 3 percent of payroll goes to secure Social Security. This ensures that workers receive their full and promised Social Security benefits and provides retirees with an average of 36 percent of their pre-retirement income.

Second, according to the Social Security Administration, an additional 0.02 percent of payroll would raise the special minimum benefit, which would bring almost every elder above the poverty line. This particular benefit places a floor (the maximum is $886.40 in 2019) and is not properly indexed to inflation—it is indexed to wage growth, and wages have rarely kept up with the cost of living—so it has eroded over time, and almost no new claimants qualify.

Another 3 percent of payroll would go to fund mandatory individual savings accounts for retirement. By itself, this contribution is unlikely to permit all workers to maintain their living standards in retirement. However, as a supplement to retirees' monthly Social Security benefit, these accounts will help ensure that even low-income older Americans can live well clear of poverty or near poverty. The program will also allow those who want to contribute more to do so. Workers approaching retirement without adequate savings would have to increase their savings by considerably more than 3 percent. Still, these workers would be better off than they are today with universal access to a low-cost savings retirement program.

BOX 10.1 Why Not Just Expand Social Security?

Why not just expand Social Security to solve the retirement crises? If we expanded Social Security to provide adequate retirement for most American workers, payroll taxes would rise to about 30 percent of pay—up from the current FICA payroll tax of 12.4 percent, which is split evenly between employer and employee. Such a move is bad for four reasons: depending on only a payroll tax means the payroll tax is high and fluctuates wildly depending upon how large and productive the current worker cohort is relative to the retired cohort. Second, with payroll taxes that high, businesses and employees avoid paying them. Third, taxing workers at such a high percentage only encourages off-the-books work and a growing informal and unregulated labor force. Fourth, a hybrid system is more resilient and efficient.

Nations that achieve widespread retirement security do so with hybrid systems, not one that just relies on a PAYGO system like Social Security. Rare cases like France and Spain that started out with just a PAYGO system have very high payroll taxes—37 percent and 28 percent, respectively—compared to 12.4 percent in the US. To keep those taxes from going any higher and to scale them back, France and Spain are both developing advance-funded systems composed of mandated hybrids blending defined-benefit and 401(k)-type plans.

And by not forcing Social Security to meet all retirement needs, we keep tax rates low. The relatively low US Social Security system payroll tax of 12.4 percent means almost everyone pays the Social Security tax.

Nobel Prize winner Peter Diamond and economist Nicholas Barr and others argue a blend of PAYGO and advance-funded plans is more efficient, meaning administrative costs and risks are smaller, a large government plan can manage economic and demographic shocks better than a pure PAYGO system or a totally capitalized system. Households can fund their retirement more cheaply with a combination of regulated advanced funded pension accounts and Social Security.

An improved US retirement system would fully fund Social Security, mandate employer and employee contributions to invest in the market, professionally manage the investments, and pay out annuities.

Best Practices in Other Nations

Most effective national retirement systems have common features. The outlier is America's voluntary, commercial, financialized, do-it-yourself system, which departs from the common pension design features found in other OECD nations. The US employer-based pension system is voluntary—other nations insist on universal coverage and rely on fewer tax incentives. No other nation allows workers to withdraw government-subsidized retirement funds or borrow against them before retirement, and unlike in many other nations, annuity options are scarce in America beyond the government sector.[4]

Models that mix a government-run, pay-as-you-go element with an advance-funded program for accumulation, investment, and annuitization have been successful. These hybrid systems—for example, in the Netherlands, Israel, Australia, and Denmark—are best in class for retirement security and sustainable design.

A report by Mercer, a global management consulting firm, ranked Denmark and the Netherlands especially high in all three years.[5] Why? For one thing, the Danish and Dutch hybrid public-private design provides flexibility to adjust to economic changes. Benefits and revenue can change to keep the system fiscally balanced and benefits adequate. The adjustments are baked into the rules, the adjustments are transparent, and a centralized administration and oversight keep the system relatively free of corruption. These systems are based on a primary layer of public pensions funded by tax revenue and a second tier of near-universal, advance-funded occupational pensions or plans for self-employed people, with the ability to lower benefits slightly if revenues from investments fall significantly. In the Netherlands, pensions can be reduced if the system does not receive enough returns—which was a challenge in 2021 because the recession kept interest rates low. Employers, workers, and the government share the risk of financial underperformance, the vulnerable are protected, and the system is highly regulated.

Australia and Denmark are also highly ranked because they have high rates of coverage, sound investment vehicle choices, and practical ways to annuitize and create lifelong income. A basic requirement for a good pension system is universal access to a savings plan. Only 44 percent of American workers have access to a retirement savings plan at work, whereas in Denmark, the rate of access is 85 percent; in the Netherlands it is 88 percent; and in Australia, it's over 75 percent. The United States has one of the highest elderly poverty rates of any of our developed country counterparts. The United States falls behind in having an adequate pension. According to the International Mercer Global Pension Index of 2021,[6] the United States gets a C– for adequacy, with a score of 61 out of 100. The United Kingdom has an adequacy score of 74 percent; Canada, 69 percent; the Netherlands, 83 percent; Denmark, 82 percent; and Australia, 67 percent. The most adequate pensions in the world come from Iceland and the Netherlands, with scores of 83 percent and 82 percent.

Another top criterion for a good pension system is its ability to achieve economic growth and equity. A welfare state that assures safety nets and household income during recessions provides long-term capital as well as efficient ways to smooth consumption from one period to the next, helping workers and firms take risks and find patient capital. Good pension systems provide smooth off-ramps from work to retirement and help incentivize hard work and investment in employees who know there is assured old-age income. A pension system that helps workers and businesses accumulate talent, skills, and capacity and that smooths transitions can bolster economic growth and equity.

By arranging to have retirement savings invested in long-term savings vehicles, the economy would have more patient finance capital available for long-term investments. Today, retirement savings in 401(k)s and IRAs are in liquid asset vehicles and thus cannot be invested in infrastructure or other long-term ventures. GRA accounts, in contrast, are nonliquid and can be invested in long-term accounts, like DB plans.

Replacing the Working-Longer Consensus

What distinguishes a progressive, leftist, or liberal vision of a working-longer consensus from a conservative, right-wing work-longer position? Not much. My proposal for a fully funded, adequate, and equitable pension system does not preclude the goal of allowing every older adult to work if they want. At heart, welfare states determine who has a claim to income without working for pay. In doing so, they provide those who want to work with more bargaining power. A pension system that provides adequate income and allows older workers to work is one that maximizes equity, adequacy, and economic growth.

Increasing elderly people's labor-force participation and providing a generous pension system encourages work. In such a system, older workers may choose to work because of attractive pay, working conditions, and hours. A liberal system leans toward outcomes in which elderly employees are working more on their own terms than those of an employer. Denmark, Sweden, and Norway have robust rates of elderly labor-force participation (ranging from 9 percent to 18 percent) and low elder poverty rates. However, when more than one out of five older people is working, the dynamic changes, and the elderly poverty rate—an indication of less generous pensions—goes up. In the OECD, the twelve nations with elder labor-force participation rates higher than the 20 percent of the United States are those with weak pension systems and high rates of elder poverty.

The dynamics of pension arrangements remain at the center of the emerging working-longer consensus. Since pensions are a large part of the welfare state, they help to regulate the size of the labor force (and whose time is commodified). The generosity of the welfare state is highly vulnerable to shifts in political will, such as the rise of austerity in the past ten years, which has fundamentally redefined who deserves income without working.

Secure retirements are an extension of workplace norms such as bargained paid time off benefits that give us the weekend, sick leave, holidays, and vacations. The working-longer consensus marks a reversal in paid time off provisions. It has eroded the weekend and evenings and time off and is attacking retirement. A liberal welfare state allows a job to any adult who wants to work—without regard to age, color, creed, sex, national origin, gender identification, or religious affiliation—and provides a high universal basic income to everyone after a lifetime of work so that people's ability to work and retire will pressure employers to improve jobs and productivity to the benefit of all.

To understand our economic problems, we should look at the lives of real people who are navigating the system. The reporter Greg Iacurci interviewed a couple in their 80s, Don and Grace Porter, at the beginning of 2021 after they lost their restocking jobs at Target, jobs they were happy to have after they lost their wallpaper business in 2008. With no part-time work, they were living on $1,700 a month in combined Social Security benefits, minus $570 that goes to a Medicare supplemental health plan. "It's tight," Grace said. "We're very frugal." The Portes are officially poor. Iacurci focused on the vulnerability of older workers in downturns. I focus on why this married couple of sixty-three years—who worked their whole lives—in their 80s had to work at Target to stay out of poverty.[7]

Grace and Dan's story is not exceptional. In May 2020, I told *CNBC News* that older workers went down market, desperate for any job after the Great Recession of 2008; we saw "the phenomenon of Granny working in McDonald's" ramping up.[8] But in the 2020 recession, employers laid off older workers faster than prime-age workers. Three million older workers and their spouses may have been forced into semipermanent poverty or near poverty over the coming ten years because of the unexpected retirements caused by the recession—though about 1 million of the youngest older workers had returned to work by 2022.[9]

The COVID-19 recession and lax labor law enforcement by the Trump administration may have provided a once-in-a-lifetime chance for employers to shed older workers to cut costs.[10] And shed they did—millions of older workers will likely never come back to work.

The United States prides itself in upholding the values that any adult who wants to work can do so free of judgment and barriers in characteristics not related to their productivity, such as national origin, religion, race, gender, and age. But strict age discrimination enforcement won't make the working-longer consensus. Although I don't want a mandatory retirement age to come back, a worthy thought experiment is this: if we didn't have a mandatory age, would the poor have better pensions?

It's Time for a Gray New Deal

As we face our future, we also face a choice and an opportunity for change. We can continue pushing older people to work longer out of sheer necessity—risking their health, keeping them precarious, and destabilizing the larger economy—or we can embrace and reinvigorate a universal pension system that enables old folks to retire in dignity and comfort if they wish.

Today's system is stuck somewhere in between, holding up the illusion of pensions and retirement while tilting heavily toward "work longer" economic coercion. A national pension system functions well when workers can consistently, over the course of their working lives, accumulate claims to income when they retire. But America's pension system has fallen short for most people because coverage is spotty and uneven: most workers in the bottom 80 percent of the income distribution do not have employers that contribute or sponsor a plan.

Because of our system's poor design, most workers don't voluntarily save for retirement because it is simply not economically feasible. Exacerbating this inequality, government subsidies—the tax benefits—mostly go to upper-income groups.

The shame of our system is that we think a good retirement comes about because of decisions made around the kitchen table, but the fact is that most people cannot retire well without government coordination. Nobody does it on their own. And this government coordination not only enables individual retirement but also helps sustain a healthy economy. Coordinating a public option for a universal supplement to Social Security will not harm the government financially, and the new system could raise wages and productivity. A public-option pension system will plug gaps in today's voluntary, commercial, individual-directed, do-it-yourself system.

We likely will have a chance to replace the working-longer consensus in the next recession and election. The policy window—when ideas, politics, and a pressing problem all come together—may finally be open for a Gray New Deal.

Remember what happened in the last recession? The value of older workers' retirement accounts fell. Some stayed on the job instead of exiting the labor force with secure pensions, and cut their spending drastically, making it difficult for younger workers to find work. Having a system that forces residents to cut their spending and cling to their jobs even more than they would during a recession is really bad economic policy. In contrast, modern economic policies have done the opposite. Economic programs—like income-support insurance systems—that stabilize spending and income during a recession automatically stabilize the economy. Social Security, unemployment insurance, income-support payments—all serve as automatic stabilizers. So do traditional pension plans. When times got tough, workers with DB plants retired instead of preventing a job opening or raising unemployment. When they collected their DB and Social Security, they maintained their spending power, to the delight of the local grocer and their mortgage holder. But the finance-based 401(k) system works in the opposite direction. People feel poor and panicked when their 401(k) loses value. They stay working and cut their spending. The recession was made even worse due to financialized pensions—we destabilized our automatic stabilizers.[11] Retirement-income security soared to the top in polls asking American families about their deepest fears.

And yet the working-longer consensus and its advocates perpetuate myths and falsehoods about work and old age. There is no evidence that working longer into old age improves people's retirement financial preparedness, especially when so many elderly workers are low paid and people must collect their Social Security while working. There is no evidence that having adequate income and control over the pace and content of your time is detrimental. On the contrary, control over your time and adequate finances promote well-being. The only evidence that is unassailable about working longer is that it makes retirement time more unequal. Retirement time is the new contested struggle for American workers.

After nearly forty years dominated by the working-longer consensus, to the detriment of millions of old folks and of our society, it's time for change. A Gray New Deal that mandates pensions, expands Social Security, and finances long-term care will increase workers' bargaining power, strengthen labor markets, and make workers better off.

Most importantly, good pensions could prevent a humanitarian disaster. Without robust off-ramps from work to retirement, or to part-time jobs that are appropriate for elders, the only option this growing cohort will have is downward mobility and old-age poverty.[12] And while old folks will suffer the most, we'll all pay for that in the end.

The truth is that we can afford a Gray New Deal. Contrary to what many say, we can afford to pay for voluntary retirements for old people who want to retire as long as we plan for it and as long as everyone contributes.

A nation's economic health depends on how it deals with an aging population and superannuation—the obsolescence of workers' skills due to changing technology and consumer demands. Considering all the human and economic benefits, paying for retirement-income security is well worth it.

The good news is that providing adequate pensions could pay for itself. Fortunately, the United States is a wealthy nation, and its population is relatively young; it can afford to restore Social Security benefits and provide universal advance-funded retirement accounts. For a relatively small price, we can ensure a secure retirement for all and nearly eradicate elder poverty in America, by saving 6 percent or more of pay in the form of a slightly higher Social Security tax and more in your own retirement savings account.

If you're still on the fence about this, consider the huge costs of not providing secure retirement to all American workers. Taxpayers will pay for the continued downward mobility of middle-class workers as millions more elders line up for public assistance. Through sheer economic coercion and necessity, millions of Americans will migrate from planned retirement to reluctant (and often dangerous) low-paid work. Consider the many negative and harmful effects of 8 million precarious elders—depressing wages, labor standards, and productivity. Meanwhile, working longer could worsen the health of many older workers, adding more suffering and medical costs. We simply cannot afford to continue in this direction.

Promising change is on the horizon and within reach. In 2021, three members of Congress introduced a bill to create an Older Workers' Bureau at the US Department of Labor. Much like the Women's Bureau formed back in the 1920s, this new body would investigate the conditions of older workers and formulate standards and policies to promote the welfare of wage-earning older people; and would advance their opportunities for appropriate and profitable employment, dignity, security, and bargaining power.

Republicans and Democrats in both the Senate and the House introduced the Retirement Savings for Americans Act which implements a TSP-for-Most type plan.[13]

If you take one lesson from this book, I hope it is this: adequate and sustainable retirement income is the key to better jobs for older workers, and it helps all workers. Stronger Social Security and a universal pension system would enable and empower older workers to make a choice they've earned through a lifetime of work. Talk about a worthwhile investment that pays massive and essential dividends.

....

BOX 10.2 How to Plan for Your Retirement While Waiting for Congress

As I write, Congress has not acted to ensure that all Americans have a decent retirement. What can you do to minimize your risk of poverty, financial instability, and working until you drop dead? Think of yourself as working on five fronts aligned with your five identities: consumer, saver, investor, worker, and voter.

If you're going to have less than ten or eleven times your target annual spending when you retire, here are five areas you can work on to make your retirement more secure. As a consumer, know how much you are spending, know how much you need to spend, and know what you can stop spending on and be just fine. Start creating a monthly budget and analyze where your money goes. Once you have a target spending—don't forget to save room for emergencies: inflate your budget by 10 percent for emergencies—consider how much you must save to be able to have enough to live on once you retire. Saving $1,000 a month for twenty-eight years should yield about $600,000—which with Social Security maintains the living standards of someone making $60,000 per year. If you earn more and want more than $600,000, then save more per month and for more years. If you want to save less per month and still have $600,000 (all figures are adjusted for inflation), then you must save longer than twenty-eight years. (I am assuming a net-of-fee return of 4 percent.)

Third, if you can't possibly save enough to get to that target, and even if you can, make your saved dollar go further by having a smart, diversified, low-fee portfolio. Make sure you pay only wholesale fees when investing in index funds. As of this writing, I recommend you consider Vanguard funds. Vanguard is the only company that has a fiduciary responsibility for your money. Because it's mutually owned by the account holders, all the profits go to the account holders in the form of better service and lower fees. Other money-management companies must make profits to pay outside shareholders. (I have no relationship with Vanguard except as an account holder.)

The fourth dimension to manage is your work life. This is hard because age discrimination and low-paid jobs pose challenges for older workers. Try to join a union and negotiate for the highest pay you can possibly get. Follow all the tips to have a robust résumé. Don't compound the age discrimination by making any senior-moment jokes.

Last, you can mobilize your role as a voter. Make sure the candidates you vote for are dedicated to adding more revenue to Social Security and Medicare and not in favor of raising the retirement age or otherwise cutting benefits. The federal government is one of your most important financial partners in retirement.

Notes

CHAPTER ONE

1. Mast, "82-Year-Old Walmart Cashier."

2. Papadopoulos et al., "Recession Increases Downward Mobility in Retirement."

3. Using the US Bureau of Labor Statistics numbers, Guy Burdick, in "Fatal Injuries," sums up the data well: fatal occupational injuries among workers of all ages decreased by 17 percent from 1992 to 2017, but for older workers, the increase in fatal injuries was 56 percent from 1992 to 2017. And it was worse for workers in the oldest group, those aged 65 and over.

4. The COVID-19 recession (as well as federal policies that have kept interest rates low) has made accumulating retirement savings even tougher. A spring 2020 survey—Berger, "3 in 10 Americans Withdrew Money from Retirement Savings"—found that 30 percent of Americans paid for groceries and housing out of their retirement accounts. Other data suggest that people who withdrew most from their savings were in the bottom of the income distribution. The issue is structural gaps between soaring costs of living and dwindling economic security, not individual spending habits; we shouldn't criticize people for dipping into their retirement funds for emergency savings and groceries in a recession, even if their future costs will be high.

5. Cooper and Davis, "Premiums and Employee Contributions."

6. Rae, Cubanski, and Damico, *Health Spending for 60-64 Year Olds*; Burtless, "Age Related Health Costs and Job Prospects of Older Workers"; Scott, Berger, and Garen, "Do Health Insurance and Pension Costs Reduce the Job Opportunities of Older Workers?"

7. *NBC Nightly News*, "Pandemic Draining Older Americans' Savings, Leaving Workers Behind," October 11, 2021, https://www.nbcnews.com/nightly-news/video/pandemic-draining-older-americans-savings-leaving-workers-behind-123290181600.

8. Smialek and Casselman, "Retirees Are One Reason the Fed Has Given Up on a Big Worker Rebound."

9. Before the pandemic, we were already looking at a trend of older workers not doing as well relative to younger workers. Gosselin, "If You're over 50, Chances Are the Decision to Leave a Job Won't Be Yours"; Farmand and Ghilarducci, "Why American Older Workers Have Lost Bargaining Power."

10. Jacobson, Feder, and Radley, "COVID-19's Impact on Older Workers: Employment, Income, and Medicare Spending."

11. Low-income workers are less likely to be able to work from home. The original source for this data comes from the St. Louis Federal Reserve and the Bureau of Labor Statistics Occupational Employment Statistics.

12. Papadopoulos et al., "Recession Increases Downward Mobility in Retirement."

13. The COVID-19 recession caused more unemployment among low- and middle-income older workers than among those with better jobs and more education. Davis et al., "A First in Nearly 50 Years, Older Workers Face Higher Unemployment Than Mid-Career Workers."

14. Most middle earners postpone claiming Social Security benefits until age 65. Low earners are more likely to claim benefits at age 62, whereas middle and high earners typically postpone retirement and claim Social Security benefits at age 65 or older. While workers can increase their retirement income by claiming at older ages, many low earners—who are less likely to find adequate employment and have little savings—cannot afford to postpone claiming. In the COVID-19 recession, even more workers who lose their jobs will claim their Social Security benefits at 62. However, we do not include the possible change in claim age or the earnings gradient in our model. On how retirement ages vary by class, see Ghilarducci and Webb, "The Distribution of Time in Retirement."

15. Clingman, Burkhalter, and Chaplain, "Replacement Rates for Hypothetical Retired Workers."

16. Ghilarducci, Papadopoulos, and Webb, "Larger Birth Cohort Lowers Wages."

17. Karamcheva, *Is Household Debt Growing for Older Americans?*

18. Morrissey, "The State of American Retirement Savings"; Mutchler et al., "The Elder Economic Security Standard Index"; Graham, "True Cost of Aging." The Elder Index is a public data set available at https://elderindex.org.

19. For the standard American description of elderly poverty, see US Department of Health and Human Services, "Poverty Definition Federal Register under the authority of 42 U.S.C. 9902(2)"; Zhe and Dalaker, "Poverty among the Population Aged 65 and Older." Note, though, the American definition is stingy compared to the rest of the OECD countries.

20. *The Economist*, "People Are Working Longer for Reasons of Choice and Necessity."

21. Beier, Torres, and Gilberto, "Determinants of Activities and Their Effect on Mental and Physical Well-Being and Retirement Expectations."

22. Skocpol, "Targeting within Universalism," 411–36.

23. The labor-force participation rates of those over age 65 by education is calculated using the BLS Consumer Population Survey in various months. Federal Reserve Bank of St. Louis (FRED), "Labor Force Participation Rate."

24. Projection of workers and share of labor force by age is updated annually by the US Department of Labor, Bureau of Labor Statistics.

25. A persistent myth is that Germany's old Otto Von Bismarck—by "old," he was 74 at the time—adopted age 65 as a standard retirement age in 1889. Germany initially set the age for mandatory retirement at 70. Von Herbay, "Otto Von Bismarck Is Not the Origin of Old Age at 65," 5.

26. In *Working Longer*, Munnell and Sass argue that, without working longer, one will fall short of a secure retirement.

27. Working longer for practical reasons is anchored in several "spreadsheet studies," which are mechanistic models based on ideal behavior. One such study, Munnell, Orlova, and Webb, "Asset Allocation," was very optimistic about the benefits of working longer. Tony Webb found that the Munnell model used assumptions about human behavior that turn out not to be true. The conclusion that people would be better off retiring at age 70 depended on the assumption that older people working had delayed claiming Social Security to get the big reward of a larger monthly benefit. That assumption was incorrect. Most people claim benefits while they are working. See Ghilarducci, Papadopoulos, and Webb, "The Illusory Benefit of Working Longer."

28. Rosenberger, "A Top Retirement Expert Weighs In."

29. National Research Council, "Labor Force Participation and Retirement." This chapter calls for much longer work lives for Americans because "with advancing age, large fractions of the population who are not working have no impairment. For example, among men aged 65–69 who are not working, more than half have no impairment. Even at ages 70–74, half of men not working have no impairment. These data suggest that the capacity to work is substantially greater than the proportion working at older ages" (93).

30. Keynes, "The Economic Possibilities for Our Grandchildren."

31. The OECD calculates effective average ages that people actually withdraw from the labor force using various methods described by a technical OECD paper: Keese, "A Method for Calculating the Average Age of Effective Retirement." To estimate how people typically work in each nation, twenty-two years is subtracted from that calculated average retirement age. For instance,

if 62 is the estimated average retirement age, then forty is the number of work years.

32. Ideally, the average number of years worked is computed with actual data and stratified by socioeconomic status. Those with fewer years of formal education usually start work at early ages and retire at early ages. However, the OECD may be missing some years. The OECD computes the average effective age of retirement as the average age of exit from the labor force during a five-year period. Keese, "A Method for Calculating."

33. There are thirty-seven OECD nations, but the OECD reports data for only thirty.

34. Older workers withdraw from the labor force at far younger ages than they had intended to or had wanted to because they were laid off, forced out, or their health or their spouse's health forced them out. See Forden et al., "Physically Demanding Jobs and Involuntary Retirement Worsen Retirement Insecurity for Older Workers"; Newport, "Snapshot: Average American Predicts Retirement Age of 66."

35. In 1978, Congress outlawed mandatory retirement before age 70, and in 1986, mandatory retirement was abolished altogether.

36. Adler, "Leading Climate Change Activist Looks to Mobilize Older Americans."

37. Social Security Administration, "Table 6.B5.1."

38. The 1983 law raised the full retirement age from 65 to 66 for people born between 1943 and 1954; to 66 and 2 months for those born in 1955; to 66 and 4 months for someone born in 1956; to 66 and 6 months for those born in 1957; 66 and 8 months for those born in 1958; to 66 and 10 months for those born in 1959 until age 67 for people born in 1960.

39. On the undeserving poor, see Katz, "The Undeserving Poor." On the "do-it-yourself" retirement system, I am one of the coiners of the term. See Ghilarducci, "The Do-It-Yourself Retirement System."

40. See the 2018 festival program *90 Is the New 50: The Science of Longevity.*

41. AARP, "World's Oldest Yoga Teacher." To feel good about Alice, see Feldman, "What a 90-Year-Old Who Works at McDonald's Can Teach Us about Happiness."

42. Johnson and Gosselin, How Secure Is Employment at Older Ages?

43. More and more people said they were retired when they were pushed out of their jobs in the pandemic, so this idea of involuntary retirement rather than voluntary retirement is key for all researchers. Whether or not you retired voluntarily or involuntarily predicts the quality of the rest of your life. We developed the numbers in 2018 and in 2020. See Forden et al., "Physically Demanding Jobs and Involuntary Retirement Worsen Retirement Insecurity for Older Workers."

44. Nicolas Barr, in "Social Insurance as an Efficiency Device," discusses why public insurance provides this type of insurance rather than private insurance. Public insurance is superior to private insurance because public or social insurance is efficient, less costly, and fairer.

45. You can see this evocative poster at the DeviantArt website (https://www.deviantart.com/party9999999/art/Thank-You-Orgainsed-Labour-4209 35154).

46. Alesina, Glaeser, and Sacerdote, "Work and Leisure in the United States and Europe."

47. Costa, *The Evolution of Retirement.*

48. Jacobs and Gerson, *Overworked Individuals or Overworked Families.*

49. Boushey and Clemens, "Disaggregating Growth: Who Prospers When the Economy Grows."

50. Estes, *Social Policy.* For more on older women's precarity, see chapter 5.

51. I prefer to rely on noneconomists for views on life stages, including retirement. Dora Costa, in *The Evolution of Retirement,* is the rare economist exploring the history of the idea of retirement time. But economists don't explore the idea of retirement as a deserving and "expectable" life stage for poor, middle class, and rich had developed in advanced economies. Goleman, "Erickson in His Own Old Age, Expands His View of Life."

52. Business Wire, "New Voya Survey Finds Half of Employed Americans Plan to Work in Retirement as a Result of COVID-19."

53. SimplyWise, "Retirement Confidence Index."

54. In the OECD, the average increase in life expectancy after the official retirement age (average normed retirement time) since 1958 is 6.08 years for women and 5.27 years for men. The US increase in expected retirement time is much less—4.4 years for women and 4.5 years for men. The explosion in retirement time has not occurred in the US. The life expectancy increase in Canada since 1958 is 7.8 years for women and 8.4 for men. In addition, the average length of life expectancy after pensionable age is lower in the US. The US ranks third from the bottom of thirty-one nations in the OECD. See OECD, *Pensions at a Glance 2019.*

55. Tina Reed, "US Life Expectancy Fell Again in 2021 amid Pandemic, Opioid Crisis."

56. The Gray New Deal is based on a powerful economic dynamic. Policies promoting working longer and providing good pensions are not mutually exclusive; they are complements. Strong pensions can help the economy create good jobs by leveraging worker bargaining power to push for higher wages and decent working conditions. Without solid pensions to fall back on, older people are compelled to work on terms that reflect employers' wants rather than older workers' needs.

CHAPTER TWO

1. Beier, Torres, and Gilberto, "Activities Matter," 67–78.

2. Munnell, Hou, and Webb, "National Retirement Risk Index," 34–42. Congressional Budget Office, *Measuring the Adequacy of Retirement Income.*

3. Bivens and Mishel, Understanding the Historic Divergence between Productivity.

4. Saez and Zucman, "Wealth Inequality in the United States," 519–78.

5. Solow, "Thomas Piketty Is Right."

6. Quinn et al, "Challenges and Opportunities of Living and Working Longer."

7. Scholarly work shows that defined-benefit (DB) plans are structured so the value is high at relatively younger ages compared to peak value in DC plans, which always increase over time. Switching from DB to DC boosted elderly work effort. There are several classic articles on this point. See Friedberg and Webb, "Retirement and the Evolution." If more businesses and employers followed this path back to traditional DB plans, far more elderly Americans would be economically secure. See also the work of the powerful research duo Gustman and Steinmeier, "How Changes in Social Security Affect Recent Retirement Trends," and research from Alicia Munnell's research shop, Hou, Munnell, Sanzenbacher, and Li, "Why Are US Households Claiming Social Security Later?"

8. They conclude with enthusiastic endorsement of older people working longer. They write: "to the extent that workers are physically able to work longer, their additional labor supply can be beneficial to these individuals, to their employers, and to society as a whole, as more goods and services are produced to be distributed over an aging population." Cahill, Giandrea, and Quinn, "Retirement Patterns from Career Employment."

9. OECD, *Pensions at a Glance 2019.*

10. Bender, "An Analysis of Well-Being in Retirement."

11. The labor movement was always ambivalent about lifting mandatory retirement ages and was not at the vanguard of antidiscrimination rules compared to its efforts on civil rights. See Ferrelli, "Tracing the Conception and Meaning of the Age Discrimination in Employment Act." Union contracts often contained mandatory retirement clauses. It helped secure their seniority rights and pension benefits. Additionally, Ron Ehrenberg feared that middle-aged employees would be discouraged from being hired or that wages for older workers would fall when the permissible mandatory retirement age was raised from 65 to 70 in 1975 (he did not foresee mandatory retirement ages would essentially disappear by 1986). This neoclassical economics answer assumed some individuals would postpone their retirement and that their marginal productivities would be falling. Employers may respond by lowering wages for older workers.

He also assumed the number of new hires would be reduced, because each employee would work longer. He also thought that employers worried they could not discharge older workers for fear of being accused of age discrimination would be discouraged from hiring middle-aged employees. Ehrenberg, "Retirement Policies, Employment, and Unemployment."

12. Women and children's labor force participation in the US often exceeded that of other rich nations. In 2023, the average labor-force participation rate for men in the G7 was 7 percent; in the US, it was about the same at 76 percent. The country with the highest labor-force participation for men is Japan, at 80 percent. The story changes for women. The G7 OECD average labor-force participation rate for women was only 62.5 percent, but the US exceeded that rate at 67.16 percent. Germany had the highest women's labor-force participation rate, at 73 percent. For teenagers and young adults the United States was also far above average. The labor-force participation rate for 15- to 24-year-olds was 52 percent in the United States and only 43 percent in the G7. The highest labor force participation rate for this young group was Canada, at 59 percent. OECD, "Employment Rate."

13. Mitchell, "Wage Pressures and Labor Shortages."

14. That changed as workers wanted more of a life and sought cultural changes in what expected end of life could be. Costa, *The Evolution of Retirement.*

15. Joe Glazer, "Too Old to Work and Too Young to Die."

16. Lammi, "Labor Undersecretary Malcolm Lovell Jr. Wednesday Urged Congress."

17. In various statistical analysis that decompose the factors that boost the labor force participation of the elderly the conclusion is that education matters, but improved health does not. Lain, *Reconstructing Retirement.* Coile, "The Evolution of Retirement Incentives in the US."

18. The Social Security Administration (SSA) uses language that confuses *retirement* with *claiming.* The SSA should stop using the word *retirement* because all it has control over is when a person claims. The SSA interchanges the word *retirement* when it means *claim* age, not retirement age. The SSA should not even use the word *retired* in describing who doesn't have disability or spousal pensions. The other complaint I have is the way Social Security describes the reduction in benefits before age 70. Claiming Social Security benefits at age 62 results in substantial reductions in monthly benefits from age 62 to the so-called full retirement age of 67 (for someone born in 1960). The monthly benefit reduction is 30 percent. But that is such a weird way to express it. The more straightforward way is that someone who is born in 1960 and makes $60,000 a year in 2021 dollars they will get $1,183 per month at 62 or almost double that, $2,281, at age 70. You can run your own calculator at https://www.ssa.gov

/cgi-bin/benefit6.cgi. Some economists think that the way Social Security expresses the choices changes people's behavior. Behaghel and Blau, "Framing Social Security Reform."

19. The poverty guidelines are updated periodically in the *Federal Register* by the US Department of Health and Human Services under the authority of 42 U.S.C. 9902(2).

20. The erosion of DB plans also started in the early 1980s with the widespread adoption of 401(k) plans—the consultant identified as being responsible for its spread, Ted Benna, has called the 401(k) something negative that referred to an abnormal and threatening structure. He used the word *monster*. Olshan, "Ted Benna Has Called the 401(k) a Monster."

21. For most employers DB plans are more expensive that DC plans. See Ghilarducci and Sun, "How Defined Contribution Plans and 401(k)s Affect Employer Pension Costs." Because of this, employers replaced DB plans with defined contribution, 401(k)-type plans that often less generous—so retirees won't be as comfortable—which alone induces work. DCs also encourage longer work lives because workers can continue to accrue benefits as long as they work and contribute to the 401(k)-type plan. The waning of DB plans and the waxing of DC plans induced people to work longer. See Coile, "The Evolution of Retirement Incentives in the US."

22. In April 2000, President Clinton signed into law the Senior Citizens Freedom to Work Act of 2000, which eliminated the earnings test that applied to those over the Social Security normal age of retirement. A version of the test still applies to those age 62–64. The new provision reduces immediate payments to beneficiaries whose labor income exceeds a given threshold but gives the benefits back when the worker retires. The earnings test is poorly understood. See Slavov, "It's Time to Do Away with the Social Security Earnings Test." The Social Security earnings test probably does not inhibit labor supply significantly. Gruber and Orszag, "Does the Social Security Earnings Test Affect Labor Supply and Benefits Receipt?"

23. The Social Security Statistical Supplement only publishes age of claiming benefits by men and women. I calculated the weighted average of the percentage of retired work beneficiaries claiming at certain ages. Seven percent of retired worker benefits who are women claim at age 70 for the first time and 5.7 percent of men do. Social Security Administration, "Table 6.B5.1."

24. If more businesses and employers followed this path back to traditional DB plans, far more elderly Americans would be far more economically secure.

25. Malcolm Lovell warned Congress (and all of us really) in 1982 that retirement can cause financial difficulty for older people. See Lain, *Reconstructing Retirement*, 56.

26. The Washington Consensus spread as a frame of reference and authority

used by powerful institutions to make difficult political and economic decisions. Williamson, "A Short History of the Washington Consensus."

27. Gruber and Wise, *Social Security and Retirement around the World*.

28. OECD, *Pensions at a Glance: Income and Poverty of Older People*.

29. Murakami, "Japan's Part-Time Workers Need Tighter Reforms."

30. "I do not think the reform as it was originally envisaged can go ahead as such," Macron told reporters in June 2021. De Clercq, "Macron Says France's Pension Reform Cannot Go Ahead as Planned." But in winter 2023, newly re-elected Macron advanced the proposal to raise the retirement age to 64. Nussbaum, "Macron Plows Ahead with Pension Reform as More Protests Loom."

31. Jones, "Economists Fret as Italian Politicians Promise to Scrap Pension Cuts."

32. Campanella, "Making Retirement Work."

33. OECD, "Employment Rate by Age Group," and also Cassandro et al., "What Drives Employment-Unemployment Transitions?"

34. Bureau of Labor Statistics, "Employment Projection, Table 3.1." Home and personal health care—an occupation with a disproportionately high shares of older workers—will add almost one million jobs in the ten years between 2021 and 2031. Bureau of Labor Statistics, "Occupations with the Most Job Growth."

35. Federal Reserve of St. Louis, online economic statistics, "Employment Level—55 Years and Over."

CHAPTER THREE

1. Gothelf, *Forever Employable*.

2. A moving book reminding us of the nation's youth culture—one of my inspirations. Jacoby, *Never Say Die*.

3. Only 10 percent of people aged 62–70 are retired and financially stable. These 62- to 70-year-olds have the highest levels of well-being especially if their health is stable and they retired voluntarily, meaning they weren't forced out because of layoffs. Agency is vital. Ghilarducci, Papadopoulos, and Webb, "The Illusory Benefit of Working Longer."

4. About 60 percent of boomers (aged 57–70) who were still working said they needed and wanted to delay retirement because of COVID-19. SimplyWise, "Retirement Confidence Index."

5. I am writing this chapter right after the COVID-19 pandemic. In fall 2020, for the first time in fifty years, older workers had a higher unemployment rate than midcareer workers (aged 35–54). Forden et al., "Physically Demanding Jobs and Involuntary Retirement Worsen Retirement Insecurity for Older Workers." Papadopoulos et al., "Recession Increases Downward Mobility in Retirement." Older workers do not have the advantage in recessions they once had in being

the "first hired last fired." See Johnson and Mommaerts, "Age Differences in Job Displacement, Job Search, and Reemployment"; Ghilarducci, "When Loyalty No Longer Pays, What's an Older Worker to Do?"

6. Berkman and Truesdale, "Working Longer and Population Aging in the US."

7. AARP, "World's Oldest Yoga Teacher."

8. Levitin, *Successful Aging.*

9. People in 401(k)-type retirement plans work longer than those in defined benefit plans, because one more hour, day, or year of work increases income in a 401(k) plan, but not in most defined benefit plans. See Friedberg and Webb, "Retirement and the Evolution of Pension Structure." Maestas and Zissimopoulos, in "How Longer Work Lives Ease the Crunch of Population Aging," found other obvious reasons people are working longer. Older people are more educated, and more older people have more education (because they are generally better paid). They also posit technological changes have made jobs better for elders (I take that convenient untruth up elsewhere in this book).

10. Clark and Newhouse, "Incentives and Limitations of Employment Policies on Retirement Transitions." It's worth noting that Tony Webb, coauthor of the Boston College study, later repudiated that work, in a paper coauthored with me and Michael Papadopoulos. Ghilarducci, Papadopoulos, and Webb, "The Illusory Benefit of Working Longer."

11. About 24 percent of men and women working at age 62 were collecting Social Security, and by age 65 a large majority are.

12. If you must work at 68, you probably will not tell a researcher. It is more dignified to say you are doing so for the love and not the money. We need research on response bias—people give answers to please the surveyor. This case may also involve cognitive dissonance because saying you are working for love and stimulation feels better than working because you have no real financial options. Cognitive dissonance means saying or believing something is true when it is not because changing your mind to feel psychologically comfortable is often easier than changing your situation.

13. More than 10 percent of older workers are the working poor. They work full-time and their incomes still meet the definition of de facto poverty.

14. Ghilarducci, Papadopoulos, and Webb, "The Illusory Benefit of Working Longer."

15. Lacey et al., "Projections Overview and Highlights, 2016–26."

16. Schwartz Center for Economic Policy Analysis, "20+ Years of Older Workers' Declining Bargaining Power."

17. Ghilarducci and Farmand, "Older Workers on the COVID-19-Frontlines without Paid Sick Leave."

18. Schwartz Center for Economic Policy Analysis, "10+ Years of No Wage Growth: The Role of Alternative Jobs and Gig Work."

19. Topel, "Specific Capital, Mobility, and Wages." The boost in compensation called the "returns to tenure" predicts the financial returns from experience are especially high for workers who stay in the same occupation because they have mastered "job-specific" skills, internalized their organization's culture, and made productive contacts. Union strength often codified these gains to productivity.

20. Kambourov and Manovskii, "Occupational Specificity of Human Capital."

21. Foster, "With Age Comes Fewer Raises."

22. Farmand and Ghilarducci, "Why American Older Workers Have Lost Bargaining Power."

23. Johnson and Mommaerts, "Age Differences in Job Displacement, Job Search, and Reemployment."

24. Bender, "An Analysis of Well-Being in Retirement."

CHAPTER FOUR

1. *Harvard Health Letter*, "Working Later in Life Can Pay off in More Than Just Income."

2. Shiller, *Narrative Economics*.

3. Enron hearings, https://www.c-span.org/video/?168571-1/enron-bankruptcy.

4. Levitan, *Successful Aging*, 197.

5. The article posed twelve reasons—assertions, really—that one should work past age 65.

6. Dhaval, Rashad, and Spasojevic, "The Effects of Retirement on Physical and Mental Health Outcomes."

7. Hershey and Henkens, "Impact of Different Types of Retirement Transitions on Perceived Satisfaction with Life."

8. Diamond, "Forced Retirement."

9. In 2017, life expectancy of American men at age 50 is 79.5.

10. Dutch researchers found health deteriorates after twenty-five years of work. Lindeboom and Kerkhofs, "Health and Work of the Elderly."

11. Pilipiec, Groot, and Pavlova, "The Effect of an Increase of the Retirement Age on the Health, Well-Being, and Labor Force Participation of Older Workers."

12. Dhaval, Rashad, and Spasojevic, "The Effects of Retirement on Physical and Mental Health."

13. Van den Bogaard and Henkens, "When Is Quitting an Escape?"

14. Van den Bogaard and Henkens, "When Is Quitting an Escape?"

15. Van den Bogaard and Henkens, "When Is Quitting an Escape?" Back in 2008, researchers found job dissatisfaction to be a major cause of early

retirement. See Von Bonsdorff et al., "Employee Well-Being, Early-Retirement Intentions, and Company Performance."

16. Eyjólfsdóttir, "Prolongation of Working Life and Its Effect on Mortality and Health in Older Adults."

17. The Netherlands, Sweden, and Switzerland have, on average, a high share of good jobs—those that provide high reward to effort—whereas Greece and Poland have a high concentration of low-quality jobs. Börsch-Supan et al., "Retirement, Health and the Quality of Work in Europe."

18. Berg, Elders, and Burdorf, "Influence of Health and Work on Early Retirement"; Calvo, Sarkisian, and Tamborini, "Causal Effects of Retirement Timing."

19. Wahrendorf et al., "Working Conditions in Mid-Life and Mental Health in Older Ages."

20. Gorry et al., "Does Retirement Improve Health and Life Satisfaction?"

21. Insler, "The Health Consequences of Retirement."

22. Horner, "Subjective Well-Being and Retirement."

23. Adversity is a functional limitation; life getting worse in the domains of health, stress, and general living circumstances; and experiencing a negative life event. Hildon et al., "Examining Resilience of Quality of Life in the Face of Health-Related and Psychosocial Adversity at Older Ages."

24. Edge, Cooper, and Coffey, "Barriers and Facilitators to Extended Working Lives in Europe."

25. Geyer and Welteke, "Closing Routes to Retirement for Women."

26. Choi, "Relationship between Life Satisfaction and Postretirement Employment among Older Women."

27. Neuman, "Quit Your Job and Get Healthier?"

28. Schmitz, "Do Working Conditions at Older Ages Shape the Health Gradient?"

29. Motegi, Nishimura, and Oikawa, "Retirement and Health Investment Behaviors."

30. Xiao, Goryakin, and Cecchini, "Physical Activity Levels and New Public Transit."

31. Pedron et al., "The Effect of Retirement on Biomedical and Behavioral Risk Factors."

32. Coe and Zamarro, "Retirement Effects of Health in Europe."

33. Grøtting and Lillebø, "Health Effects of Retirement."

34. No author has inferred that work itself is causing the good outcome. People who are happier and connected have more income and education may work, but the intervening reason for the higher well-being for older workers is their choice to work, not that they are working per se.

35. Van den Bogaard and Henkens, "When Quitting Is an Escape."

36. Moore, Ghilarducci, and Webb, "The Inequitable Effects of Raising the Retirement Age on Blacks and Low-Wage Workers."

37. Ghilarducci et al., "Gender and Racial Disparities in Physical Job Demands of Older Workers."

38. Bersin and Chamorro-Premuzic, "The Case for Hiring Older Workers," 9.

39. Bruder, *Nomadland*.

40. Schwandt, "Wealth Shocks and Health Outcomes."

41. Rohe et al., "The Impacts of Individual Development Accounts, Assets, and Debt on Future Orientation and Psychological Depression."

42. Zurlo, "Unsecured Consumer Debt and Mental Health Outcomes in Middle-Aged and Older Americans."

43. Coe and Zamarro, "Retirement Effects of Health in Europe."

44. Coile, Milligan, and Wise, "Health Capacity to Work at Older Ages: Evidence from the United States n Social Security Programs and Retirement around the World."

45. Dufouil et al., "Older Age at Retirement Is Associated with Decreased Risk of Dementia."

46. Messe and Wolff, "Healthier When Retiring Earlier?"

47. Rohwedder and Willis, "Mental Retirement."

48. Rohwedder and Willis, "Mental Retirement."

49. Tumino, "Retirement and Cognitive Abilities."

50. Bingley and Martinello, "Mental Retirement and Schooling."

51. Oi, "Does Gender Differentiate the Effects of Retirement on Cognitive Health?"

52. Cho, "Bridge Employment and Health."

53. Carrino, Glaser, and Avendano, "Later Retirement, Job Strain, and Health."

54. Schroeder, "Retirement Wisdom."

55. On the podcast, Schroeder said: "One of the key pieces of work for them is it's something they can go lose themselves in or get a distraction or say, Hey, I have to go into work for a little while today. So suddenly when there's no place that they have to be, there's nothing that they're responsible for accomplishing, that can really drop people into a really challenging place. So, spending more time with a spouse or kids, or even themselves, is another big challenge that I see a lot. And the other big one, although there's lots of other little kind of nuanced experiences, is finding ways to create meaning, to have meaning, to reach meaning in their lives. That's a big one too. Again, so many people get so much out of work where they get so much of their meaning. And so suddenly when that's no longer there, it kind of, it drops them big time for a loop."

56. Schroeder, "Retirement Wisdom."

CHAPTER FIVE

1. See the rich history on leisure studies in anthropology and sociology. Veal, "Is There Enough Leisure Time?"

2. Biggs et al., "Work, Health, and the Commodification of Life's Time," 4.

3. Dudel et al., "A Lost Generation?"; Dudel and Myrskylä, "Working Life Expectancy at Age 50 in the United States."

4. In a July 2019 *Guideline* interview, well-respected Boston College retirement researcher Alicia Munnell advocates for 70 as the new retirement age: "If you can add eight years to your work life by delaying retirement, suddenly the ratio of work to retirement years changes dramatically. 70 should be the goal now."

5. Coile, "The Evolution of Retirement Incentives in the US"; Coile et al., Social Security and Retirement around the World. Coile measures incentive behavior through the implicit tax rate on work (ITAX). Her study calculates what she cites as a key behavioral variable, ITAX, which measures the tax rate on working longer. She calculates the ITAX under given Social Security rules each year from 1980 to 2016, generating a time series of retirement incentives that show only the variation in Social Security rules. She calculates the ITAX for different earners, splitting them among into high, median, and low earners; male and female; and single and married. If the ITAX is negative, then Social Security wealth is rising with additional years of work. If it is positive, then Social Security wealth is shrinking. Coile controls for age and estimates that, since 1983, changes in Social Security rules have caused a 15-percentage-point drop in the ITAX of workers over age 65. In short, work is more valuable for people over age 65 than ever before. The incentives to work longer aren't that impactful for workers under age 65, most of whom have been forced out of their primary jobs before reaching that age.

6. Chou and Choi, "Prevalence and Correlates of Perceived Workplace Discrimination among Older Workers in the United States of America."

7. Because our sample is a synthetic cohort, we carefully constructed our measure of socioeconomic status by using a ranking of educational attainment that considers changes over time in markers of socioeconomic status. We justify using educational attainment rather than income as a measure of socioeconomic status because it is determined early in life before the onset of chronic disease that may affect labor market outcomes. Because average educational attainment has increased dramatically across the three birth cohorts—those with less than a high school education have become a much smaller and select group—we control for improvements in educational attainment over time by sorting participants into three education terciles rather than using the convention of categorizing educational attainment by whether participants have

completed high school, have some college-level education, or have a four-year degree or more. Pre-retirement, the sizes of the terciles are equal. At older ages, we adjust their relative sizes to reflect the socioeconomic mortality gradient.

8. First, we are confident our spliced sample reflects important relationships reported in the demography and health literatures: our sample means confirm studies showing women live longer, on average, but have an earlier age of onset of needing assistance with activities of daily living (ADLs) limitations. We also confirm other studies that find educational gradients in health—those with higher levels of educational attainment live longer. Good resources on differences in life expectancy are: Brown and Hargrove, "Multidimensional Approaches to Examining Gender and Racial/Ethnic Stratification in Health"; Bosworth and Burke, "Differential Mortality and Retirement Benefits in The Health and Retirement Study"; Olshansky et al., "Differences in Life Expectancy Due to Race and Educational Differences Are Widening, and Many May Not Catch Up."

9. We don't have enough data points to tease out differences across race/ethnicity.

10. Bor, Cohen, and Galea, "Population Health in an Era of Rising Income Inequality."

11. These projections are based on period life tables so the growing gap should grow a bit smaller over time. I thank Anthony Webb for this point. The University of Southern California study confirmed what many suspected and dreaded. Andrasfay and Goldman, "Reductions in 2020 US Life Expectancy due to COVID-19 and the Disproportionate Impact on the Black and Latino Populations."

12. Bosworth, Burtless, and Zhang, "Later Retirement, Inequality in Old Age, and the Growing Gap in Longevity between Rich and Poor."

13. Sanzenbacher et al., "Calculating Neutral Increases in Retirement Age by Socioeconomic Status."

14. Retirement duration is computed using retirement and death ages. Death age is straightforward, computing retirement age is more complicated. Self-reports about retirement age are insufficient: many who self-report being retired work. To solve this problem—one that bedevils all researchers attempting to identify the age of retirement—we use the composite variable "labor force status" created by RAND: a person is in the labor force if working full- or part-time, unemployed, or on temporary layoff. RAND codes people as "retired" if they are not working, not looking for a job, and mention retirement. Therefore, we have an expanded version of *retired*. A person is in the labor force if working full- or part-time, unemployed, or on temporary layoff. People are "retired" if they are not working, not looking for a job, and mention retirement in the survey. We reclassify people on disability as retired at age 66 because at younger ages they are subject to return-to-work programs and an expectation

they attempt to work. Although unretirement is not uncommon we classify workers as retired when they quit their last job. Maestas, "Cohort Differences in Retirement Expectations and Realizations."

15. See Ghilarducci and Webb, "The Distribution of Time in Retirement."

16. Because our sample is a synthetic cohort, we carefully constructed our measure of SES by using a ranking of educational attainment that considers changes over time in markers of SES. We use educational attainment rather than income as a measure of SES because it is determined early in life before the onset of chronic disease that may affect labor market outcomes. We control for improvements in educational attainment over time by sorting participants into three education terciles rather than using the convention of categorizing educational attainment since average educational attainment has increased dramatically across the three birth cohorts. Pre-retirement, the sizes of the terciles are equal. At older ages, we adjust their relative sizes to reflect the socioeconomic mortality gradient.

17. If we take away our multivariate analysis and controls for a moment, the data don't reveal the class differences so clearly. Viewed through that blurry uncontrolled lens, men in the top third and middle third of educational attainment have 14.3 years in retirement, while those at the bottom have 1.7 fewer years, at 12.6. Men in the bottom third retire 2.3 years earlier than men at the top, but they also die four years younger. In this same limited lens, women in the top third of educational attainment have 19.7 years of retirement time, which is 2.2 more years than the middle third and 3.8 more years than women in the bottom third. Higher-educated women get their advantage in retirement time by living longer and are more likely to be in good health.

18. Crystal and Shea, "Cumulative Advantage, Cumulative Disadvantage, and Inequality among Elderly People"; Coe and Zamarro, "Retirement Effects on Health in Europe."

19. Radl, "Too Old to Work, or Too Young to Retire?"

20. Friedberg and Webb, "Retirement and the Evolution of Pension Structure"; Munnell et al., "How Has the Shift to 401(k) Plans Affected Retirement Income?"

21. We created a sample to identify correlates of retirement duration and the disability status of those in retirement. the data should be reanalyzed when more HRS participants have lived natural human spans. More longitudinal research on the relationships between gender, work characteristics, health, and longevity are also needed. Arias, Heron, and Xu, "United States Life Tables, 2013."

22. O'Connor, "Living Longer Does Not Mean We Should All Work Longer."

23. Auerbach et al., "How the Growing Gap in Life Expectancy May Affect Retirement Benefits and Reforms."

CHAPTER SIX

1. Zoll, "Working Longer Can Be a Win-Win for Investors."

2. Munnell and Sass, *Working Longer the Solution to the Retirement Income Challenge.*

3. See Sass's interview in Zoll, "Working Longer Can Be a Win-Win for Investors."

4. Policy makers imagined that when they raised the Social Security full retirement age to 70 that people would work longer to get larger Social Security benefits. That did not happen. Many older workers work for such low wages they collect Social Security as a low-wage supplement—indirectly helping employers keep pay low for older workers.

5. For this calculation we use a comprehensive earlier model written by my coauthor Tony Webb as a benchmark. See Munnell et al., "How Important Is Asset Allocation to Financial Security in Retirement?"

6. These scholars are very aware that some people cannot work so they always propose ways people could be exempted from having to wait until 70 to get full pensions with an expanded disability programs to manage those with age-related physical or mental decline to work. But making retiring at age 65 a matter of disability and making retiring at age 70 the norm would stigmatize those who retire before age 70.

7. I fear that low-wage older workers collecting Social Security is an indirect incentive for low-wage employers of older workers to keep wages low. There is considerable evidence that the EITC lowers wages. See Farmand, "Impacts of the Earned Income Tax Credit on Wages of Ineligible Workers"; Leigh, "Who Benefits from the Earned Income Tax Credit?"; Rothstein, "The Unintended Consequences of Encouraging Work."

8. Social Security benefits provide a supplement to low pay so that these income sources together maintain a workers' household with a standard of living reached before retirement.

9. Ghilarducci, Papadopoulos, and Webb, "The Illusory Benefit of Working Longer," 6.

10. These data are for the 1943–47 birth cohort, the most recent cohort for which we possess claims histories that are most complete and mostly based on administrative data and therefore can be compared with data for previous cohorts.

11. About 25 percent of workers in the 1943–47 birth cohort had claimed at age 63, compared with 24 percent of workers in the 1931–37 birth cohort who had claimed at age 63. Among the 1931–37 birth cohort, claiming spiked at age 65—89 percent of workers and 98 percent of retirees had claimed by that age. Among the 1943–47 cohort, who faced a full retirement age of 66, the spike in

claiming occurred one year later, 89 percent of workers and 99 percent of retirees had claimed by that age.

12. In 2021, Congress allowed eligible childless workers and workers over
65 to collect the Earned Income Tax Credit. It will be interesting to see if that
reduces claiming Social Security receipt while working.

13. Improving the way Social Security comminates is part of a big discussion. In the pamphlet "When to Start Receiving Retirement Benefits," the Social
Security Administration communicates a complicated rule. It would be best
to change the entire language and just call age 70 the maximum benefit.

14. Ghilarducci, Radpour, and Webb, "New Evidence on the Effect of Economic Shocks on Retirement Plan Withdrawals," 6.

15. The dynamic duo Annamaria Lusardi and Olivia Mitchell with coauthor
N. Oggero, in Lusardi, Mitchell, and Oggero, "The Changing Face of Debt and
Financial Fragility at Older Ages," investigated changes in older individuals'
financial fragility as they stand on the verge of retirement and found that over
time older Americans close to retirement are holding more and more debt than
earlier generations because they bought more expensive homes with smaller
down payments.

16. The advice to work longer in personal finance blogs often assumes that
older workers delay claiming and save more. See Elkins, "Here's How Much
Money You'd Have If You Delayed Retirement until 70." And the advice to work
longer pops up in the academic literature because all academic projections
of the benefit of working at older ages use some combination of optimistic
assumptions to project significant increases in retirement readiness. We just
don't see these assumptions holding up when we examine real people's behavior. Specifically, all but one of these papers, Bajtelsmit, Foster, and Rappaport,
"Strategies for Mitigating the Risk of Outliving Retirement Wealth," assumes
that older workers delay claiming Social Security. They all assume increases
in financial wealth, and only one Butrica and colleagues considers that earnings do not generally increase at older ages. Since the models use optimistic
assumptions about claiming and saving it is not a surprise the studies project
substantial increases in all good things: increases in replacement rates—ranging
from 5 percent to 9 percent a year; reductions in the share at risk of outliving
their wealth; and reductions in target savings rates; and substantial increases
in the share of households able to achieve replacement rate targets. See Bronshtein et al., "The Power of Working Longer"; Butrica et al., "Does Work Pay at
Older Ages?"; Butrica, Smith, and Steuerle, "Working for a Good Retirement";
Munnell, Webb, and Golub-Sass, "How Much to Save for a Secure Retirement?";
Munnell, Hou, and Sanzenbacher, "Women Retirement and the National Retirement Risk Index"; Munnell, Orlova, and Webb, "How Important Is Asset
Allocation to Financial Security in Retirement?" Target incomes are defined as

target replacement rates. A target replacement rate is about 60 percent–80 percent of pre-retirement earnings after retirement. The lower income groups need a higher percentage of post-retirement income.

17. Ghilarducci et al., "Working Longer Cannot Solve the Retirement Income Crisis."

18. Our method isolates the effect of independent factors on outcomes, in this case, financial retirement readiness. Using gold-standard data we found what independent factor of factor explains a person's changes (increases or decreases) in financial preparedness for retirement year to year. Our statistical technique allows us to control for educational attainment, race, birth cohort, health at age 62, marital status at age 62, and widowhood or divorce between ages 62 and 70. (We experimented with specifications that included industry, occupation, firm size, and union membership. None of these variables was statistically significant and thus we do not report results.)

19. We report in 2008 dollars throughout the study, to align with Palmer, "The 2001 GSU/AON Retire Project Report." Aon Consulting, *Real Deal*.

20. I and many other researchers in life-cycle studies use educational attainment as stable marker for class position in old age, because that status does not change over a person's lifetime. At older ages, using only income as a marker could not indicate the retired surgeon who took a year off to meditate.

21. As noted in our technical paper, when we are using the federal poverty line for the definition of low status instead of educational attainment or pay and conducting a multiple regression analysis, it reveals that the type of pension plan is even more important than pay or education.

CHAPTER SEVEN

1. Bruder, *Nomadland*.

2. Papadopoulos et al., "Recession Increases Downward Mobility in Retirement."

3. Radpour, Papadopoulos, and Ghilarducci, "Trends in Employer-Sponsored Retirement Plan Access and Participation Rates."

4. Dunlop and Higgins, "'Bargaining Power' and Market Structures."

5. Aaron, "Nudged, Pushed, or Mugged."

6. These wage numbers are adjusted for inflation and hours, I am reporting real median weekly earnings for full-time male workers calculated from the BLS, CPS numbers.

7. Radpour, Papadopoulos, and Ghilarducci, "Trends in Employer Sponsored Retirement Plan Access and Participation Rates."

8. Morrissey, Radpour, and Schuster. The Older Workers and Retirement Chartbook.

9. Davis and Webb, "Extreme Retirement Inequality Persists, Even among Those with Similar Earnings."

10. On average, middle-class households need $600,000 to maintain their pre-retirement living standards in retirement, yet the median retirement balance for families reaching retirement age is $0, and the average is just $15,000.

11. One of the best sources for trends in retirement plan coverage at work is explained in this memo describing how the different data sets work together. Ghilarducci, Papadopoulos, and Webb, "Inadequate Retirement Savings for Workers Nearing Retirement"; Munnell and Bleckman, "Is Pension Coverage a Problem in the Private Sector?"

12. There is no reason to believe the relative expected income has gotten much better since coverage didn't improve. It is also important to note that income from Social Security is not increasing. Moreover, increases in the Social Security full retirement age cut benefits by 13 percent directly. Workers can claim Social Security benefits at any age after 62, with reduced benefits for those claiming before (ranging from 5.0 to 6.7 percent per year) and increased benefits for those claiming after the full retirement age (8.0 percent). Thus, an increase in the full retirement age acts as a cut in benefits for all workers. The full retirement age is currently in the process of being raised from 65 to 67, cutting Social Security benefits as much as 13 percent for early retirees and 16 percent for late retirees. Butrica et al., "The Disappearing Defined Benefit Pension and Its Potential Impact on the Retirement Incomes of Baby Boomers."

13. In the stylized versions of competitive markets in textbooks worker compensation is determined by the value of the marginal product of workers. Kaufman and Hotchkiss, *The Economics of Labor Markets*.

14. Bahn, *Understanding the Importance of Monopsony Power in the US Labor Market*.

15. Flood et al., *Integrated Public Use Microdata Series, Current Population Survey*.

16. Papadopoulos, "Reservation Wages and Work Arrangements."

17. Ghilarducci, Papadopoulos, and Webb, "Larger Birth Cohort Lowers Wages."

18. Ghilarducci, Webb, and Papadopoulos, "The Growth of Unstable and Low-Wage Work among Older Workers."

19. Weaver, "Worker's Expectations about Losing and Replacing Their Jobs."

20. Farber, "Employment Insecurity"; Hollister and Matissa, "Employment Stability in the US Labor Market."

21. The sample of workers who are older than 64 is special; they are the workers who stayed in the market and are likely to have longer tenure.

22. Bidwell, "What Happened to Long-Term Employment?"; Chan and Stevens, "Job Loss and Employment Patterns of Older Workers"; Munnell, Soto, and Zhivan, "Has the Displacement of Older Workers Increased?"

23. Sass and Webb, "Is the Reduction in Older Workers' Job Tenure a Cause for Concern?"

24. Lalé, "Turbulence and the Employment Experience of Older Workers."

25. Yamashita et al., "Adult Competencies and Employment Outcomes among Older Workers in the United States."

26. US Bureau of Labor Statistics. "Labor Statistics from the Current Population Survey: Table 36."

27. Davis et al., "The Stalled Jobs Recovery Pushed 1.1 Million Older Workers out of the Labor Force."

28. Neumark, Burn, and Button, "Is It Harder for Older Workers to Find Jobs? New and Improved Evidence from a Field Experiment."

29. Collinson, "Striking Similarities and Disconcerting Disconnects."

30. Gosselin and Tobin, "Cutting 'Old Heads' at IBM."

31. Clark et al., "Employer Concerns and Responses to an Aging Workforce."

32. Molloy et al., "Understanding Declining Fluidity in the US Labor Market."

33. Chetty et al., "Where Is the Land of Opportunity?"; and Bergman et al., "Creating Moves to Opportunity."

34. Shambaugh, Nunn, and Liu, "How Declining Dynamism Affects Wages."

35. From 2008 to 2014, at least 52 percent of retirees over 55 left their last job involuntarily, the result of job loss or deterioration in health. Farmand, "Involuntary Unemployed by Class."

36. Nichols and Rothstein, "The Earned Income Tax Credit."

37. In 2020, the maximum credit for a childless adult between the ages of 25 and 65 was $538, phasing out fully at $15,820. After the passage of the American Rescue Plan in March 2021, benefits for childless adults were roughly tripled and eligibility was temporarily expanded to workers older than 65 and workers 19 to 25 who are not students. For students who are attending school at least part-time, the age limit is temporarily reduced from 25 to 24.

38. Davis and Farmand, "Who Does the Earned Income Tax Credit Benefit?"; Maag and Werner, "Expanding the Earned Income Tax Credit Could Provide Financial Security for Millions of Workers without Children"; and Rothstein, "Is the EITC as Good as an NIT?"

39. Lacey et al., "Projections Overview and Highlights 2016-26."

40. Estimated elasticities of wages with respect to the relative size of one's own cohort generally fall between –0.05 and –0.10 and are of similar magnitude for men and for women. Papadopoulos, Patria, and Triest, "Population Aging, Labor Demand, and the Structure of Wages."

41. Ghilarducci, Papadopoulos, and Webb, "Larger Birth Cohort Lowers Wages."

42. Goux and Maurin, "Persistence of Interindustry Wage Differentials."

43. Autor et al., "The Fall of the Labor Share and the Rise of Superstar Firms."

44. There was a non-significant correlation of –0.31 between median age and unemployment rate in each occupation. Additionally, correlations between the percentage change of value added per industry (between 2007 and 2017) and median age of that industry produces the same results.

45. Farmand and Ghilarducci, "Why American Older Workers Have Lost Bargaining Power."

46. Morrissey, Radpour, and Schuster, "Older Workers and Retirement Chartbook," chart 1H.

47. The Center for Retirement Research and Brookings Institution document that older workers are more educated, which accounts for almost half of the increase in older worker labor force participation. In 1985, less than 20 percent of workers between the ages of 60 and 64 had college degrees. In 2013, 35 years later, over 36 percent did. (In a remarkable testament to aggressive public policy to improve K-12 education—including desegregation and keeping girls in high school—the share of older workers without high school degrees fell from over 26 percent in 1985 to about 7 percent in 2013.) Burtless, "Can Educational Attainment Explain the Rise in Labor Force Participation at Older Ages?"

48. The United States is among the few rich countries—those that make up the group of 36 countries in the Organisation for Economic Co-operation and Development—that ban mandatory retirement as a form of age discrimination. Americans sophisticated legal infrastructure supports workers suing for age discrimination. With few exceptions, Americans cannot be banned from work—or paid, promoted, or trained less—because of their age. OECD, "Working Better with Age."

49. Smith, "What Is the Ideal Retirement Age for Your Health?"

50. Weil, "Understanding the Present and Future of Work in the Fissured Workplace Context."

<h3 style="text-align:center">CHAPTER EIGHT</h3>

1. Economic Innovation Group, 2021.

2. Kiplinger-Alliance for Lifetime Income, poll; Ghilarducci, "Why Do We Make It So Easy to Steal Seniors' Money?"

3. States where work and retirement plans with high labor-force participation among the elderly and higher levels of workplace retirement coverage (all correlated with more education among the elderly) were much more likely to vote. I calculate a positive correlation between older voter turnout and workplace

pensions—for 45- to 64-year-olds—of 18 percent. The correlation between older voters engaged in the labor force by either working or looking for worker and turnout among those over 65 is also quite high at 29 percent.

4. Doonan and Kenneally, *Generational Views of Retirement in the United States*.

5. Tergenson, "How COVID-19 Will Change Aging and Retirement," T1.

6. Burtless, "The Impact of Population Aging and Delayed Retirement on Workforce Productivity."

7. Vargas, "Oregon Grocery Store Worker, 91, Retires after Raising More Than $80,000 Online."

8. Morrissey, "How Many Older Workers Have Difficult Jobs?"

9. National Research Council, "Labor Force Participation and Retirement."

10. Pampel and Williamson, *Age, Class, Politics, and the Welfare State*. See also Ghilarducci and James, "Americans Haven't Saved Enough for Retirement."

11. Ghilarducci and James, "Americans Haven't Saved Enough for Retirement."

12. Gruber and Wise, Social Security and Retirement around the World.

13. I found among forty-two OECD nations the correlation between pension generosity—the amount of money spent per old person and the average time a person spends in retirement was 12 percent in 2005 and 16 percent in 2015. I find weak support for Gruber and Wise's (2000) supply-side argument.

14. McDonough, "Job Insecurity and Health"; Scott-Marshall, "The Social Patterning of Work-Related Insecurity and Its Health Consequences."

15. Burman, Geissler, and Toder, "How Big Are Total Individual Income Tax Expenditures, and Who Benefits from Them?"; Megan, "Federal Retirement Tax Benefits Mostly Go to the Wealthy"; Toder, Berger, and Powers, *Distributional Effects of Individual Income Tax Expenditures*.

CHAPTER NINE

1. Bureau of Labor Statistics, "Employment Projection, Table 3.1."

2. Ghilarducci and Cook, "Op-Ed: Pushed to Retire and to Keep Earning, Older Americans Face a Peculiar Vise."

3. McGahey, "America Needs an Older Workers Bureau."

4. Beyer, "Newman Introduce Legislation To Establish Older Workers' Bureau."

5. Davis et al., "The Pandemic Retirement Surge Increased Retirement Inequality."

6. Ghilarducci and Farmand, "Older Workers on the COVID-19-Frontlines without Paid Sick Leave."

7. The financial incentives and the labor market environment would have to change to ensure old people are not too expensive to hire. Employment protection and employment development would have to change so that older people

are given flexibility they might need and continued training. Social norms, especially ageism, as well as a passion to end illegal age discrimination, would have to change so that older people could work. And last any collateral damage from increasing disability and morbidity caused by older people working to age 70 and must be acknowledged. What are the carrots and sticks faced by employers who may consider older workers and people over age 62 or so who would consider working?

8. Goldmacher and Ember, "Biden, Seeking Democratic Unity, Reaches Left toward Sanders's Ideas"; Ghilarducci, "The Time Is Now to Lower The Medicare Age to 50."

9. Reyes, "'It's Like We are Just a Piece of Garbage.'"

10. McWilliams et al., "Health of Previously Uninsured Adults after Acquiring Medicare Coverage."

11. Bonnie, Stroud, and Breiner, "Safety Committee on Improving the Health, Youth Board on Children."

12. Kirzinger, Muñana, and Brodie, "KFF Health Tracking Poll—January 2019."

13. Docteur et al., *Examining Approaches to Expand Medicare Eligibility*.

14. Since 61 million people receive Social Security benefits, and recipients are a significant source of aggregate demand raising Social Security by $200 a month would have stimulated demand and made up for the isolation felt deeply by elders during the pandemic. We could have sent the enhanced direct deposits—most Social Security beneficiaries have it—on May 1 to those receiving worker benefits under the median. Ghilarducci, "Teresa Ghilarducci on Social Security Fixes to Protect the Poorest."

15. See these articles about what older workers want. Burke and Cooper, *The Fulfilling Workplace*; Marvell and Cox, *Fulfilling Work*; Allan et al., "Conceptualizing Well-Being in Vocational Psychology."

16. Our calculation defined workers as self-employed but not incorporated; wage/salary, private; federal government employees; state government employees; and local government employees. Not included are self-employed who are incorporated; members of the armed forces; unpaid family workers; and those who retired during the previous year or were not in the labor force for other reasons for part of the year. *Working poor* is defined as those with earnings below two-thirds of the US median annual hourly wage in 2020 (as calculated for all workers). Two-thirds of the median annual hourly wage is $15.29 in 2020. About one-fifth of older workers—6.9 million workers over 55—earn less than the equivalent of $15.29 per hour. The share of younger, prime age workers who are between age 35 and 54 is 19 percent—11 million prime-age workers earn less than two-thirds median wage. Ghilarducci and Schuster, "Working Longer Not a Panacea Considering the Number of Low-Wage Work Options."

17. Davis and Farmand, "Who Does the Earned Income Tax Credit Benefit? A Monopsony View."

18. Ghilarducci et al., "How Expanding EITC Will Benefit 1.5 Million Low-Income."

19. Truesdale, "Better Jobs, Longer Working Lives."

20. Abraham and Houseman, *Policies to Improve Workforce Services for Older Americans*.

21. Vogel, Ludwig, and Börsch-Supan, "Aging and Pension Reform: Extending the Retirement Age and Human Capital Formation." A quote from their paper: "Our quantitative finding is that endogenous human capital formation in combination with an increase in the retirement age has strong implications for economic aggregates and welfare, in the open economy. These adjustments reduce the maximum welfare losses of demographic change for households alive in 2010 by about 2.2 percentage points in terms of consumption equivalent variation."

22. Erikson and Erikson, *The Life Cycle Completed*.

23. Ageist jokes include these from *Reader's Digest*: "My husband can't activate our Amazon Echo, because he keeps forgetting its name, Alexa. 'Just think of the car Lexus and add an a at either end,' I suggested. The next time he wanted to use our new toy, he looked a bit puzzled. Then he remembered what I'd said and confidently called out, "Acura!'" *Reader's Digest*, "Old Age Jokes."

24. Neumark and Song, "Do Stronger Age Discrimination Laws Make Social Security Reforms More Effective?" 13; McLaughlin, "Age Discrimination Laws, Physical Challenges, and Work Accommodations for Older Adults."

25. Neumark, "Strengthen Age Discrimination Protections to Help Confront the Challenge of Population Aging."

26. Forden et al., "Physically Demanding Jobs and Involuntary Retirement Worsen Retirement Insecurity for Older Workers."

27. Auerbach et al., "Is Uncle Sam Inducing the Elderly to Retire?"

28. Goda, Shoven, and Slavov, "Removing the Disincentives in Social Security for Long Careers."

29. US Department of Labor, "Older Workers."

CHAPTER TEN

1. Economic Policy Institute, American Federation of Teachers, and Schwartz Center for Economic Policy Analysis. *Breathe Easy—How Guaranteed Retirement Accounts Could Change Your Life*.

2. Ghilarducci et al., "Extreme Retirement Wealth Inequality Persists, Even Among Those with Similar Earnings"; Ghilarducci, Radpour, and Webb, "Social

Security Reduces Retirement Wealth Inequality"; Radpour, Ghilarducci, and Webb, "Expanding Social Security Benefits to Help All Workers."

3. Economic Innovation Group, "Bipartisan Pair of Economists Propose Bold New Wealth Building Program for the Bottom 50 Percent of American Workers."

4. Berger, "3 in 10 Americans Withdrew Money from Retirement Savings amid the Coronavirus Pandemic—and the Majority Spent It on Groceries."

5. Melbourne Mercer, *Global Pension Index*.

6. Melbourne Mercer, *Global Pension Index*.

7. Iacurci, "They Went Bust in the Great Recession."

8. Novie, "For Millions of Americans, the Coronavirus Pandemic Will Make Retiring Harder."

9. Novie, "For Millions of Americans, the Coronavirus Pandemic Will Make Retiring Harder."

10. Right about the time the country was shutting down for the pandemic the ultraconservative magazine the *National Interest* publishing article connecting lax enforcement of age discrimination laws with activism with the Trump administration. The Trump administration cited with an employer, in the case here it was the Veterans Administration that an employee needs a strict standard of proof to prove age discrimination. Harnois and Roscigno, "Trump Is Making It Harder for Older Americans to Prove Workplace Discrimination."

11. Ghilarducci and Saad-Lessler, "How 401(k) Plans Make Recessions Worse."

12. Ghilarducci, Papadopoulos, and Webb, "40% of Older Workers and Their Spouses Will Experience Downward Mobility in Retirement."

13. Hickenlooper, "Hickenlooper, Tillis, Sewell, Smucker Introduce Bill to Expand Retirement Savings for Working Americans."

Bibliography

Aaron, Henry J. "Nudged, Pushed, or Mugged: Policies to Encourage Older Workers to Retire Later." In *Closing the Deficit: How Much Can Later Retirement Help?*, edited by Henry J. Aaron Henry and Gary Burtless, 36–45. Washington, DC: Brookings Institution Press, 2013.

AARP: The Magazine. "World's Oldest Yoga Teacher." https://www.aarp.org /health/healthy-living/info-2016/yoga-worlds-oldest-teacher/.

Aon Consulting. *The Real Deal: 2018 Retirement Income Adequacy Study*. https:// insights-north-america.aon.com/retirement/aon-the-real-deal-2018-retire ment-income-adequacy-study-report.

Abraham, Katharine G., and Susan N. Houseman. *Policies to Improve Workforce Services for Older Americans*. Washington, DC: Brookings Institution. September 2020. https://www.brookings.edu/wp-content/uploads/2020/11 /ES-11.19.20-Abraham-Houseman.pdf.

Adler, Ben. "Leading Climate Change Activist Looks to Mobilize Older Americans." *Yahoo News*, November 29, 2021. https://www.aol.com/leading -climate-change-activist-looks-204334903.html.

Age Discrimination in Employment Act of 1967. 29 U.S.C. §§ 621–634 (1967).

Alesina, Alberto, Edward Glaeser, and Bruce Sacerdote. "Work and Leisure in the United States and Europe: Why So Different?" *NBER Macroeconomics Annual* 20 (2005): 1–64.

Allan, Blake A., Rhea L. Owens, Haley M. Sterling, Jessica W. England, and Ryan D. Duffy. "Conceptualizing Well-Being in Vocational Psychology: A Model of Fulfilling Work." *Counseling Psychologist* 47, no. 2 (2019): 266–90.

Andrasfay, Theresa, and Noreen Goldman. "Reductions in 2020 US Life Expectancy Due to COVID-19 and the Disproportionate Impact on the Black and Latino Populations." *Proceedings of the National Academy of Sciences* 118, no. 5 (2021): e2014746118.

Arias, E., M. Heron, and J. Q. Xu. "United States Life Tables, 2013." *National Vital Statistics Reports* 66, no. 3 (2017).

Aston, David. "What's Your Magic Number?" *MoneySense*, August 29, 2013. https://pmac.org/wp-content/uploads/2014/05/07-02-series-aritcle-1-Aston-David-What-s-Your-Magic-Number.pdf.

Auerbach, Alan J., Kerwin K. Charles, Courtney C. Coile, William Gale, Dana Goldman, Ronald Lee, Charles M. Lucas, et al. "How the Growing Gap in Life Expectancy May Affect Retirement Benefits and Reforms." *Geneva Papers on Risk and Insurance-Issues and Practice* 42 (2017): 475–99.

Auerbach, Alan J., Laurence J. Kotlikoff, Darryl Koehler, and Manni Yu. "Is Uncle Sam Inducing the Elderly to Retire?" *Tax Policy and the Economy* 31, no. 1 (2017): 1–42.

Autor, David, David Dorn, Lawrence F. Katz, Christina Patterson, and John Van Reenen. "The Fall of the Labor Share and the Rise of Superstar Firms." Working Paper No. 23396, National Bureau of Economic Research, Cambridge, MA, May 2017.

Bahn, Kate. *Understanding the Importance of Monopsony Power in the US Labor Market.* Washington, DC: Washington Center for Equitable Growth, July 5, 2018.

Bajtelsmit, Vickie, J. D. Foster, Ottem Le Andra, and Anna Rappaport. "Strategies for Mitigating the Risk of Outliving Retirement Wealth." *Financial Services Review* 22, no. 4 (2013): 311–29.

Barr, Nicholas. "Social Insurance as an Efficiency Device." *Journal of Public Policy* 9, no. 1 (1989): 59–82.

Beardsley, Eleanor. "Labor Unrest Is Growing in Europe." *All Things Considered*, January 28, 2023. https://www.npr.org/2023/01/28/1152353140/labor-unrest-is-growing-in-europe.

Behaghel, Luc, and David M. Blau. "Framing Social Security Reform: Behavioral Responses to Changes in the Full Retirement Age." *American Economic Journal: Economic Policy* 4, no. 4 (2012): 41–67.

Beier, Margaret E., W. Jackeline Torres, and Jacqueline M. Gilberto. "Activities Matter: Personality and Resource Determinants of Activities and Their Effect on Mental and Physical Well-Being and Retirement Expectations." *Work, Aging and Retirement* 4, no. 1 (2018): 67–78.

———. "Determinants of Activities and Their Effect on Mental and Physical Well-Being and Retirement Expectations." *Work, Aging and Retirement* 4, no. 1 (2018): 67–78.

Bender, Keith A. "An Analysis of Well-Being in Retirement: The Role of Pensions, Health, and 'Voluntariness' of Retirement." *Journal of Socio-Economics* 41, no. 4 (2012): 424–33.

Berger, Sarah. "3 in 10 Americans Withdrew Money from Retirement Savings amid the Coronavirus Pandemic—and the Majority Spent It on Groceries." *Money Matters*, May 13, 2020.

Bergman, Peter, Raj Chetty, Stefanie DeLuca, Nathaniel Hendren, Lawrence Katz, and Christopher Palmer. "Creating Moves to Opportunity: Experimental Evidence on Barriers of Neighborhood Choice." Working Paper No. 26164, National Bureau of Economic Research, Cambridge, MA, 2019.

Berkman, Lisa F., and Beth C. Truesdale. "Working Longer and Population Aging in the US: Why Delayed Retirement Isn't Practical Solution for Many." *Journal of the Economics of Ageing* 24 (2023): 100438.

Bernt, Lisa J. "Workplace Transparency beyond Disclosure: What's Blocking the View?" *Marquette Law Review* 105 (2021): 73.

Bersin, Josh, and Tomas Chamorro-Premuzic. 2019. "The Case for Hiring Older Workers." *Harvard Business Review*, September 26, 2019. https://hbr.org/2019/09/the-case-for-hiring-older-workers.

Beyer, Newman. "Introduce Legislation to Establish Older Workers' Bureau Washington." Press release, November 18, 2022.

Bidwell, Matthew J. "What Happened to Long-Term Employment? The Role of Worker Power and Environmental Turbulence in Explaining Declines in Worker Tenure." *Organization Science* 24, no. 4 (2013): 1061–82.

Biggs, Simon, Michael McGann, Dina Bowman, and Helen Kimberley. "Work, Health and the Commodification of Life's Time: Reframing Work-Life Balance and the Promise of a Long Life." *Ageing & Society* 37, no. 7 (2017): 1458–83.

Bingley, Paul, and Alessandro Martinello, "Mental Retirement and Schooling." *European Economic Review* 63 (2013): 292–98.

Bivens, Josh, and Lawrence Mishel. *Understanding the Historic Divergence between Productivity and a Typical Worker's Pay: Why It Matters and Why It's Real*. Washington, DC: Economic Policy Institute, 2015. https://www.epi.org/files/2015/understanding-productivity-pay-divergence-final.pdf.

Bonnie, Richard J., Clare Stroud, Heather Breiner, Safety Committee on Improving the Health, Youth Board on Children, Institute of Medicine, and National Research Council. *The Health Care System: Investing in the Health and Well-Being of Young Adults*. Washington, DC: National Academies Press, 2015.

Bor, Jacob, Gregory H. Cohen, and Sandro Galea. "Population Health in an Era of Rising Income Inequality: USA, 1980–2015." *Lancet* 389, no. 10077 (2017): 1475–90.

Börsch-Supan, Axel, Agar Brugiavini, Enrica Croda, and Johannes Siegrist. "Retirement, Health, and the Quality of Work in Europe." *Four Pillars* 45 (2009): 1–7.

Bosworth, Barry, and Kathleen Burke. "Differential Mortality and Retirement Benefits in the Health and Retirement Study." Brookings Institution, Washington, DC, 2014. https://www.brookings.edu/research/differential-mortal ity-and-retirement-benefits-in-the-health-and-retirement-study/.

Bosworth, Barry, Gary Burtless, and Kan Zhang. "Later Retirement, Inequality in Old Age, and the Growing Gap in Longevity between Rich and Poor." *Economic Studies at Brookings* 87 (2016): 1–166.

Boushey, Heather, and Austin Clemens. "Disaggregating Growth: Who Prospers When the Economy Grows?" Washington Center for Equitable Growth, Washington, DC, March 2018. https://equitablegrowth.org/research-paper /disaggregating-growth/.

Bronshtein, Gila, Jason Scott, John B. Shoven, and Sita Nataraj Slavov. "The Power of Working Longer." *Journal of Pension Economics and Finance* 18, no. 4 (2019): 623–44.

Brown, Tyson H., and Taylor W. Hargrove. "Multidimensional Approaches to Examining Gender and Racial/Ethnic Stratification in Health." *Women, Gender, and Families of Color* 1, no. 2 (2013): 180–206.

Bruder, Jessica. *Nomadland: Surviving America in the Twenty-First Century.* New York: W. W. Norton, 2017.

Bureau of Labor Statistics. "Labor Force Share, by Age Group, 2000, 2010, 2020, and Projected 2030." September 2021. https://www.bls.gov/emp/graphics /labor-force-share-by-age-group.htm.

———. "Median Usual Weekly Earnings of Full-Time Wage and Salary Workers by Age and Sex." September 2021.

Burke, Ronald J., and Cary L. Cooper. *The Fulfilling Workplace: The Organization's Role in Achieving Individual and Organizational Health.* London: Routledge, 2016.

Burman, Leonard E., Christopher Geissler, and Eric J. Toder. "How Big Are Total Individual Income Tax Expenditures, and Who Benefits from Them?" *American Economic Review* 98, no. 2 (2008): 79–83.

Burtless, Gary. "Age Related Health Costs and Job Prospects of Older Workers." October 30, 2016. Available at SSRN. https://doi.org/10.2139/ssrn.4121660.

———. "Can Educational Attainment Explain the Rise in Labor Force Participation at Older Ages?" Brief No. 13-13, Center for Retirement Research at Boston College, Boston, September 2013.

———. "The Impact of Population Ageing and Delayed Retirement on Workforce Productivity." Available at SSRN. https://doi.org/10.2139/ssrn.2275023.

Business Wire. "New Voya Survey Finds Half of Employed Americans Plan to Work in Retirement as a Result of COVID-19." November 15, 2022. https:// www.businesswire.com/news/home/20221115005243/en/Amid-the-war-for -talent-don%E2%80%99t-forget-the-retirement-plan-Voya-survey-finds.

Butrica, Barbara A., Howard Iams, Karen E. Smith, and Eric J. Toder. "The Disappearing Defined Benefit Pension and Its Potential Impact on the Retirement Incomes of Baby Boomers." *Social Security Bulletin* 69, no. 3 (2009): 1–28.

Butrica, Barbara A., Richard W. Johnson, Karen Elizabeth Smith, and Eugene C. Steuerle. "Does Work Pay at Older Ages?" Working Paper No. 30, Center for Retirement Research, Boston College, Chestnut Hill, MA, 2004.

Butrica, Barbara A., Karen E. Smith, and Howard Iams. "This Is Not Your Parents' Retirement: Comparing Retirement Income across Generations." *Social Security Bulletin* 72, no. 1 (2012): 37–58.

Butrica, Barbara A., Karen Elizabeth Smith, and Eugene C. Steuerle. "Working for a Good Retirement." In *Government Spending on the Elderly*, edited by Dimitri B. Papadimitriou, 141–74. London: Palgrave Macmillan, 2007.

Cahill, Kevin E., Michael D. Giandrea, and Joseph F. Quinn. "Retirement Patterns from Career Employment." *Gerontologist* 46, no. 4 (August 2006): 514–23.

Calvo, Esteban, Natalia Sarkisian, and Christopher R. Tamborini. "Causal Effects of Retirement Timing on Subjective Physical and Emotional Health." *Journals of Gerontology Series B: Psychological Sciences and Social Sciences* 68, no. 1 (2013): 73–84.

Campanella, Edoardo. "Making Retirement Work." *Project Syndicate*, December 12, 2018.

Carlsson, Magnus, and Stefan Eriksson. "Age Discrimination in Hiring Decisions: Evidence from a Field Experiment in the Labor Market." *Labour Economics* 59 (August 19): 173–83.

Carrino, Ludovico, Karen Glaser, and Mauricio Avendano. "Later Retirement, Job Strain, and Health: Evidence from the New State Pension Age in the United Kingdom." *Health Economics* 29, no. 8 (2020): 891–912.

Cassandro, Nicola, Marco Centra, Dario Guarascio, and Piero Esposito. "What Drives Employment-Unemployment Transitions? Evidence from Italian Task-Based Data." *Economia Politica* 38 (2021): 1109–47.

Chan, Sewin, and Ann Huff Stevens. "Job Loss and Employment Patterns of Older Workers." *Journal of Labor Economics* 19, no. 2 (April 2001): 484–521.

Chetty, Raj, Nathaniel Hendren, Patrick Kline, and Emmanuel Saez. "Where Is the Land of Opportunity? The Geography of Intergenerational Mobility in the United States." *Quarterly Journal of Economics* 129, no. 4 (November 2014):1553-1623.

Cho, Jihyun. "Bridge Employment and Health." University of Michigan, 2016. https://deepblue.lib.umich.edu/bitstream/handle/2027.42/135855/jhacho_1 .pdf?sequence=1&isAllowe.

Choi, Namkee. "Relationship between Life Satisfaction and Postretirement Employment among Older Women." *International Journal of Aging and Human Development* 52, no. 1 (2001): 45–70.

Chou, Rita Jing-Ann, and Namkee G. Choi. "Prevalence and Correlates of Perceived Workplace Discrimination among Older Workers in the United States of America." *Ageing and Society* 31, no. 6 (2011): 1051–70.

Clark, Robert L., and Joseph P. Newhouse. "Incentives and Limitations of Employment Policies on Retirement Transitions." *Journal of Pension Economics and Finance* 18, no. 4 (2019): 495–99.

Clark, Robert L., Steven Nyce, Beth Ritter, and John B. Shoven. "Employer Concerns and Responses to an Aging Workforce." Working Paper Series No. 25572, National Bureau of Economic Research, Cambridge, MA, February 2019.

Clingman, Michael, Kyle Burkhalter, and Chris Chaplain. "Replacement Rates for Hypothetical Retired Workers." Actuarial Note Social Security No. 2020.9. Baltimore: Social Security Administration Office of the Chief Actuary, 2020.

Coe, Norma B., and Gema Zamarro, "Retirement Effects of Health in Europe." *Journal of Health Economics* 30, no. 1 (2011): 77–86.

Coile, Courtney C. "The Evolution of Retirement Incentives in the US." In *Social Security Programs and Retirement around the World: Reforms and Retirement Incentives*. Chicago: University of Chicago Press, 2018.

Coile, Courtney, Kevin Milligan, and David A. Wise. "Health Capacity to Work at Older Ages: Evidence from the United States." In *Social Security Programs and Retirement around the World: The Capacity to Work at Older Ages*, 359–94. Chicago: University of Chicago Press, 2017.

Collinson, Catherine. "Striking Similarities and Disconcerting Disconnects: Employers, Workers and Retirement Security, 18th Annual Transamerica Retirement Survey." *Transamerica Center for Retirement Studies* 18 (August 2018): 24–38.

Congressional Budget Office. "Measuring the Adequacy of Retirement Income: A Primer." October 2017. https://www.cbo.gov/system/files/115th-congress -2017-2018/reports/53191-retirementadequacy.pdf.

Cooper, Philip F., and Karen E. Davis. "Premiums and Employee Contributions to Employer-Sponsored Health Insurance by Workforce Gender and Firm Size, Private Industry, 2018." Statistical Brief No. 525, Agency for Healthcare Research and Quality, Rockville, MD, September 2019.

Costa, Dora. *The Evolution of Retirement: An American Economic History, 1880– 1990*. Chicago: University of Chicago Press, 1998.

Coxwell, Kathleen. "What Is Another Word for Retirement? There Has Got to Be Something Better!" *New Retirement*, July 24, 2019. https://www.new retirement.com/retirement/another-word-for-retirement/.

Crystal, Stephen, and Dennis Shea. "Cumulative Advantage, Cumulative Disadvantage, and Inequality among Elderly People." *Gerontologist* 30, no. 4 (1990): 437–43.

C-SPAN. Enron hearings, 2002. https://www.c-span.org/video/?168571-1/enron-bankruptcy.

Dave, Dhaval, Inas Rashad, and Jasmina Spasojevic. "The Effects of Retirement on Physical and Mental Health Outcomes." *Southern Economic Journal* 75, no. 2 (2008): 497–523.

Davis, Owen, and Aida Farmand. "Who Does the Earned Income Tax Credit Benefit? A Monopsony View." Working Paper No. 1, Schwartz Center for Economic Policy Analysis, New School for Social Research, New York, 2021.

Davis, Owen, Bridget Fisher, Teresa Ghilarducci, and Siavash Radpour. *A First in Nearly 50 Years, Older Workers Face Higher Unemployment Than Mid-Career Workers.* Policy Brief No. 2020-05, Schwartz Center for Economic Policy Analysis and Department of Economics, New School for Social Research, New York, 2020.

———. "The Stalled Jobs Recovery Pushed 1.1 Million Older Workers out of the Labor Force." Brief, Schwartz Center for Economic Policy Analysis and Department of Economics, New School for Social Research, New York, February 2021.

Davis, Owen, and Siavash Radpour. "The Pandemic Retirement Surge Increased Retirement Inequality." Brief No. 2021-03, Schwartz Center for Economic Policy Analysis and Department of Economics, New School for Social Research, New York, 2021.

De Clercq, Geert. "Macron Says France's Pension Reform Cannot Go Ahead as Planned." *Reuters,* June 3, 2021. https://www.reuters.com/world/europe/frances-pension-reform-cannot-go-ahead-planned-macron-2021-06-03/.

Desilver, Drew. "The Politics of American Generations: How Age Affects Attitudes and Voting Behavior." *Pew Research Center* (blog). https://www.pewresearch.org/short-reads/2014/07/09/the-politics-of-american-generations-how-age-affects-attitudes-and-voting-behavior/.

Diamond, Phyllis. 2019. "Forced Retirement: What Is It and What Can You Do about It?" *Chasing the Dream,* Next Avenue, March 19, 2019. https://www.pbs.org/wnet/chasing-the-dream/stories/forced-retirement/.

Docteur, Elizabeth, Renée M. Landers, Bethany Cole, Marilyn Moon, and Cori Uccello. "Examining Approaches to Expand Medicare Eligibility: Key Design Options and Implications." National Academy of Social Insurance, Washington, DC, March 2020. https://www.nasi.org/research/examining-approaches-to-expand-medicare-eligibility-key-design-options-and-implications/.

Doonan, Dan, and Kelly Kenneally. *Generational Views of Retirement in the United States.* Washington, DC: National Institute on Retirement Security. https://www.nirsonline.org/reports/generations/.

Dudel, Christian, María Andrée López Gómez, Fernando G. Benavides, and Mikko Myrskylä. *A Lost Generation? The Financial Crisis and the Length of*

Working Life in Spain. Rostock, Germany: Max Planck Institute for Demographic Research, 2016.

Dudel, Christian, and Mikko Myrskylä. "Working Life Expectancy at Age 50 in the United States and the Impact of the Great Recession." *Demography* 54, no. 6 (2017): 2101–23.

Dufouil, Carole, Edwige Pereira, Geneviève Chêne, M. Maria Glymour, Annick Alpérovitch, Elodie Saubusse, Mathilde Risse-Fleury, et al. "Older Age at Retirement Is Associated with Decreased Risk of Dementia." *European Journal of Epidemiology* 29, no. 5 (2014): 353–61.

Dunlop, John T., and Benjamin Higgins. "'Bargaining Power' and Market Structures." *Journal of Political Economy* 50, no. 1 (1942): 1–26.

Economic Innovation Group. "Bipartisan Pair of Economists Propose Bold New Wealth Building Program for the Bottom 50 Percent of American Workers." Press release, March 25, 2021.

Economic Policy Institute, American Federation of Teachers, and Schwartz Center for Economic Policy Analysis. *Breathe Easy—How Guaranteed Retirement Accounts Could Change Your Life*. Washington, DC: Economic Policy Institute, American Federation of Teachers, and Schwartz Center for Economic Policy Analysis, 2019.

The Economist. "People Are Working Longer for Reasons of Choice and Necessity: The Long and Winding Career." September 17, 2019.

Edge, Clare Ellen, Anna Mary Cooper, and Margaret Coffey. "Barriers and Facilitators to Extended Working Lives in Europe: A Gender Focus." *Public Health Reviews* 38, no. 1 (2017): 2–12.

Ehrenberg, Ronald G. "Retirement Policies, Employment, and Unemployment." *American Economic Review* 69, no. 2 (1979): 131–36.

Elkins, Kathleen. "Here's How Much Money You'd Have If You Delayed Retirement until 70, According to Stanford Researchers." *CNBC*, August 26, 2019.

Employment Analysis and Policy Division, Directorate for Employment. *Labour and Social Affairs*. Paris: OECD.

Erikson, Erik H., and Joan M. Erikson. *The Life Cycle Completed (Extended Version)*. W. W. Norton, 1998.

Estes, Carroll L. "Christopher R. Phillipson, Capitalism and the Construction of Old Age." *Ageing & Society* 11, no. 3 (1991): 349–52.

———. *Social Policy and Aging: A Critical Perspective*. Thousand Oaks, CA: Sage Publications, 2001.

Eyjólfsdóttir, Harpa Sif, Isabel Baumann, Neda Agahi, Johan Fritzell, and Carin Lennartsson. "Prolongation of Working Life and Its Effect on Mortality and Health in Older Adults: Propensity Score Matching." *Social Science and Medicine* 226 (2019): 77–86.

Farber, Henry S. "Employment Insecurity: The Decline in Worker-Firm Attachment in the United States." Working Paper No. 172, Center for Economic Policy Studies, Washington, DC, June 2008.

Farmand, Aida. "Impacts of the Earned Income Tax Credit on Wages of Ineligible Workers." Schwartz Center for Economic Policy Analysis, New School for Social Research, New York, 2019.

———. "Involuntary Unemployed by Class." Research Note Series No. 2, Schwartz Center for Economic Policy Analysis, New School for Social Research, New York, August 2021. https://www.economicpolicyresearch.org/events/up coming-events/older-workers-are-forced-out-of-the-workforce.

Farmand, Aida, and Teresa Ghilarducci. "Why American Older Workers Have Lost Bargaining Power." Schwartz Center for Economic Policy Analysis, New School for Social Research, New York, 2019.

Federal Reserve Bank of St. Louis. "COVID-19 Workers Higher Unemployment Risk." 2020. https://www.stlouisfed.org/on-the-economy/2020/march /covid-19-workers-highest-unemployment-risk.

———. "Economic Statistics: Employment Level—55 Years and Over." https:// fred.stlouisfed.org/graph/?g=SfdZ.

———. "Moody's Seasoned AAA Corporate Bond Yield," January 7, 2021. https:// fred.stlouisfed.org/series/AAA.

Feldman, Jamie. "What A 90-Year-Old Who Works at McDonald's Can Teach Us about Happiness." *Huffington Post*, May 17, 2018. https://www.huffpost .com/entry/90-year-old-mcdonalds-happiness_n_5af9c43be4b09a94524af527.

Ferrelli, Monica. "Tracing the Conception and Meaning of the Age Discrimination in Employment Act: Where Are We with Mandatory Retirement." *Journal of Sociology & Social Welfare* 12 (1985): 326.

Fidelity. "Online Retirement Readiness Calculator." https://digital.fidelity .com/prgw/digital/financial-checkup/survey/7.

Fisher, Gordon M. "The Development and History of the Poverty Thresholds." *Social Security Bulletin* 55, no. 4 (1992): 3–14.

Flood, Sarah, Miriam King, Renae Rodgers, Steven Ruggles, and J. Robert Warren. *Integrated Public Use Microdata Series, Current Population Survey: Version 8.0, Annual Social and Economic Supplement 1991–2018*. Minneapolis: https://www.ipums.org/projects/ipums-cps/d030.v8.0.

Forden, Jessica, Siavash Radpour, Eva Conway, Christopher Cook, and Teresa Ghilarducci. "Physically Demanding Jobs and Involuntary Retirement Worsen Retirement Insecurity." Status of Older Workers Report Series, Schwartz Center for Economic Policy Analysis, New School for Social Research, New York, 2022.

Foster, Sarah. "With Age Comes Fewer Raises: Here's Why Many Americans Aren't Receiving Higher Pay." *Bankrate*, February 4, 2020.

Friedberg, Leora, and Anthony Webb. "Retirement and the Evolution of Pension Structure." *Journal of Human Resources* 40, no. 2 (2005): 281–308.

Geyer, Johannes, and Clara Welteke. "Closing Routes to Retirement for Women How Do They Respond?" *Journal of Human Resources* 56, no. 1 (2021): 311–41.

Ghilarducci, Teresa. "The Do-It-Yourself Retirement System Is Not Working." *Wealthtrack*, March 8, 2019. https://wealthtrack.com/the-do-it-yourself -retirement-system-isnt-working-retirement-pro-teresa-ghilarducci-has -solutions/.

———. "Older Workers' Bureau Gains Momentum in Congress." *Forbes*, December 12, 2022. https://www.forbes.com/sites/teresaghilarducci/2022/12/12 /older-workers-bureau-gains-momentum-in-congress/?sh=3666dda853a8.

———. "Teresa Ghilarducci on Social Security Fixes to Protect the Poorest." *Bloomberg Opinion*, March 27, 2020.

———. "The Time Is Now to Lower the Medicare Age to 50." *Forbes*, April 10, 2020. https://www.forbes.com/sites/teresaghilarducci/2020/04/10/now -more-than-ever-is-time-to-lower-medicares-age-to-50/.

———. "United States Congress Joint Economic Committee Hearing on Building a Better Labor Market: Empowering Older Workers for a Stronger Economy," US Joint Economic Committee, 2022. https://www.jec.senate.gov /public/index.cfm/2022/2/building-a-better-labor-market-empowering -older-workers-for-a-stronger-economy.

———. "When Loyalty No Longer Pays, What's an Older Worker to Do?" *Forbes*, September 16, 2020. https://www.forbes.com/sites/teresaghilarducci/2020 /09/16/when-loyalty-doesnt-pay-whats-an-older-worker-to-do/?sh=74c7ac 217d24.

———. "Why Do We Make It So Easy to Steal Seniors' Money?" *Bloomberg Opinion*, December 22, 2022.

Ghilarducci, Teresa, and Christopher D. Cook. "Op-Ed: Pushed to Retire and to Keep Earning, Older Americans Face a Peculiar Vise." *Los Angeles Times*, September 27, 2021.

Ghilarducci, Teresa, and Aida Farmand. "Older Workers on the COVID-19- Frontlines without Paid Sick Leave." *Journal of Aging and Social Policy* 32, nos. 4–5 (2020): 471–76.

Ghilarducci, Teresa, Aida Farmand, Bridget Fisher, and Siavash Radpour. "How Expanding EITC Will Benefit 1.5 Million Low-Income Older Workers." *Schwartz Center for Economic Policy Analysis Insights* (blog), September 8, 2021. https://www.economicpolicyresearch.org/insights-blog/how-expand ing-eitc-will-benefit-1-5-million-low-income-older-workers.

Ghilarducci, Teresa, Bridget Fisher, Kyle Moore, and Anthony Webb. "Gender and Racial Disparities in Physical Job Demands of Older Workers." Policy

Note Series, Schwartz Center for Economic Policy Analysis, New School for Social Research, New York, 2016.

Ghilarducci, Teresa, and Tony James. "Americans Haven't Saved Enough for Retirement: What Are We Going to Do about It? "*Harvard Business Review,* March 28, 2018. https://hbr.org/2018/03/americans-havent-saved-enough -for-retirement-what-arewe-going-to-do-about-it.

Ghilarducci, Teresa, M. Papadopoulos, B. Fisher, and A. Webb. "Working Longer Cannot Solve the Retirement Income Crisis." Policy Note Series, Schwartz Center for Economic Policy Analysis, New School for Social Research, New York, 2021.

Ghilarducci, Teresa, Michael Papadopoulos, and Anthony Webb. "40% of Older Workers and Their Spouses Will Experience Downward Mobility in Retirement." Policy Note Series, Schwartz Center for Economic Policy Analysis, New School for Social Research, New York, 2018. https://www.economic policyresearch.org/images/docs/research/retirement_security/Downward _Mobility_in_Retirement_P_N.pdf#:~:text=Older%20workers%20-%20ages %2050-60%20and%20their%20spouses,than%20twice%20the%20Federal %20Poverty%20Level%20in%20retirement.

———. "The Illusory Benefit of Working Longer on Retirement Financial Preparedness: Rethinking Advice That Working Longer Increases Retirement Income." *Journal of Retirement* 10, no. 4 (2022): 7–26.

———. "Inadequate Retirement Savings for Workers Nearing Retirement." Policy Note Series, Schwartz Center for Economic Policy Analysis, New School for Social Research, New York, 2017.

———. "Larger Birth Cohort Lowers Wages." Policy Note Series No. 1, Schwartz Center for Economic Policy Analysis, New School for Social Research, New York, 2017.

Ghilarducci, Teresa, Siavash Radpour, Owen Davis, and Anthony Webb, "Extreme Retirement Inequality Persists, Even among Those with Similar Earnings." Policy Note Series 2019-01, Schwartz Center for Economic Policy Analysis, New School for Social Research, New York, 2019. https://ideas .repec.org/p/epa/cepapn/2019-01.html.

Ghilarducci, Teresa, Siavash Radpour, and Anthony Webb. "New Evidence on the Effect of Economic Shocks on Retirement Plan Withdrawals." *Journal of Retirement* 6, no. 4 (2019): 7–19.

———. "Retirement Plan Wealth Inequality: Measurement and Trends." *Journal of Pension Economics and Finance* 21, no. 1 (2022): 119–39.

———. "Social Security Reduces Retirement Wealth Inequality." Policy Note Series No. 1, Schwartz Center for Economic Policy Analysis, New School for Social Research, New York, January 2020.

Ghilarducci, Teresa, and Joelle Saad-Lessler. "How 401(k) Plans Make Recessions Worse." *Inequality, Uncertainty, and Opportunity* (2015): 9.

Ghilarducci, Teresa, and Barbara Schuster. "Working Longer Not a Panacea Considering the Number of Low-Wage Work Options." *Generations*, November 16, 2021.

Ghilarducci, Teresa, and Wei Sun. "How Defined Contribution Plans and 401(k)s Affect Employer Pension Costs." *Journal of Pension Economics and Finance* 5, no. 2 (2006): 175–96.

Ghilarducci, Teresa, and Anthony Webb. "The Distribution of Time in Retirement: Evidence From the Health and Retirement Survey." *Work, Aging and Retirement* 4, no. 3 (July 2018): 251–61.

Ghilarducci, Teresa, Anthony Webb, and Michael Papadopoulos. "The Growth of Unstable and Low-Wage Work among Older Workers." Policy Note Series, Schwartz Center for Economic Policy Analysis, New School for Social Research, New York, 2018.

Goda, Gopi Shah, John B. Shoven, and Sita Nataraj Slavov. "Removing the Disincentives in Social Security for Long Careers." Working Paper Series No. 21588, National Bureau of Economic Research, Cambridge, MA, May 2007.

Goldmacher, Shane, and Sydney Ember. "Biden, Seeking Democratic Unity, Reaches Left toward Sanders's Ideas." *New York Times*, April 9, 2020.

Goleman, Daniel. "Erickson in His Own Old Age, Expands His View of Life." *New York Times*, June 14, 1988.

Gorry, Aspen, Devon Gorry, and Sita Nataraj Slavov. "Does Retirement Improve Health and Life Satisfaction?" *Health Economics* 27, no. 12 (December 2018): 2067–86.

Gosselin, Peter. "If You're Over 50, Chances Are the Decision to Leave a Job Won't Be Yours." ProPublica and Urban Institute, December 28, 2018. https://www.propublica.org/article/older-workers-united-states-pushed-out-of-work-forced-retirement.

Gosselin, Peter, and Ariana Tobin. "Cutting 'Old Heads' at IBM." ProPublica, March 22, 2018.

Gothelf, Jeff. *Forever Employable: How to Stop Looking for Work and Let Your Next Job Find You.* New Jersey: Gothelf Corp., 2020.

Goux, Dominique, and Eric Maurin. "Persistence of Interindustry Wage Differentials: A Reexamination Using Matched Worker-Firm Panel Data." *Journal of Labor Economics* 17, no. 3 (1999): 492–533.

Graham, Judith. 2022. "'True Cost of Aging' Index Shows Many U.S. Seniors Can't Afford Basic Necessities." CBS News, July 27, 2022. https://www.cbs news.com/news/retirement-many-seniors-cant-afford-basic-necessities/.

Grøtting, Maja Weemes, and Otto Sevaldson Lillebø. "Health Effects of Retirement: Evidence from Survey and Register Data." *Journal of Population Economics* 33, no. 2 (2020): 671–704.

Gruber, Jonathan, and Peter Orszag. "Does the Social Security Earnings Test Affect Labor Supply and Benefits Receipt?" *National Tax Journal* 56, no. 4 (2003): 755–73.

Gruber, Jonathan, and David A. Wise, eds. *Social Security and Retirement around the World: The Relationship to Youth Employment.* Chicago: University of Chicago Press, 2000.

Gustman, Alan L., and Thomas L. Steinmeier. "How Changes in Social Security Affect Recent Retirement Trends." *Research on Aging* 31, no. 2 (March 2009): 261–90.

Harnois, Catherine, and Vincent Roscigno. "Trump Is Making It Harder for Older Americans to Prove Workplace Discrimination." *National Interest,* March 20, 2020.

Harris, Kelly, Sarah Krygsman, Jessica Waschenko, and Debbie Laliberte Rudman. "Ageism and the Older Worker: A Scoping Review." *Gerontologist* 58, no. 2 (April 2018): e1–e14.

Harvard Health Letter. "Working Later in Life Can Pay Off in More Than Just Income." June 2018. https://www.health.harvard.edu/staying-healthy/working-later-in-life-can-pay-off-in-more-than-just-income#:~:text=There's%20increasing%20evidence%20that%20the, with%20better%20health%20and%20longevity.

Hershey, Douglas A., and Kène Henkens. "Impact of Different Types of Retirement Transitions on Perceived Satisfaction with Life." *Gerontologist* 54, no. 2 (2014): 232–44.

Hickenlooper, John. "Hickenlooper, Tillis, Sewell, Smucker Introduce Bill to Expand Retirement Savings for Working Americans." Press release, December 8, 2022. https://www.hickenlooper.senate.gov/press_releases/Hickenlooper-tillis-sewell-smucker-introduce-bill-to-expand-retirement-savings-for-working-americans/.

Hildon, M. A., Scott M. Montgomery, David Blane, Richard D. Wiggins, and Gopalakrishnan Netuveli. "Examining Resilience of Quality of Life in the Face of Health-Related and Psychosocial Adversity at Older Ages: What Is 'Right' about the Way We Age?" *Gerontologist* 50, no. 1 (2010): 36–47.

Hollister, Matissa. "Employment Stability in the US Labor Market: Rhetoric versus Reality." *Annual Review of Sociology* 37, no. 1 (August 2011): 305–24.

Horner, Elizabeth Mokyr. "Subjective Well-Being and Retirement: Analysis and Policy Recommendations." *Journal of Happiness Studies* 15, no. 1 (2014): 125–44.

Hou, Wenliang, Alicia H. Munnell, Geoffrey T. Sanzenbacher, and Yinji Li. "Why Are US Households Claiming Social Security Later?" Center for Retirement Research at Boston College, Boston, April 2017.

Iacurci, Greg. 2021. "They Went Bust in the Great Recession. Now, in Their 80s, the Pandemic Took Their Jobs." CNBC, February 6, 2021. https://www.cnbc.com/2021/02/06/how-covid-led-to-unemployment-for-older-amer icans.html.

Insler, Michael. "The Health Consequences of Retirement." *Journal of Human Resources* 49, no. 1 (2014): 195–233.

Jacobs, Jerry A., and Kathleen Gerson. "Overworked Individuals or Overworked Families? Explaining Trends in Work, Leisure, and Family Time." *Work and Occupations* 28, no. 1 (2001): 40–63.

Jacobson, Gretchen, Judith M. Feder, and David C. Radley. "COVID-19's Impact on Older Workers: Employment, Income, and Medicare Spending." Commonwealth Fund, New York, October 2020.

Jacoby, Susan. *Never Say Die: The Myth and Marketing of the New Old Age.* New York: Vintage Books, 2011.

Johnson, Richard W., and Peter Gosselin. *How Secure Is Employment at Older Ages?* Washington, DC: Urban Institute, 2018.

Johnson, Richard W., and Corina Mommaerts. "Age Differences in Job Displacement, Job Search, and Reemployment." Working Paper No. 2011-3, Center for Retirement Research, Boston College, Chestnut Hill, MA, 2010.

Jones, Gavin. "Economists Fret as Italian Politicians Promise to Scrap Pension Cuts." *Reuters*, November 29, 2017. https://www.reuters.com/article/italy -politics-pensions/economists-fret-as-italian-politicians-promise-to-scrap -pension-cuts-idUSL8N1NY5R5.

Kambourov, Gueorgui, and Iourii Manovskii. "Occupational Specificity of Human Capital." *International Economic Review* 50, no. 1 (2009): 63–115.

Karamcheva, Nadia S. *Is Household Debt Growing for Older Americans?* Report No. 2013-33. Program on Retirement Policy, Urban Institute, Washington, DC, 2013.

Katz, Michael. *The Undeserving Poor: America's Enduring Confrontation with Poverty.* Princeton, NJ: Princeton University Press, 2013.

Kaufman, Bruce E., and Julie L. Hotchkiss. *The Economics of Labor Markets.* Mason, OH: Thomson South-Western, 2006.

Keese, Mark. "A Method for Calculating the Average Age of Effective Retirement." OECD Publication, Employment Analysis and Policy Division, Directorate for Employment, Labour and Social Affairs, Paris. https://www.oecd.org/els/emp/39371923.pdf.

Keynes, John Maynard. "Economic Possibilities for Our Grandchildren." In *Essays in Persuasion*, 358–74. 1930; New York: W. W. Norton, 1963.

Kiplinger–Alliance for Lifetime Income Poll. *Americans & Retirement Security.* https://www.kiplinger.com/retirement/social-security/601262/a-kiplinger -alliance-for-lifetime-income-poll-americans.

Kirzinger, Ashley, Cayley Muñana, and Mollyann Brodie. "KFF Health Tracking Poll—January 2019: The Public on Next Steps for the ACA and Proposals to Expand Coverage." News release, Kaiser Family Foundation, January 23, 2019. https://www.kff.org/health-reform/poll-finding/kff-health-tracking -poll-january-2019/.

Lacey, T. Alan, Mitra Tosi, Kevin S. Dubna, and Andrea B. Gensler. "Projections Overview and Highlights, 2016–26." *Monthly Labor Review* 140 (2017): 1.

Lael, Étienne. "Turbulence and the Employment Experience of Older Workers." *Quantitative Economics* 9, no. 2 (2018): 735–84.

Lain, David. *Reconstructing Retirement: Work and Welfare in the UK and USA.* Bristol, UK: Public Policy Press, 2018.

Lalé, Étienne. "Turbulence and the Employment Experience of Older Workers." *Quantitative Economics* 9, no. 2 (2018): 735–84.

Lammi, Elmer W. "Labor Undersecretary Malcolm Lovell Jr. Wednesday Urged Congress . . ." United Press International, August 18, 1992. https://upi.com /5953619.

Lee, Chungsup, Laura L. Payne, and Liza Berdychevsky. "The Roles of Leisure Attitudes and Self-Efficacy on Attitudes toward Retirement among Retirees: A Sense of Coherence Theory Approach." *Leisure Sciences* 42, no. 2 (March 2020): 152–69.

Leigh, Andrew. "Who Benefits from the Earned Income Tax Credit? Incidence among Recipients, Coworkers and Firms." *B. E. Journal of Economic Analysis & Policy* 10, no. 1 (2010): 1–43.

Levitin, Daniel J. *Successful Aging: A Neuroscientist Explores the Power and Potential of Our Lives.* New York: Penguin, 2020.

Lindeboom, Maarten, and Marcel Kerkhofs. "Health and Work of the Elderly: Subjective Health Measures, Reporting Errors and Endogeneity in the Relationship between Health and Work." *Journal of Applied Econometrics* 24, no. 6 (2009): 1024–46.

Lusardi, Annamaria, Olivia S. Mitchell, and Noemi Oggero. "The Changing Face of Debt and Financial Fragility at Older Ages." In *AEA Papers and Proceedings*, 108:407–11. Nashville, TN: American Economic Association, 2018.

Maag, Elaine, and Kevin Werner. "Expanding the Earned Income Tax Credit Could Provide Financial Security for Millions of Workers without Children." Urban Institute, Washington, DC, February 1, 2021.

Maestas, Nicole. "Cohort Differences in Retirement Expectations and Realizations." In *Redefining Retirement: How Will Boomers Fare*, edited by Brigitte

Madrian, Olivia S. Mitchell, and Beth J. Soldo, 13–35. New York: Oxford University Press, 2007.

Maestas, Nicole, and Julie Zissimopoulos. "How Longer Work Lives Ease the Crunch of Population Aging." *Journal of Economic Perspectives* 24, no. 1 (2010): 139–60.

Manning, Allee. "Where Are All the Sex Toys for Older Adults?" *Mashable*, January 19, 2018.

Marvell, Rosa, and Annette Cox. *Fulfilling Work: What Do Older Workers Value about Work and Why?* Brighton, UK: Institute for Employment Studies and Centre for Ageing Better, February 2017.

Mast, Ferozan. "82-Year-Old Walmart Cashier Can Finally Retire after Good Samaritan Raises $108,000 from Online Donors." *Best Life* (blog), January 12, 2023. https://bestlifeonline.com/news-elderly-walmart-cashier-retirement -after-fundraising/#:~:text=A%20Walmart%20cashier%20was%20finally ,awareness%20for%20Warren%20Marion%2C%2082.

Max, Sarah. "Nobel Prize-Winning Economist on How to Solve the 'Nastiest, Hardest Problem' in Retirement." *Barron's*, November 15, 2019. https://www .barrons.com/articles/william-sharpe-how-to-secure-lasting-retirement -income-51573837934.

McDonough, Peggy. "Job Insecurity and Health." *International Journal of Health Services* 30, no. 3 (2000): 453–76.

McGahey, Richard. "America Needs an Older Workers Bureau." *Forbes*, June 11, 2021. https://www.forbes.com/sites/richardmcgahey/2021/06/11/america -needs-an-older-workers-bureau/?sh=5972c3291179.

McLaughlin, Joanne Song. "Age Discrimination Laws, Physical Challenges, and Work Accommodations for Older Adults." *Generations: Journal of the American Society on Aging* 43, no. 3 (2019): 59–62.

McNamee, David. "Working to Survive." *Lancet* 343, no. 8903 (1994): 930.

McWilliams, J. Michael, Ellen Meara, Alan M. Zaslavsky, and John Z. Ayanian. "Health of Previously Uninsured Adults after Acquiring Medicare Coverage." *JAMA* 298, no. 24 (December 26, 2007): 2886–94.

Megan, Kenneth. "Federal Retirement Tax Benefits Mostly Go to the Wealthy— Here's How to Make Them Work for Everyone," Economic Innovation Group, November 3, 2021. https://inclusivewealth.eig.org/federal-retirement-tax -benefits-are-mostly-used-by-the-wealthy-heres-how-to-make-them-work -for-everyone/.

Melbourne Mercer. *Global Pension Index 2019*. Melbourne: Mercer Institute and Monash University. https://info.mercer.com/rs/521-DEV-513/images /MMGPI%202019%20Full%20Report.pdf.

———. *Global Pension Index 2021*. Mercer CFA Institute. https://www.africa .mercer.com/our-thinking/global-pension-index-2021.html#contactForm.

Messe, Pierre-Jean, and François-Charles Wolff. "Healthier When Retiring
Earlier? Evidence from France." *Applied Economics* 51, no. 47 (2019): 5122–43.

Mitchell. Daniel J. B. "Wage Pressures and Labor Shortages: The 1960s and
1980s." *Brookings Papers on Economic Activity*, no. 2 (1989): 191–231.

Molloy, Raven, Christopher L. Smith, Riccardo Trezzi, and Abigail Wozniak.
"Understanding Declining Fluidity in the US Labor Market." *Brookings
Papers on Economic Activity*, no. 15 (2016): 183–259.

Moore, Kyle, Teresa Ghilarducci, and Anthony Webb. "The Inequitable Effects
of Raising the Retirement Age on Blacks and Low-Wage Workers." *Review
of Black Political Economy* 46, no. 1 (2019): 22–37.

Morrissey, Monique. *How Many Older Workers Have Difficult Jobs?* Washington,
DC: Economic Policy Institute.

———. "The State of American Retirement Savings: How the Shift to 401(k)s
Has Increased Gaps in Retirement Preparedness Based on Income, Race,
Ethnicity, Education, and Marital Status." *Economic Policy Institute* (2019):
https://files.epi.org/pdf/136219.pdf.

Morrissey, Monique, Siavash Radpour, and Barbara Schuster. "Older Workers
and Retirement Chartbook." Economic Policy Institute and Schwartz Center for Economic Policy Analysis, November 16, 2022. https://www.epi.org
/publication/chapter-1-older-workers/.

Motegi, Hiroyuki, Yoshinori Nishimura, and Masato Oikawa. "Retirement and
Health Investment Behaviors: An International Comparison." *Journal of the
Economics of Ageing* 16 (2020): 100267.

Munnell, Alicia H. *The Future of Social Security*. Washington, DC: Brookings
Institution, 1977.

Munnell, Alicia H., and Dina Bleckman. "Is Pension Coverage a Problem in
the Private Sector?" Issues in Brief No. 7, Center for Retirement Research,
Boston College, Boston, 2014.

Munnell, Alicia, Wenliang Hou, and Geoffrey T. Sanzenbacher. "Do Households Have a Good Sense of Their Retirement Preparedness?" Issues in Brief
No. 4, Center for Retirement Research, Boston College, Boston, 2017.

———. "Women Retirement and the National Retirement Risk Index." Issues in
Brief No. 10, Center for Retirement Research, Boston College, Boston, 2019.

Munnell, Alicia H., Wenliang Hou, and Anthony Webb. "National Retirement
Risk Index (NRRI) Update Shows Half of Working-Age Americans Still Falling Short." *Journal of Retirement* 3, no. 2 (Fall 2015): 34–42.

Munnell, Alicia H., Wenliang Hou, Anthony Webb, and Yinji Li. "How Has the
Shift to 401(k) Plans Affected Retirement Income?" Issue Brief 17-5, Center
for Retirement Research, Boston College, Boston, 2017.

Munnell, Alicia H., Natasha Orlova, and Anthony Webb. "How Important Is
Asset Allocation to Financial Security in Retirement?" In *The Market for*

Retirement Financial Advice, edited by O. S. Mitchell and K. Smetters, 89–106. Oxford: Oxford University Press, 2013.

Munnell, Alicia H., and Steven A. Sass. *Working Longer: The Solution to the Retirement Income Challenge*. Washington, DC: Brookings Institution Press, 2009.

Munnell, Alicia H., Steven Sass, Mauricio Soto, and Natalia Zhivan. "Has the Displacement of Older Workers Increased?" Working Paper No. 17, Center for Retirement Research, Boston College, Chestnut Hill, MA, September 2006.

Munnell, Alicia H., Anthony Webb, and Francesca Golub-Sass. "How Much to Save for a Secure Retirement?" Issues in Brief No. 13, Center for Retirement Research, Boston College, Boston, 2011.

Murakami, David. "Japan's Part-Time Workers Need Tighter Reforms." *East Asia Forum*, November 2, 2019.

Mutchler, J. E., Yao-Chi Shih, Jiyoung Lyu, Ellen A. Bruce, and Alison Gottlieb. "The Elder Economic Security Standard Index: A New Indicator for Evaluating Economic Security in Later Life." *Social Indicators Research* 120 (2015): 97–116.

National Research Council. "Labor Force Participation and Retirement." In *Aging and the Macroeconomy: Long-Term Implications of an Older Population*, 75–105. Washington, DC: National Academies Press, 2012.

Neuman, K. "Quit Your Job and Get Healthier? The Effect of Retirement on Health." *Journal of Labor Research* 29 (2008): 177–201.

Neumark, David. "Strengthen Age Discrimination Protections to Help Confront the Challenge of Population Aging." Brookings Institution, Washington, DC, November 19, 2020.

Neumark, David, Ian Burn, and Patrick Button. "Is It Harder for Older Workers to Find Jobs? New and Improved Evidence from a Field Experiment." *Journal of Political Economy* 127, no. 2 (April 2019): 922–70.

Neumark, David, and Joanne Song. "Do Stronger Age Discrimination Laws Make Social Security Reforms More Effective?" Working Paper Series No. 17467, National Bureau of Economic Research, Cambridge, MA, September 2011.

Newport, Frank. "Snapshot: Average American Predicts Retirement Age of 66." Gallup, May 10, 2018.

Nichols, Austin, and Jesse Rothstein. "The Earned Income Tax Credit." In *Economics of Means-Tested Transfer Programs in the United States*, edited by Robert A. Moffitt, 1:137–218. Chicago: University of Chicago Press, 2016.

Novie, Annie. "For Millions of Americans, the Coronavirus Pandemic Will Make Retiring Harder." *CNBC News*, May 16, 2020. https://www.cnbc.com /2020/05/16/why-the-coronavirus-recession-makes-retiring-harder-for -millions.html.

Nussbaum, Ania. "Macron Plows Ahead with Pension Reform as More Protests Loom." *Yahoo*, January 23, 2023. https://finance.yahoo.com/news
/macron-plows-ahead-pension-reform-115404059.html?fr=sycsrp_catchall.

O'Connor, Sarah. "Living Longer Does Not Mean We Should All Work Longer."
Financial Times, March 30, 2021.

OECD. *Employment Outlook 2021: Building Back More Inclusive Labor Markets.*
Paris: OECD Publishing, 2021. https://doi.org/10.1787/084f32c7-en.

———. "Employment Rate." *OECD Employment Outlook 2023*. https://data.oecd
.org/emp/employment-rate.htm#indicator-chart.

———. *Pensions at a Glance: Income and Poverty of Older People*. Paris: OECD Publishing, 2019. https://stats.oecd.org/index.aspx?queryid=69414.

———. *Working Better with Age*. Paris: OECD Publishing, 2019.

Oi, Katsuya. "Does Gender Differentiate the Effects of Retirement on Cognitive Health?" *Research on Aging* 41, no. 6. (July 2019): 575–601.

Olshan, Jeremy. "Ted Benna Has Called the 401(k) a Monster." *MarketWatch*,
September 26, 2016.

Olshansky, S. J., T. Antonucci, L. Berkman, R. H. Binstock, A. Börsch-Supan,
J. T. Cacioppo, B. A. Carnes, L. L. Carstensen, L. P. Fried, D. P. Goldman,
J. Jackson, M. Kohli, J. Rother, Y. Zheng, and J. Rowe. "Differences in Life
Expectancy Due to Race and Educational Differences Are Widening, and
Many May Not Catch Up." *Health Affairs* 31, no. 8 (2012): 1803–13.

Overall, Christine. *Aging, Death, and Human Longevity: A Philosophical Inquiry.*
Berkeley: University of California Press, 2003.

Palmer, Bruce A. "The 2001 GSU/A on Retire Project Report." *Journal of Financial Service Professionals* 56, no. 1 (January 2002): 35–43.

Pampel, Fred C., and John B. Williamson. *Age, Class, Politics, and the Welfare
State*. Cambridge: Cambridge University Press, 1989.

Papadopoulos, Michael. "Reservation Wages and Work Arrangements: Evi-
dence from the American Life Panel." Working Paper Series No. 1, Schwartz
Center for Economic Policy Analysis, New School for Social Research, New
York, 2020.

Papadopoulos, Michael, Bridget Fisher, Teresa Ghilarducci, and Siavash Radpour. "Over Half of Unemployed Older Workers at Risk of Involuntary Retirement." Publication Series 2020-04, Schwartz Center for Economic Policy
Analysis, New School for Social Research, New York, 2020.

———. "Recession Increases Downward Mobility in Retirement: Middle Earn-
ers Hit From Both Sides." Status of Older Workers Report Series, Schwartz
Center for Economic Policy Analysis, New School for Social Research, New
York, 2020.

Papadopoulos, Michael, Margarita Patria, and Robert K. Triest. "Population

Aging, Labor Demand, and the Structure of Wages." Working Paper No. 17-1, Federal Reserve Bank of Boston, 2017.

Pedron, Sara, Werner Maier, Annette Peters, Birgit Linkohr, Christine Meisinger, Wolfgang Rathmann, Peter Eibich, and Lars Schwettmann. "The Effect of Retirement on Biomedical and Behavioral Risk Factors for Cardiovascular and Metabolic Disease." *Economics and Human Biology* 38 (2020): 100893.

Pilipiec, P., W. Groot, and M. Pavlova. "The Effect of an Increase of the Retirement Age on the Health, Well-Being, and Labor Force Participation of Older Workers: A Systematic Literature Review." *Population Ageing* (2020).

Quinn, Joseph F., Kevin E. Cahill, R. Clark, R. Maurer, and O. S. Mitchell. "Challenges and Opportunities of Living and Working Longer." In *How Persistent Low Returns Will Shape Saving and Retirement*, edited by O. Mitchel, R. Clark, and R. Maurer, 101–19. Oxford: Oxford University Press, 2018.

Radl, Jonas. "Too Old to Work, or Too Young to Retire? The Pervasiveness of Age Norms in Western Europe." *Work, Employment and Society* 26, no. 5 (2012): 755–71.

Radpour, Siavash, Teresa Ghilarducci, and Michael Papadopoulos. "Trends in Employer-Sponsored Retirement Plan Access and Participation Rates: Reconciling Different Data Sources." No. 2021-02, Schwartz Center for Economic Policy Analysis, New School for Social Research, New York, 2021.

Radpour, Siavash, Teresa Ghilarducci, and Anthony Webb. "Expanding Social Security Benefits to Help All Workers." Policy Note Series No. 1, Schwartz Center for Economic Policy Analysis and Department of Economics, New School for Social Research, New York, March 2020.

Rae, M., J. Cubanski, and A. Damico. *Health Spending for 60–64 Year Olds Would Be Lower under Medicare Than under Large Employer Plans*. San Francisco: Kaiser Family Foundation, 2021.

Reader's Digest. "Old Age Jokes: Old People Jokes and Jokes for Seniors." https://www.rd.com/jokes/old-age/.

Reed, Tina. 2022. "U.S. Life Expectancy Fell Again in 2021 amid Pandemic, Opioid Crisis." *Axios*, December 22, 2022. https://www.axios.com/2022/12/22/us-life-expectancy-fell-again-in-2021-amid-pandemic-opioid-crisis.

Reyes, Juliana Feliciano. "'It's Like We Are Just a Piece of Garbage': Laid-Off Philly Workers Face Life without Health Insurance." *Philadelphia Inquirer*, April 2, 2020. https://www.inquirer.com/jobs/labor/coronavirus-layoffs-health-insurance-hourly-workers-philadelphia-20200402.html.

Rohe, William, Clinton Key, Michal Grinstein-Weiss, Mark Schreiner, and Michael Sherraden. "The Impacts of Individual Development Accounts, Assets, and Debt on Future Orientation and Psychological Depression." *Journal of Policy Practice* 16, no. 1 (2017): 24–45.

Rohwedder, Susann, and Robert J. Willis. "Mental Retirement." *Journal of Economic Perspectives* 24, no. 1 (2010): 119–38.

Rosenberger, Jeff. "A Top Retirement Expert Weighs in about How to Strengthen the US Retirement System." *Guideline*, July 24, 2019.

Rothstein, Jesse. "Is the EITC as Good as an NIT? Conditional Cash Transfers and Tax Incidence." *American Economic Journal: Economic Policy* 2, no. 1 (2010): 177–208.

———. *The Unintended Consequences of Encouraging Work: Tax Incidence and the EITC*. Princeton, NJ: Center for Economic Policy Studies, Princeton University, 2008.

Saez, Emmanuel, and Gabriel Zucman. "Wealth Inequality in the United States since 1913: Evidence from Capitalized Income Tax Data." *Quarterly Journal of Economics* 131, no. 2 (2016): 519–78.

Sanzenbacher, Geoffrey, Anthony Webb, Candace Cosgrove, and Natalia Orlova. "Calculating Neutral Increases in Retirement Age by Socioeconomic Status." August 1, 2015. Available at SSRN. http://dx.doi.org/10.2139/ssrn.2658191.

Sass, Steven, and Anthony Webb. "Is the Reduction in Older Workers' Job Tenure a Cause for Concern?" Working Paper No. 20, Center for Retirement Research, Boston College, Chestnut Hill, MA, 2010.

Schmitz, Lauren. "Do Working Conditions at Older Ages Shape the Health Gradient?" *Journal of Health Economics* 50 (2016): 183–97.

Schroeder, Kate. "The Emotional Side of Retiring." *Retirement Wisdom* (podcast), June 27, 2022. https://www.retirementwisdom.com/the-retirement-wisdom-podcast/.

Schwandt, Hannes. "Wealth Shocks and Health Outcomes: Evidence from Stock Market Fluctuations." *American Economic Journal: Applied Economics* 10, no. 4 (2018): 349–77.

Schwartz Center for Economic Policy Analysis. "10+ Years of No Wage Growth: The Role of Alternative Jobs and Gig Work." Status of Older Workers Report Series, Schwartz Center for Economic Policy Analysis, New School for Social Research, New York, May 2019.

———. "20+ Years of Older Workers' Declining Bargaining Power." Status of Older Workers Report Series No. 2, Schwartz Center for Economic Policy Analysis, New School for Social Research, New York, 2019.

Scott, Frank A., Mark C. Berger, and John E. Garen. "Do Health Insurance and Pension Costs Reduce the Job Opportunities of Older Workers?" *Industrial and Labor Relations Review* 48, no. 4 (1995): 775–91.

Scott-Marshall, Heather. "The Social Patterning of Work-Related Insecurity and Its Health Consequences." *Social Indicators Research* 96 (2010): 313–37.

Seibold, Arthur. "Reference Points for Retirement Behavior: Evidence from

German Pension Discontinuities." *American Economic Review* 111, no. 4 (2021): 1126–65.

Shambaugh, Jay, Ryan Nunn, and Patrick Liu. "How Declining Dynamism Affects Wages." *Hamilton Project*, February 2018. https://www.hamiltonpro ject.org/papers/how_declining_dynamism_affects_wages.

Shiller, Robert J. "Narrative Economics." *American Economic Review* 107, no. 4 (2017): 967–1004.

Siegrist, Johannes, and Morten Wahrendorf. 2009. "Quality of Work, Health, and Retirement | Elsevier Enhanced Reader." *Lancet* 374 (9705): 1872–73. https://doi.org/10.1016/S0140-6736(09)61666-4.

SimplyWise. "Retirement Confidence Index: January 2021." https://www .simplywise.com/blog/retirement-confidence-index/.

Skocpol, Theda. "Targeting within Universalism: Politically Viable Policies to Combat Poverty in the United States." In *The Urban Underclass*, edited by Christopher Jencks and Paul E. Peterson, 411–36. Washington, DC: Brookings Institution, 1991.

Slavov, Sita. "It's Time to Do Away with the Social Security Earnings Test." *Bloomberg Tax Journal*, April 9, 2021.

Smialek, Jeanna, and Ben Casselman. "Retirees Are One Reason the Fed Has Given Up on a Big Worker Rebound." *New York Times*, December 27, 2022. https://www.nytimes.com/2022/12/27/business/economy/labor-shortage -retirees-boomers.html.

Smith, Dana G. "What Is the Ideal Retirement Age for Your Health?" *New York Times*, April 3, 2023. https://www.nytimes.com/2023/04/03/well/live/retire ment-age-health.html.

Social Security Administration. "Table 6.B5.1—Number and Average Age of Retired-Worker Awardees, and Percentage Distribution by Age at Entitlement: By Sex and Year of Entitlement, 1998–2020." Annual Statistical Supplement, 2021. https://www.ssa.gov/policy/docs/statcomps/supplement/2021/6b.pdf.

——. Bulletin EN-05010147. https://www.ssa.gov/pubs/EN-05-10147.pdf.

——. "Period Life Table, 2019, as Used in the 2022 Trustees Report in 2017." https://www.ssa.gov/oact/STATS/table4c6.html.

——. "When to Start Receiving Retirement Benefits." https://www.ssa.gov /pubs/EN-05-10147.pdf.

Solow, Robert M. 2021. "Thomas Piketty Is Right: Everything You Need to Know about 'Capital in the Twenty-First Century.'" *New Statesman*, June 9, 2021. https://www.newstatesman.com/business/economics/2014/04/thomas -piketty-right-everything-you-need-know-about-capital-twenty-first-century.

Tergenson, Anne. "How Covid-19 Will Change Aging and Retirement." *Wall Street Journal*, November 15, 2020.

Toder, Eric, Daniel Berger, and Yifan Powers. *Distributional Effects of Individual Income Tax Expenditures: An Update*. Washington, DC: Brookings Tax Policy Center, 2016.

Topel, Robert. "Specific Capital, Mobility, and Wages: Wages Rise with Job." *Journal of Political Economy* 99, no. 1 (1991): 145–76.

Truesdale, Beth C. "Better Jobs, Longer Working Lives: Proposals to Improve the Low-Wage, Labor Market for Older Workers." Brookings Institution, November 2020.

Tumino, Alberto. "Retirement and Cognitive Abilities." ISER Working Paper Series No. 2016-06, Institute for Social and Economic Research, University of Essex, Colchester, UK, 2016.

"2019 Poverty Guidelines." n.d. Assistant Secretary for Planning and Evaluation. https://aspe.hhs.gov/topics/poverty-economic-mobility/poverty-guide lines/prior-hhs-poverty-guidelines-federal-register-references/2019-poverty -guidelines.

US Bureau of Labor Statistics. "Labor Statistics from the Current Population Survey: Table 36, A-36. Unemployed Persons by Age, Sex, Race, Hispanic or Latino Ethnicity, Marital Status, and Duration of Unemployment." 2021.

US Bureau of Labor Statistics and US Department of Labor. "Employment Projection Five Major Occupational Groups." https://www.bls.gov/emp/tables /emp-by-major-occupational-group.htm.

US Congress, Senate, Special Committee on Aging. *America's Aging Workforce: Opportunities and Challenges*. December 6, 2017. 115th Cong., 1st sess. https://www.aging.senate.gov/imo/media/doc/Aging%20Workforce%20 Report%20FINAL.pdf.

US Department of Health and Human Services. "Poverty Definition Federal Register under the Authority of 42 U.S.C. 9902(2)."

US Department of Labor, Bureau of Labor Statistics. "Civilian Labor Force by Age, Sex, Race, and Ethnicity Projections." https://www.bls.gov/emp/tables /civilian-labor-force-summary.htm.

US Department of Labor, Office of Disability Employment Policy. "Older Workers." 2021. https://www.dol.gov/agencies/odep/program-areas/indivi duals/older-workers.

Van den Berg, Tilja I. J., Leo A. M. Elders, and Alex Burdorf. "Influence of Health and Work on Early Retirement." *Journal of Occupational and Environmental Medicine* (2010): 576–83.

Van den Bogaard, Levi, and Kène Henkens. "When Is Quitting an Escape? How Different Job Demands Affect Physical and Mental Health Outcomes of Retirement." *European Journal of Public Health* 28, no. 5 (2018): 815–19.

Veal, A. J. "Is There Enough Leisure Time? Leisure Studies, Work-Life Balance, the Realm of Necessity, and the Realm of Freedom." *World Leisure Journal* 62, no. 2 (2020): 89–113.

Vogel, Edgar, Alexander Ludwig, and Axel Börsch-Supan. "Aging and Pension Reform: Extending the Retirement Age and Human Capital Formation." Working Paper Series No. 18856, National Bureau of Economic Research, Cambridge, MA, February 2013.

von Bonsdorff, Monika E., Sinikka Vanhala, Jorma Seitsamo, Minna Janhonen, and Päivi Husman. "Employee Well-Being, Early-Retirement Intentions, and Company Performance." *Journal of Occupational and Environmental Medicine* 52, no. 12 (December 2010): 1255–61.

von Herbay, Axel, "Otto Von Bismarck Is Not the Origin of Old Age at 65." *Gerontologist* 54, no. 1 (February 2014): 5.

Wahrendorf, Morten, David Blane, Mel Bartley, Nico Dragano, and Johannes Siegristc. 2013. "Working Conditions in Mid-Life and Mental Health in Older Ages." *Advances in Life Course Research* 18, no. 1 (March 2013): 16–25.

Weaver, Charles N. "Worker's Expectations about Losing and Replacing Their Jobs: 35 Years of Change." *Monthly Labor Review* (January 2015).

Wei, Sun, and Anthony Webb. "Valuing the Longevity Insurance Acquired by Delayed Claiming of Social Security." *Journal of Risk and Insurance* 78, no. 4 (2010): 907–30.

Weil, David. "Understanding the Present and Future of Work in the Fissured Workplace Context" *RSF: The Russell Sage Foundation Journal of the Social Sciences* 5, no. 5 (December 2019): 147–65.

Williamson, John. "A Short History of the Washington Consensus." *Law and Business Review of the Americas* 15, no. 1 (2009): 7–26.

World Science Festival. *90 Is the New 50: The Science of Longevity*. June 1, 2008. https://www.worldsciencefestival.com/programs/90_is_the_new_50_the _science_of_longevity/.

Vargas, Ramon Antonio. "Oregon Grocery Store Worker, 91, Retires after Raising More Than $80,000 Online." *The Guardian*, April 27, 2023. https://www .theguardian.com/us-news/2023/apr/27/oregon-winco-betty-grocery-store -worker-retire.

Xiao, Christina, Yevgeniy Goryakin, and Michele Cecchini. "Physical Activity Levels and New Public Transit: A Systematic Review and Meta-analysis." *American Journal of Preventive Medicine* 56, no. 3 (2019): 464–73.

Yamashita, T., P. A. Cummins, A. Arbogast, and R. J. Millar. "Adult Competencies and Employment Outcomes among Older Workers in the United States: An Analysis of the Program for the International Assessment of Adult Competencies." *Adult Education Quarterly* 68, no. 3 (2018): 235–50.

Zhe, Li and Joseph Dalaker. "Poverty among the Population Aged 65 and Older." *Congressional Research Service*. https://crsreports.congress.gov.

Zoll, Adam "Working Longer Can Be a Win-Win for Investors." Morningstar, January 21, 2013. https://www.morningstar.com/articles/581570/working -longer-can-be-a-win-win-for-investors.

Zurlo, Karen A., Wonah Yoon, and Hyungsoo Kim. "Unsecured Consumer Debt and Mental Health Outcomes in Middle-Aged and Older Americans." *Journals of Gerontology* 69, no. 3 (2014): 461–69.

Index

Note: The italic letters *b*, *f*, and *t* following a page number indicate a box, figure, or table, respectively, on that page.